HISTORIC
WALKS
OF EDMONTON

HISTORIC
WALKS
OF EDMONTON

KATHRYN IVANY

Red Deer PRESS

Published by
Red Deer Press
813 MacKimmie Library Tower
2500 University Drive N.W.
Calgary Alberta Canada T2N 1N4

Credits
Edited by Jill Fallis
Cover and text design by Erin Woodward
All photographs taken by the author unless otherwise noted
Printed and bound in Canada by Friesens for Red Deer Press

Acknowledgments
Financial support provided by the Canada Council, the Department of
Canadian Heritage, the Alberta Foundation for the Arts, a beneficiary of the
Lottery Fund of the Government of Alberta, and the University of Calgary.

THE CANADA COUNCIL | LE CONSEIL DES ARTS
FOR THE ARTS | DU CANADA
SINCE 1957 | DEPUIS 1957

National Library of Canada Cataloguing in Publication
Ivany, Kathryn
Historic walks of Edmonton / Kathryn Ivany.
Includes bibliographical references.
ISBN 0-88995-298-1
1. Historic buildings—Alberta—Edmonton—Guidebooks.
2. Walking—Alberta—Edmonton—Guidebooks. 3. Edmonton (Alta.)—
Tours. 4. Edmonton (Alta.)—History. I. Title.
FC3696.7.I92 2004   917.123'34044   C2004-903522-3

5 4 3 2 1

Contents

Acknowledgements

As I write these walking tours, I am very aware that I am walking in the footsteps of many local public historians who have researched and compiled some of these stories before me. This work rests on the work of numerous people who have gathered the history, preserved the buildings, and documented both processes for future generations.

When I started doing the walking tour of the Edmonton Cemetery, I was really following the example of my friend Marcel Dirk, who told me of the popularity of his cemetery tours in Medicine Hat. Judy Berghofer of the Old Strathcona Foundation started a similar project for the Mount Pleasant Cemetery at about the same time, so I knew it was a good idea. The neighborhood tours grew from my involvement in the Edmonton and District Historical Society. I was contacted by a number of community groups that were looking for ways to celebrate anniversaries of their league or organization.

The dedication and enthusiasm of those volunteers—who realized how enjoyable and accessible history could be through the medium of a walking tour—was infectious. A few, like Ted Smith of the Highlands Historical Foundation, generously offered to assist me with photographs and editorial assistance for the tours of their area.

Professional historians and writers who have created and published neighborhood histories and biographies, including Shirley Lowe, Lori Yanish, Marianne Fedori, Ken Tingley, Lawrence Herzog, and our beloved Alex Mair, have all assisted me, personally and with their documents, in creating my own walking tours.

Other historians, archivists, and planners I admire, such as David Leonard, former provincial archivist; Bruce Ibsen, former city archivist; David Holdsworth of the city's heritage planner's office; and Dorothy Field of Alberta Historic Sites Services, have been doing walking tours for school groups, professional organizations, and provincial and municipal VIPs and guests for years as a way of promoting the city. Though fulfilling the duties of their jobs, their attention to detail in research, their appreciation of the people stories, and their ability to convey architectural nuances have been inspirational.

I am grateful to all those colleagues and friends, and hope I have not forgotten anyone. I am, however, most thankful to my mother, Joan Ivany, and my family, Bob, Joan, and Stewart Wyatt, who have graciously, for the most part, given up my attention so that I could devote time to the researching and writing of this book. They have listened to my stories, been dragged about communities, cemeteries, and churches, and politely not moaned excessively whenever I launched into yet another lecture about the origin of that name or that building's architectural style.

Introduction

Why a walking tour book? I am a great proponent of studying history by going out and looking, and asking questions. Really good stories often come from seeing something interesting and asking, "How did this get here?" In the case of downtown Edmonton, the more relevant question may be "How did this manage to survive here?"

I came late to the study of history, firmly believing that history of great civilizations and great men was boring and irrelevant to me. What I discovered, however, was that history, especially of my own country, town, and neighbors was quite fascinating, and it explained a lot about how things work in my own life and community. I have chosen, therefore, to work as a public historian who concentrates on local history and local people, and I often use nontraditional methods of sharing that information, such as walking tours.

Walking tours add another dimension to the study of history: the participants are fully engaged physically as well as mentally. The material being studied has a tangible, three-dimensional aspect not usually found in the classroom or textbook. While photographs, especially archival or historic ones, can give a good sense of what it was like before, there is nothing like actually seeing a building or community to help realize the essence of the stories being told about it. Even better, historic walking tours help people learn and explore while enjoying a healthy, outdoor activity.

While it is impossible for a walking-tour book to give the complete story, I hope that the material presented will be enough for an introduction and basic understanding. If the material piques your interest, you may wish to consult the references listing included in this book which provides some sources for further research. A glossary of architectural terms can also be found at the back of this book.

WARNING

Please remember that the majority of buildings and objects in these tours are not public places, but rather are private homes and businesses. They should be viewed from the street, and the property respected.

Also a note to walkers: these tours will involve activity on your part. Some, like the Archeological Tour, involve a considerable amount of walking up and down hills; others, like the Cemetery Tour, require walking over some rough terrain. Even walking about downtown Edmonton on good streets can be tiring and hard on your feet and back if you are not wearing comfortable walking shoes.

In most cases, walkers will find nice little stopping places along the way where a snack and a break can occur. In other tours, you may have to hike a bit farther to reach such a place. In any case, be prepared—carry water and light snack.

Most of all I hope you enjoy the walking tours.

Archeological Tour

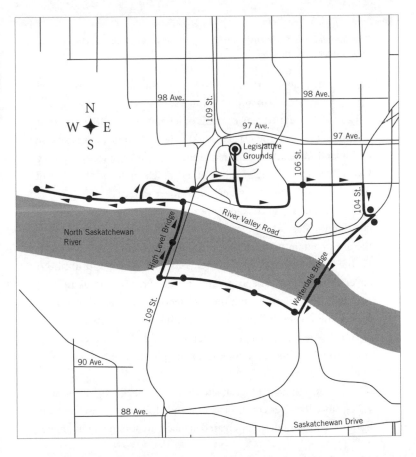

The flat lands beside the river provided space for industry and residences in the past and for recreation today.

Until about 12,000 years ago, the area between Fort Saskatchewan and Drayton Valley was covered by a glacial lake trapped between hills of ice and debris to the northeast and the southwest. The glaciers and the lake ensured a large expanse of flat land. When the ice melted at the end of the last ice age and the lake started to drain, it initially cut a deep channel and then spread out to widen the North Saskatchewan River valley.

Layers of silt and sand were deposited as the water receded, creating the flats which, handily for the later human inhabitants of the area, contain material that is highly suitable for making bricks. Farther west the river cut into igneous rock which had not been covered by the glacial deposits, and its waters carried out particles of gold that were mixed in with the silts deposited downstream around the Edmonton area. Several ravines cut into the river valley, originally having drained from sloughs left in the uplands. Now, the creeks that run through all but the Whitemud ravine in the southwest are only seasonal streams.

The earliest archeological sites are found at the top of the river valley, since the river cut down and people followed the water to the bottom. The oldest human-created artifacts are found within 1 meter of the surface, the most recent in the lowest part of the river valley. The lowest-level sites date back approximately 8,000 years. (The earliest sites in Alberta are in the Peace River area and date back about 11,000 years.) Animal fossils, on the other hand, are much older. For millions of years, various kinds of animals have lived here, which means we can include dinosaur fossils.

An almost complete skeleton of a 30.5-meter carnivorous dinosaur was discovered in the gravel beds near the Edmonton country club in 1941, and as recently as 1999, fossil bones have been pulled out of sandbars near the river. About 25,000 years ago, before the last ice age glaciation, mammoths, saber-toothed cats, camels, and musk oxen lived in the area. Their fossils have been found in the Cloverbar area.

The types of artifacts found that show evidence of human endeavour include stone points, clay pots, and scraped and cooked animal bones. They tend to be found in sites of small family camps near or in the Edmonton area. In the best-known Stony Plain and Strathcona sites, they are much larger, cover many hectares, and contain thousands of artifacts. Of course, many sites have been destroyed by the development of subsequent civilizations, and especially by road construction. However, if you know where to look, like on the edges of the river where creeks flow into it, fossils can be found.

The camping sites were used over thousands of years by related family groups. In certain areas such as Riverbend, which was explored extensively before development in the late 1960s, and other areas with high hills in Edmonton, such as Rabbit Hill and Mount Pleasant, large numbers of repeatedly used camping sites have been found. These hills were important camps because they offered good viewpoints, a cooling breeze, and well-drained ground. The hills are "kames" which were formed by glacial meltwaters depositing layers of silt and sediment (glacial drift).

Once the European settlers arrived in the area, they took up various pursuits that represented their interests. Gold panning has occurred near Edmonton since the 1880s. By 1894, over $4 million in fine gold dust had reportedly been removed from the sandbars and gravel found 160 kilometers up- and downstream from Edmonton. Once gold fever really struck in 1897, there were as many as ten dredges on the river as well as several hand miners. Eventually, in 1899, the town purchased gold rights along the river's edge to prevent undermining of the banks.

Once people started living here year-round, they needed to find fuel to burn to keep themselves warm. While there were many trees, the traders at the Hudson's Bay Company trading posts soon discovered coal along the banks of the river. It was a soft coal, lignite, which couldn't be transported very far since it crumbled easily; however, it was good for domestic use. The traders dug into the sides of the riverbanks like "gopher mines," and early settlers outside the fort did likewise—although Donald Ross did shore up the entrance and the tunnels a bit at his mine near 102nd Street in the Rossdale flats.

The first deep-shaft mine, of approximately 30 meters depth, was started in 1905 by partners John Walter, Alexander Rutherford, and William Humberstone. By 1912, the city had to put a stop to most of the mining activities under the city center since cave-ins and sinkholes started appearing in land people were trying to build on. Most of the mines within the city limits were closed by 1943, as they threatened housing and development along the river valley.

Most of the Hudson's Bay Company men who left the fort to start their own businesses ended up taking up a number of occupations to make their fortunes—several in the lumber trade. They cut timber upstream in more heavily forested areas in winter, then bundled the logs at the side of the river, waiting to be lifted by spring floods (or rolled in) and floated down to lumberyards and mills near Edmonton. John Walter had a lumber sawmill at Walterdale and Rossdale, W. H. Clark opened one at Cloverdale, and John Fraser caught the logs at Riverdale.

Other river valley industries included finishing mills, grain mills, breweries, brick makers, hide tanners, ice plants, and eventually both water works and a power plant. There was even an oil well dug in 1907. The exploration of Dingman turned out nothing but a dry hole, but the hope was there.

With all this activity at the bottom of the river valley, it was necessary to have a way of transporting the produced goods to market. Trails, of course, grew out from the river, assisted by Walter's and Humberstone's ferries, and trains crossed it as soon as bridges were built. In 1902, the Canadian Northern Railway crossed on the Low Level Bridge, built in 1900. The Canadian Pacific Railway crossed overhead in 1913, although the Calgary and Edmonton Railway had been at the top of the south-side bank since 1892. The Incline Railway (1908–12) was an attempt to assist those who were draying the goods out of the valley and up into the commercial center of Edmonton. Paddlewheelers and steamers carried goods up and down the river to other riverbound outposts, many of them started at John Walter's piers.

All the industrial activities were dependent on the river. It was not an easy dependence. The flood of 1899 brought industry there to a standstill. After the waters receded, there was a great deal of damage to be put to rights, and stock lost. The powerhouse was completely inundated, and there was no power for three weeks. The Low Level Bridge piers, still under construction at the time, were completely submerged, and the engineers decided they had to be raised by several meters.

That flood, however, was minor compared to the flood of 1915, when the water rose so quickly and kept rising—little could be done but save people. The lumber mills were destroyed; most of their stock broke free and floated away. The other industries found that their equipment was severely damaged, and the depressed economy and lack of manpower to assist meant that few started up operations again. From being a vibrant center of industry, the valley became incredibly quiet and by the 1920s reverted, in large part, back to nature.

Legislature Grounds

Location: Top of Fortway Road below the Legislature, near the bowling greens

Date(s): ca. 1830

Route: Start south of the Legislature Building, heading down the steps to the fountain. Go past towards the bowling greens then west along the walkway.

The bowling greens on the Legislature grounds hide evidence of the old Fort Edmonton.

Buried under the manicured lawns and clipped lawn-bowling greens to the south of the Legislature Building is the last site of Fort Edmonton. A plaque on the sidewalk beside the bowling greens represents the location of the northwest corner of the fort.

The fort grounds stretched southeast from there to include all of the western bowling green and diagonally intersecting the eastern green. The southern wall of the fort roughly followed the line of the roadway along the top of the riverbank, and there were some buildings found outside the walls.

Excavations during the building of the Legislature disturbed most of the shallowly buried remains; however, archeologists from the University of Alberta have been able to dig deeper to determine where the palisade walls and trenches, privies, cellars, and wooden foundations were laid. Certain buildings, such as the married men's quarters and some work areas (coopers and boat builders), were near the present-day drinking fountain and skating rink. From the eastern edge of the skating rink, you can look north and east of the Legislature to the approximate site where the last factor, Richard Hardisty, built his "Big House" in 1874, outside the protection of the fort walls.

Preliminary excavations at the Legislature site were carried out between 1977 and 1992, followed by extensive digs in the summers up to 1995. Archeologists employed ground-penetrating radar and magnetometers (they look for anomalies in readings which would indicate disturbances in the ground caused by earlier construction or the presence of "foreign" materials) in preliminary stages of the investigation. They also looked at old maps of the fort in the Hudson's Bay Company archives and old photographs.

As far as they can determine, the last fort covered over 10,000 square meters during its largest point in history, around the 1860s when it employed about 150 people. The layout changed over time. As the fort's importance grew, it required a more grandiose factor's house and ample accommodation for larger numbers of servants and officers. The archeologists excavated only 100 square meters and found 55,000 artifacts. If the whole 10,000-square-meter site could have been excavated, they expected to have found more than 5,550,000 artifacts. What's more, deeper digging might reveal more pre-European artifacts since the site was also probably used by prehistoric native peoples, given its prominent location.

The history of Fort Edmonton dates back to 1795, when Hudson's Bay Company employee William Tomlinson founded the first Edmonton House, near the North Saskatchewan River at the present site of Fort Saskatchewan, where the Sturgeon and North Saskatchewan rivers meet. This was the period of first contact with native peoples in this area. The North West Company had preceded the Hudson's Bay Company briefly with a post called Fort Augustus, which was set up to trade with the woodland and plains First Nations peoples.

In 1802, the post was moved upstream, probably to the Rossdale flats site. Some sources indicate that another move was made in 1804, downstream to Fort White Earth (present-day Victoria/Pakan), near Smoky Lake. The movement of the posts was the result of the movement of the native peoples due to hunting and tensions between bands, and the supplies of furs. By 1813, Edmonton House had returned to the Rossdale flats. The merger of the Hudson's Bay Company with the North West Company in 1821 led company officials to think that they could abandon the northern location, the "Fort des Prairies," and concentrate on the Blackfoot in the south to raise their profits. But the southern location proved not so advantageous for either transportation or safety. Then, when a decision was needed on where in the north to set the post—the Athabasca or Saskatchewan route—a party was sent along each route to see which was fastest. John Rowand proved to Governor George Simpson that the Saskatchewan route was faster than the Athabasca route, essentially saving this location.

Rowand was named chief factor in 1824, and Edmonton House became the center for the Saskatchewan district. Because it was the height of navigation from York Factory before freeze-up and it also had a recognized and well-used ford of the river, it seemed the most logical choice. The post became a depot or large fort that traded as well as collected other posts' furs and distributed supplies for posts farther west and north.

Edmonton became the hub, and the company employees cut the pack trail to northern points in the Peace River Country and along the Assiniboine. That meant they required a pack horse brigade stationed at the fort, and since they traded pemmican to those other points, they also needed a processing plant and a farm to provide the food stuffs they sent north. Floods in 1829 and 1830 forced Rowand to relocate the fort once again, but this time only to the tableland just below the top of the northern riverbank.

Once the 1830 fort was completed, Rowand suggested a name change to Sanspareil—meaning, the "peerless" fort. The name was disallowed by Hudson's Bay Company directors, and it remained Fort Edmonton. Once the post became the hub for western travel, it also saw the beginning of an influx of missionaries, initially Robert

Rundle and Father Albert Lacombe, as well as tourists like Paul Kane, Dr. Cheadle, and Lord Milton. Soon there were also new "government-sponsored" exploration parties coming in to determine the possibilities of the frontier lands.

By the 1860s, the company was noticing a decline in the fur trade and sensed that the end of its merchant empire was on the way. In 1869, the Hudson's Bay Company sold its title to Rupert's Land to the new Dominion of Canada, except for "reserves" around each post. With the transfer of land came the beginning of settlement, although some matters, like the first Riel uprising at Red River, first needed clearing up.

Settlement didn't really start around the Edmonton area until the late 1870s and early 1880s. A wagon trail to Athabasca was cleared in 1879, and the Dominion Survey conducted in 1882 under the direction of surveyor M. Deane. He laid out Jasper Avenue along the line of a trail between the McDougall mission in the west and the Anglican church on Malcolm Groat's land on the east.

The survey recorded the river lot system adopted by the first homesteaders to venture out from the fort, and the land in the middle of the settlement reserved for the Hudson's Bay Company. The main street was surveyed north from the top of the riverbank up to what is today 97th Street. When the Saskatchewan (Riel) Rebellion broke out in 1885, there were 1,800 people living in the settlement of Edmonton, and most of them tried to squeeze back inside the walls of Fort Edmonton.

By 1907, however, very little remained inside the fort, not even the Hudson's Bay Company store. The fort was decommissioned, and the City of Edmonton used two of the warehouses for telephone offices. The fort can be seen in old photographs showing the building of the High Level Bridge and the construction of the Legislature, but by 1915 the whitewashed log buildings and the old picket fence— all that was left of the fort—were dismantled.

Some timbers were used by Edmontonians for other structures and firewood, so the only evidence left of the fort is buried underground or housed in the city of Edmonton's and the university's storage.

Legislature grounds with Fort Edmonton in foreground, 1915.
CITY OF EDMONTON ARCHIVES EA-10-2942

Terrace Building

Address: 96th Avenue & 106th Street
Style: Utilitarian–Moderne
Architect: Department of Public Works
Date: 1962
Route: Go east along the roadway to the Terrace Building.

This is actually the second Terrace Building. It replaced an earlier
Terrace building on the same site. That one was the first provincial
administrative building, built in 1906—before the Legislature was
built and while Fort Edmonton was still on the grounds. The brick
building had a mansard roof and gables. It was two storeys high on
the north side and terraced down the riverbank for another two or
three storeys. The building housed all 100 employees of the government in four departments.

One of the elaborate entryways of the crescent shaped Terrace Building.

The largest department was public works, and within four years that department began to oversee its largest project to date: the construction of the Legislature Building. Alexander Cameron Rutherford, Alberta's first premier, and his successor, Arthur Sifton, had a corner office with a fireplace. Only cabinet ministers rated a fireplace; luckily, there were only four ministries. Once the Legislature was completed in 1913, most of the employees moved into their new offices. The first Terrace Building was demolished in February 1961.

The new Terrace Building was designed for the specific purpose of housing the newest computer technology available to the government of Alberta. The Terrace Building was to be the new electronic data-processing center, and the public works department was more concerned with humidity and dust control than with architectural beauty. They didn't want to block the view from the Legislature with an elevator tower, however, so they drilled 23 meters into the ground to fit the workings for a hydraulic lift.

The second Terrace Building cost $3.5 million to build. It is three storeys tall at the front and five storeys at the rear over the riverbank, like its predecessor. The building comprises 20,903 square meters, running 201 meters in length with an average width of 22 meters. This Terrace Building houses 700 government employees.

Rossdale Flats

Location: Intersection of River Road & 104th Street
Route: Turn right at the north end of the Terrace Building and head down the hill toward 104th Street. Follow 104th Street south toward the Rossdale Power Plant crossing carefully over to the east side of 103rd Street, south of 96th Avenue.

The Rossdale flats were an early commercial and residential centre of the settlement.
CITY OF EDMONTON ARCHIVES EA 10–2764

The Rossdale flats were named for Donald Ross, an early pioneer in the city and a man who contributed much to Edmonton's transition from frontier post to modern industrial center. Ross was Scottish, although raised partly in England before coming to North America. He followed various careers—hotel employee, gold prospector, miner—before coming to Edmonton about 1872.

Here he continued his checkered career, finding whatever work could support him and, after 1878, his family. He worked as a gardener for the Hudson's Bay Company in return for the land on which he gardened, west of the company's reserve land in the valley. He opened the Edmonton Hotel there and dug coal from the riverbank north of the hotel and also across the river near where the Low Level Bridge would be built. He joined the boards and the ownership of several industries in the valley by swapping land for shares.

He dabbled in real estate when the market developed after 1900, and, since his hotel was the largest gathering place in the early settlement days, he fostered the establishment of many institutions, such as the school board in 1881, various clubs, and several societies, including the Northern Alberta Old Timers Association. He also chaired many committees to serve the community, such as the civic defense committee struck during the Riel Rebellion in 1885.

The flatlands was the location of at least one of the earlier incarnations of Edmonton House, or Fort Edmonton, and Fort Augustus, the North West Company post, including a horseracing track immediately behind the power plant near the present ball stadium. Closer to the river there were also boat-landing places and probably a cemetery for post employees, their families, and First Nations people who over the years lived and died here. A great deal of the archeological record has been destroyed over the years by the construction of houses, gardens, the power plant, roadways, and railways.

East of the Walterdale Bridge, there have been found remains of palisade posts and the west walls of the first forts near the power plant. Evidence of a cemetery has been unearthed beneath the intersection of 105th Street and River Valley Road, probably directly west of the old fort walls, in which there was thought to be over 200 European and native interments. It is believed that many remains have been relocated, but it may be that the majority still lie beneath more than a meter of construction infill and river alluvium.

Archeological evidence of early industrial endeavors of Edmontonians also has been found. There are traces of early settlement plans, industrial and residential sites, and major public works to be explored. The community of Rossdale can be considered as an important artifact in the discovery of the history of Edmonton.

Rossdale Power Plant

Address: 104th Street & 94th Avenue
Style: Utilitarian with Victorian, moderne & art deco influences
Architect: Maxwell Dewar
Date: 1930–54

The Rossdale Power Plant has been compared to a ocean liner with its rows of chimney stacks seen here over the banks of the North Saskatchewan River.

The Edmonton Electric Lighting and Power Company began in 1891 as a private company, financed in the amount of $10,000 by Alex Taylor. Taylor had been instrumental in building up a variety of technological improvements in the town of Edmonton, from telegraph to telephone, and electricity was the next frontier. He served also as managing director of the new power company, and John McDougall, another prominent businessman in Edmonton, was the first president.

The first plant was built on the south side, near where the Low Level Bridge would be built. The flood of 1899 put the plant out of commission for weeks, and it cost a great deal to refurbish it. Taylor and partners sold out to Edmonton for $13,500 in 1904, the year that the town became a city, and the plant was moved to the north side.

The first city power plant building was designed by J. Martland, the city architect, and it operated with only one turbine. The plant used slack coal, the material often rejected because it was too small and brittle for transportation, and was consequently quite cheap.

During the First World War, the Alliance Power Company took over operations, but the plant was returned to city control in 1919. Growth in the city demanded more power by 1927, and Edmonton Power installed a large steam turbine that year to meet the demand of 67,000 Edmontonians using power.

The new power plant was built in stages between 1930 and 1954 as demand for newer and larger equipment continued. Although actually three buildings, the use of similar styles for each new addition maintained a uniform and cohesive appearance, and achieved considerable massing on the site. In 1939, the largest steam boiler in Canada was installed. By 1947, a water treatment center had been added, expanding the footprint of the plant to the east. A new section opened in 1953 that allowed the plant to double its capacity by 1958. The power generation had converted to gas in 1955 when prices tipped in favor of the new fuel.

Built in a utilitarian industrial style, the Rossdale Power Plant is constructed of brick over steel girders that form a load-bearing skeleton from which the brick curtain walls are suspended. The plant has thick concrete floors and foundations to support the massive equipment inside. The building is one of only five industrial sites on the municipal historical resources "A" list.

Walterdale Bridge (105th Street Bridge)
Architect: Dominion Bridge Company
Date: 1913

In 1912, tenders called for a bridge to be built across the North Saskatchewan River, just downstream of the launch site of the Walter ferry. The crossing was also one of the few fords across the river, since the distance between the two banks was comparatively short. The decision to build the bridge was made as part of the negotiated deal for Edmonton's amalgamation with Strathcona in 1911.

The Dominion Bridge Company was the successful bidder, and it built the bridge with three spans, each slightly more than 70 meters long (about 210 meters total), balanced on two piers and two abutments approximately 12 meters above mean water level. The bridge opened to foot and cart traffic in the autumn of 1913, but was not officially opened until 1914. It was the fourth bridge built in the city, preceded by the Low Level (1900), the Dawson (1905), and the High Level (1913) bridges. Streetcar tracks were run across it and into Rossdale.

The Walterdale Bridge represented progress from the Walter ferry.

By 1954, city engineers were trying to figure out how to widen the bridge or twin it. Traffic congestion was a consistent problem (a situation which remains today). Various schemes were proposed and delayed because of numerous problems. At one point in the 1960s, the city piled the excavated fill from downtown construction projects (including the new library) at the south foot of the bridge for over a year in preparation for grading a new approach to the bridge's twin. Some prankster put up a sign calling it Mount Dantzer after the incumbent mayor. The thinking then was to make the bridge part of a freeway scheme from south Edmonton to downtown, but the scheme, known as Dantzer's Folly, never materialized since costs kept rising and the city could not get enough support from other levels of government to make it viable.

Three other bridges were under construction at the same time: the Quesnell (1968), the Capilano (1969), and the James Macdonald

(1971). Citizens and aldermen couldn't help but make unfavorable comparisons. Further plans for a suggested six-lane replacement came out again in 1974, but after two years of review, that plan was also rejected. So the Walterdale Bridge, or the 105th Street Bridge (no one can agree on the name either), continues today as it has historically.

Walterdale Flats

Location: West of 105th Street; bottom of the old Fort Road, south of the North Saskatchewan River

Date: 1880s

Route: Turn west (and go under the underpass) from the south side of the bridge to follow the walking path along the river toward the John Walter Museum.

Many industries operated on the Walterdale flats as the High Level Bridge began to take shape crossing the river.
CITY OF EDMONTON ARCHIVES EA 297–08

The Walterdale flats were named after the first settler on the south side of the river and the owner of several industries that developed on this property. John Walter was an Orkneyman who came to the area in 1870 to serve the Hudson's Bay Company as a boat builder. Following his example, a number of business owners started their companies on nearby land and reaped the rewards of hard work and industry.

Just before the small cairn that recognizes John Walter (to the east of the houses), a small path leads down toward the river, where the remains of Walter's last ferry are rotting away in the bush.

Occasionally, at low water, you can also see the remains of his stern-wheeler—the *City of Edmonton,* used for Saturday-evening, 50-cent dance cruises up to Big Island—as well as old wooden piles (possibly the remains of piers). Big Island was located about where Anthony Henday Drive would intersect the river when extended south of Whitemud Drive. The last steamer working out of Edmonton was in operation until 1918.

The rotting remains of the last Walter ferry are found in the bushes at the edge of the river.

The sawmill started in 1883, and Walter added a sash and door plant a few years later. The mills produced lumber and building trim that was marketed around northern Alberta and into Saskatchewan, and it employed men from the timber lots west of the city to inside the mills through to the transporting of the finished goods by steamer and wagon.

John Walter's mine, the Strathcona Coal Company, had its pithead below 108th Street. It was the first deep-shaft mine that dug out a 1.2-meter coal seam over 30 meters underground. Over five years it produced almost 150,000 tonnes of coal. A fire in the third year, 1907, destroyed the pithead building, and six men were killed from the smoke while trapped underground. John Walter never recovered emotionally from the responsibility for those deaths. The mine was abandoned in 1911.

Walterdale was called the "Cradle of Edmonton Industry." Here, between the 1880s and 1915, there were coalmines, a sawmill, a sash and door plant, a tannery, and a brickyard. Hundreds of men were employed in those industries, and approximately 60 of their families lived on the flats in company and private housing. There was a small school, a general store, a church, and a butcher shop.

The end of this prosperous community was determined by the very river that gave it life. The first major flood of 1899 caused a setback to many of the businesses, and then the flood of 1915 was so destructive and the economy so hampered by the First World War and the Depression that none of the industries were able to recover. By 1920, the industrial center was abandoned and still.

Walterdale Residences

Address: North of the Kinsman Park parking lot
Date: 1885–1911

Transported from Scotland to the western frontier by the Hudson's Bay Company in 1870, John Walter made the York boats that were used to haul the supplies and furs of the fur trade east and west along the river, and he also built carts for the supplying of the Athabasca posts in the north.

When his five-year contract with the company expired, Walter moved to the south side of the river and commenced building his own business. There was a natural ford upstream, where the 105th Street Bridge was constructed, so the trail from the south wound down into the valley very close to where Walter settled.

He continued to build boats, including ferries. The first was oar-powered, and then, after a trip to Winnipeg to buy about 330 meters of cable in 1882, he designed the first cable-operated ferry, the *Belle*, which could transport six carts and horses across the river. Later it was called the Upper Ferry, as there was another ferry run by

One of the three Walter residences found as part of a City interpretation centre in Kinsman Park.

Humberstone called the Lower Ferry. Walter built most of the other ferries used throughout the Northwest Territories, and eventually he hired a blacksmith and added to his company's services the building of scows and wagons for settlers and prospectors, and gold dredges.

Walter also started other industries on the flats. He established a lumberyard, leased timber stands to the west, built a sawmill and a sash and door plant, and had interests in coalmines into the river-bank. Walter was a successful businessman in a number of fields and the first millionaire in Edmonton and in Strathcona as well. He was a founding member of many institutions in Strathcona, including the school board and town council, and was instrumental in the amalgamation negotiations between Edmonton and Strathcona.

Most of his empire was destroyed in the 1915 flood, and he died in 1920 of complications from appendicitis. His wife, Annie, and their children remained in the last house for several years, helped by a Métis man called Muchias, a former colleague of Walter's at the fort and an employee at the mills.

John Walter's first residence was built in 1875 outside of and almost directly across from Fort Edmonton. Once he constructed his second residence, the first house was used for a telegraph office by Alex Taylor. Although he lost his fortune in the aftermath of the flood, three of his residences remain in Walterdale (all moved to the present location) and have been used as interpretive centers by the City of Edmonton's parks and recreation department for many years. Hours for tours and interpretive programs are posted.

Kinsmen Park
Address: 9100 Walterdale Hill
Date: 1953
Route: Continue west along the road into the park.
Originally named Walterdale Park after the neighborhood that once existed here, the park was renamed after the Kinsmen Clubs of Edmonton signed the first of several agreements with the city to develop the park and its recreational facilities for the benefit of all Edmontonians.

Extensive playing fields and facilities lie in the shadow of the High Level Bridge in Kinsman Park.

The city had initially planned to develop the site for the zoo being moved from Borden Park in the 1950s. However, negotiations with the Kinsmen resulted in the promise of a $100,000 to $250,000 expenditure over fifteen years for swimming pools, playing fields, hockey arenas, and playgrounds—a sum which the city could not hope to commit on its own. The plans took a significant turn.

In 1953, the Kinsmen were granted a ten-year lease for the Kinsmen Recreation Centre. Various other groups were encouraged to use the facilities. For example, in 1957, the Edmonton Huskies Football Club moved the Noble Electric Company office and warehouse from 8631–109th Street to Kinsmen Park for use as a clubhouse. They called it the Huskies Building, and it served them until it was replaced in 1983.

The Kinsmen Club was granted an extension of the lease and more land in 1968, having met and exceeded the terms of the original lease, spending over $300,000 for the facilities provided. The five-year, renewable extension added two hectares, west of the High Level Bridge, to the park's existing 23.5 hectares. The following year, the city added another 16.6 hectares of woodland, and the Kinsmen Club was granted the proceeds of the food concessions on site to use for further development.

The facilities built by the Kinsmen Club include a field house, an aquatic center, an arena, a pitch and putt golf course, playgrounds, a fitness trail, baseball diamonds, soccer and football fields, a wading pool, tennis and handball courts, toboggan runs, and a junior ski hill, plus hockey rinks and the associated service buildings, grandstands, and clubhouses. In the wilderness area, picnic sites and natural trails have been provided, while ensuring the preservation of trees and wildlife habitat.

As with all the river flats, archeological studies have uncovered both prehistoric artifacts and evidence of historic human activities. Much of the site was disturbed during the construction of the facilities, but the latest finds were uncovered during construction of the parking lot.

Bedard Tannery & Pollard Brothers Brickyard

Location: 108th Street & 92nd Avenue (approximately)
Date: *tannery*, 1895–1915; *brickyard*, 1898–1915
Route: Proceed west along the roadway toward the LRT
     bridge.

Firmin Bedard, who was born in Quebec in 1844, came to Edmonton via Minnesota about 1895 and tried to make a living washing gold from the river. Since gold panning was not a steady way to live or support a family Bedard purchased a 0.8-hectare site for his Strathcona Tannery from Laurent Garneau (river lot 7) in November 1895, and built a gigantic water pump (bucket and crane) operation that pulled water from the river. Later he replaced it with a proper well and pump. Bedard had seven children, one of whom, Annie, caught the eye of the Bedard's neighbor Frank Pollard. The tannery prepared hides and furs for its major market in British Columbia for twenty years before being put out of business by the 1915 flood. After that, Bedard moved to Prince Albert with his wife, Clarice Farland.

John Pollard (1875–1958) came to Edmonton in early 1898 from a farm in Iowa. He was headed for the gold rush, but was distracted by talk of good brick-making clay to be found on the river's south bank. Although not trained in brick making, Pollard staked his future on the business, purchased some land from Laurent Garneau, and started making bricks by hand-baking them in the sun. He invited his brother Frank to join him, and in the fall of 1898 they established the Pollard Brothers brickyard.

The Strathcona Tannery belonging to the Bedard family was one of the industrial enterprises which operated in the river valley.
CITY OF EDMONTON ARCHIVES EA10–1425

Pollard Brothers was not the first brick maker in Edmonton. William Humberstone had started making brick at Cloverdale in 1881 and was joined there by Anderson in 1901. Pete Sandison likewise was providing brick to north Edmonton in the 1890s from the Groat flats. James Little started at Riverdale in 1893 and bought out Sandison's equipment after his death in 1905. In a growing and prosperous community, there was always a demand for good brick.

The Pollards' first project was the construction of a two-storey brick house on the flats for Frank and his new wife Annie (nee Bedard) and their soon growing family. Next to the house, which was also used as the dining room for the yard's employees, they built the plant and constructed several linear kilns, the remains of which can be seen on the north side of the roadway, west of the High Level Bridge piers.

At the height of business the plant employed 50 men, most of whom were housed on the flats, and it had over 50 buildings, including married men's quarters, livestock sheds, business offices, kilns, and drying sheds. Pollard bricks were used for many of the buildings in Strathcona and the University of Alberta area, including Holy Trinity Church (which used clinker or burnt brick), Strathcona Baptist Church, and St. Anthony's Catholic Church.

The Pollards also found green clay along the riverbank, which was used by University of Alberta fine art students for modeling. With prosperity came the opportunity to invest in real estate—timber plots for wood to be used in the kilns, an acreage at Hay Lake, and various lots in Garneau. John shrewdly negotiated with the Canadian Pacific Railway for the land for the bridge supports, and in 1909 he bought new machinery for the plant from Minneapolis. John ran for alderman in 1912, but was defeated. The war in 1914 called Frank and many of the men away from the plant for four years. John looked after Frank's eight children plus five of his own.

The flood in 1915 was a disaster for the family and the business. Annie and the children had to be evacuated from second floor of the house in the flats in the middle of the night since they stayed too long, expecting that the river wouldn't overflow its banks. Luckily, John's house was in Garneau at the top of the riverbank. The flood ruined the machinery, which rusted during the war because of a lack of manpower and resources to restart the plant. John took up work as a fireman to support the two families until Frank returned. Frank, however, had been gassed during the war, and he arrived back in Edmonton in poor health, unable to work as before.

An attempt to restart the business in 1920 was doomed. Many of the Pollard's creditors were willing to wait for the company's recovery, but the city foreclosed on the land for back taxes. Frank died in 1926. John worked at a number of businesses, including the Pollard Garage on Calgary Trail and the Princess Theatre, and his wife Edith was a music teacher. One of their sons, John "Red" Pollard, was the jockey of the racehorse Sea Biscuit, whose story was made into a movie in 2003.

Remains of the Pollard brickyard can be seen along the running trails under and to the west of the two bridges, including cellar depressions, wells, chimneys, trash deposits, brick kilns, and borrow pits (from which the clay was dug). All the remains have been heavily damaged by erosion and possibly some vandalism.

Brick slag at bottom of bank

Remains of a bricked-in well, east of the LRT bridge. An access trail, past the bridges, leads east off to the right, down to another tableflat above the river.

Here, brick slag can be seen lying where it was dumped over the riverbank. The path is unpaved and caution should be used, especially if the ground is wet. The clay can be extremely slippery.

High Level Bridge

Location: 109th Street between the banks of the North Saskatchewan River

Architect: Phillip B. Motley, CPR engineer (Montreal); Donald Carter, Dominion Bridge Company

Date(s): 1910–13

Route: Travel west on the walking / bicycle trail to two bridges.

The High Level Bridge rises above the Dudley Menzies Bridge as seen from the stairs rising from the River Road beside the Royal Glenora Club.

Although the Calgary and Edmonton Railway and their corporate sponsors, the Canadian Pacific Railway, did not consider extending the railway across the North Saskatchewan River when they first arrived in 1891, by 1907 they had determined that Edmonton and northern Alberta were important enough markets that the railway had to go there.

By 1909, the CPR had begun to secure the land for a right-of-way through Strathcona and the river valley. The City of Edmonton was delighted and determined not to miss the opportunity of securing a way to improve transportation between the two cities. The best way to achieve that, the planners felt, was to ensure that pedestrians, horse-drawn wagons, streetcars, and maybe even those new-fangled contraptions, the automobiles, should be allowed to cross on the railway bridge.

After months of negotiations with the provincial government and the CPR, and after a plebiscite that passed handily in Edmonton but only reluctantly in Strathcona, the city obtained the CPR's consent to add a floor deck for traffic under the railway deck. The amalgamation of the two separate cities of Strathcona and Edmonton was made inevitable. The cities merged in 1912, and the avenues and streets were renamed (actually, renumbered) in 1914 to eliminate duplication and make directions easier.

The total cost of $2 million was divided between the provincial government, the Canadian Pacific Railway, and the City of Edmonton. Pedestrians and vehicle traffic were accommodated on a lower road and walkway, while the upper deck was reserved for railway and streetcar use. The mayor insisted that the roadway be wide enough to accommodate the passing of two fully loaded hayracks—a farsighted move that ensured adequate room for future traffic on the bridge.

The Dominion Bridge Company won the bid to build the bridge, the largest construction job in Edmonton to that date. Construction started from the south side, erecting 32 piers and pedestals, including the two massive ones in the middle of the stream and two large ones, one on either bank. Those four piers were 1.8 meters square at the base and rose 42 meters high. Close to 8,000 tonnes of steel girders were erected on top of those piers and pedestals, 13 meters wide and stretching 755 meters across the river.

A movable crane apparatus called a "traveler rig" was run out on rails at the edges of the bridge and would swing the next steel girders into place. Track was laid between the rails of the rig for regular train flatcars, which carried the girders and other supplies. As one section was finished, the traveler rig moved out to start construction on the next piece.

More than 300,000 meters of steel was used, along with 215,000 board meters of lumber, 1.4 million rivets, and 22,730 litres of paint, to prevent rust. The top of the railway deck lies over 60 meters above the low-water level, with the seven-meter-wide traffic deck about twelve meters below that. The railway tracks ran on the inside of the bridge, and the streetcar tracks were placed on either side, balancing on the outer edges of the top deck. The sidewalks for pedestrians were suspended from above and bolted laterally into the traffic deck. The work was extremely dangerous, and four construction workers lost their lives in accidents on the construction job. The High Level Bridge remains one of the city's most inspiring engineering feats.

At the opening ceremonies on June 2, 1913, the first train across consisted of seven cars of dignitaries, railway officials, representatives of the Canada Bridge Company, and special guests. They rode across, stopped on the Edmonton side, and then returned to Strathcona—because there was no more track. The first streetcar crossed in August, establishing the fifteen-minute service to Strathcona. By September, traffic was crossing on the lower deck with ease.

In 1995, the High Level Bridge was completely refurbished in the hopes that the Light Rail Transit (LRT) system could use the upper deck. But the bridge's steel was found to be too brittle to withstand the high-speed vibrations of the electric trains, and a new overpass, the Dudley Menzies Bridge, was constructed below and slightly to the west.

Construction of both the High Level and the Dudley Menzies bridges exposed large sections of the riverbank. Investigation will show well-defined layers of soil, silt, and ash. The layer of Mazama ash was the result of a volcanic eruption 6,800 years ago. The ash layer varies in thickness from place to place but is a distinctive gray colour that can be seen apart from the darker soils surrounding it. Mount Mazama exploded with ten times the magnitude of Mount St. Helen's in 1981. Because the ash spread throughout the North American northwest, it has become a valuable gauge for archeological dating: objects found below the ash are older than 6,800 years.

Dudley Menzies Bridge

Address: 108th Street just below the High Level Bridge
Date: 1990

The access ramp to the Dudley Menzies Bridge rises to the pedestrian walkway used by multitudes daily as they enjoy Edmonton's river valley.

Dudley Menzies was a city commissioner from 1945 to 1971. He was elected alderman in 1971 and served until 1974. At 82 years of age, in November 1990, he attended the opening of his $1 million namesake bridge.

The Dudley Menzies Bridge includes a bikeway/pedway which links the north and south trails. Construction began in 1988 using a technique that had not before been used in western Canada. The pedestrian portion is suspended from the LRT bridge, and cables anchored to the bank help support it. It is 3.2 meters wide and 282 meters long. Some people claim it swings in high winds or when there is a lot of traffic on it, but the city's engineering department and outside experts have declared the pedway safe.

Excavation up the southside riverbank for the access for the Dudley Menzies Bridge exposed a profile of the floodplain sediments on the south bank of the river. Both historic (industrial) and prehistoric archeological remains were unearthed.

Royal Glenora Club

Address: 11160 River Valley Road
Style: Moderne
Architect: Rule Wynn & Rule
Date: 1961
Route: Proceed farther westward to look for remains of the
Pollard brickyard, or cross the bridge and continue with
the tour on the north side of the river.

The boxy addition to the Royal Glenora Club hides the more traditional façade.

The land on which the Royal Glenora Club is situated originally contained a lumber and grist mill operated by the Hudson's Bay Company from 1830 to 1885. It was destroyed by fire, and the debris was buried by the flood of 1889. It is possible that an early brewery was established here after the fire—possibly one of John Walter's business ventures—and it may have lasted until the early 1900s. Some of the remaining buildings were used by the market gardeners, mostly Chinese, who worked the flats until at least the 1930s.

The Royal Glenora Club was formed in 1959 when three of the oldest recreational associations in Edmonton—the Braemar

Badminton Club, the Royal Curling Club, and the Glenora Skating and Tennis Club—amalgamated, merged memberships, sold off their individual properties, and built one facility. The new club of about 450 members negotiated a lease on a site of approximately three hectares in the river valley, and for about $2 million had contractor Stuart Olsen build a facility with curling and skating rinks, and badminton and tennis courts. The official opening was held in April 1961 with the Hon. A. R. Patrick, provincial minister for industry and development, officiating.

Five years later, the club had grown and thought to renovate and expand. First they sought a longer lease with the city, then they expanded the membership base to 5,600 to help fund the expansion. By 1973, the new facility had reached 11,706 square meters for sports and recreational activities. The interior was completely redecorated with thick rugs, paneled woodwork, Scandinavian modern furniture, and open fireplaces in the lounge areas and the new 200-seat dining room.

More importantly for a sports club, there were new immense spectator galleries and 650 square meters of squash and handball courts. The club was estimated to have $2.5 million in assets. The larger space allowed the club to sponsor larger tournaments and attract players of international renown. Coaching and competitions at the Royal Glenora Club became world famous as well as important to developing local talents and skills.

In order to keep at the top of their game, another $1.6-million expansion was undertaken in 1980–81, after negotiating another lease extension. This included the boxlike addition to the east. The club celebrated its 25th anniversary in 1986.

In 1990, the club converted the curling rinks into indoor tennis courts to make the Glenora the largest indoor tennis center in Edmonton. First they had to thaw 2.4 meters of frost that had accumulated in the ground during more than twenty years of curling rinks. Another $1.6-million renovation was completed in 2000 after the city granted the club a 40-year lease. This renovation included an energy efficiency upgrade.

Victoria Park

Location: River Road
Date(s): ca. 1911
Route: At this point you have the option of following the River Road westward to view the Victoria Park and Golf Course, and Government House Park, or returning eastward up the hill and stairs to the Legislature Building via the Ezio Farone Park.

Victoria Park includes a number of recreational facilities including playing fields and ice surfaces as well as the golf course.

Victoria Park was originally known as the Hudson's Bay Flats, since it was part of the land covered by the Hudson's Bay reserve, which stretched from the river's edge to approximately 111th Avenue and from 101st Street to 122nd Street. The flats were also used as a camping ground by First Nations people when they came to trade at old forts on lower level of the riverbank.

The city and the company representatives had discussed turning the area into a public park as early as 1907, and eventually negotiations were carried through to a happy conclusion for the city. The Hudson's Bay Company had golf links near its fort, and several people in the city were interested in maintaining them and even expanding the course into the flats.

Victoria Park, renamed in 1914 for the long-reigning queen, was considered a natural amphitheater, and it was used, for example, in 1927 for a fireworks display with people sitting from the bottom of the hill to the lawns of houses above, watching fireworks burst over the river. Recreational clubs used parts of the park at various times. There was a rifle range, horse stables, and a cricket pitch as well. Although the shooters and riders have had to find other locations, the cricketers still play in the park, now near the golf course clubhouse. The park also has a skating oval south of the fairways, which is very popular in the wintertime.

The Edmonton Yukon and Pacific Railway, which grew out of the Edmonton District Railway begun in 1896, ran halfway up the hill and along almost to Groat Ravine, emerging into the Groat Estates and continuing northward until it intersected with the Canadian Northern tracks at 106th Avenue. The cut through the bank can still be walked along in places above the park.

MacKenzie and Mann, railway investors in a number of western ventures, purchased the charter from the Edmonton businessmen who had first simply wanted to bring a railway across the river from Strathcona. They changed the name after the Yukon gold rush began, but they didn't get the railway into operation until 1902, too late for the prospectors.

From Strathcona, the tracks traveled down the Mill Creek ravine across the Low Level Bridge to the base of McDougall Hill. MacKenzie and Mann built a station house there and were stalled for a few years. Finally, they built track west past the Legislature. A spur line helped convey equipment and supplies to the site of the construction of the High Level Bridge from 1910 on, and gradually climbed the grade to 123rd Street. It crossed the road that Sandison built up to 121st Street for his brickyard, which many adventurous boys also used in the wintertime for a good fast tobogganing run.

In all, it was only 7.3 kilometers of track that was eventually bought out by the Canadian Northern Railway.

Victoria Golf Course
Address: River Road
Date: 1907

The Golf Course Club house sits next to a two tiered driving range.

The original Hudson's Bay Company five-hole golf links were laid on the present site of the Legislature Building. When construction on the Provincial Building was started, the links were moved to the Hudson's Bay Flats.

At first the city leased the land, but four years later bought it for over $300,000 in order to expand the golf course and, as an American landscape architect advised, to provide for a river valley park for the citizens. The Hudson's Bay Company put a condition on the sale that the land should remain parkland in perpetuity and the city had to maintain it properly.

Edmonton's golf links were officially opened in September 1906. The club had 107 male and 70 female members. To begin with, the course offered only nine holes, but plans were soon underway for another nine-hole extension. After the city bought the land and extended the lease to the club, discussions were held to encourage the club to be open to the public. Pressure from the citizens, who had heard that Calgary might be opening a city golf course, sped the process.

In the spring of 1914, Edmonton's parks and recreation department decided to take control of the flats and make the golf course a municipal responsibility, which made it the first municipally operated golf course in Canada. The Edmonton Golf Club donated its buildings and two tournament trophies.

Sandison's brickyard was originally built in 1902, near the site of Mayfair Golf Club on the south side of the river, but it was moved to the north side, east of the Groat Ravine access to the river, in 1905 when he expanded his plant. The seventh fairway has a depression that was once the clay pit. Sandison hauled bricks up the "Brickyard Road" he made near 121st Street, and it was also used in the 1920s by the market gardeners who worked the flats until the 1930s.

Sandison's yard was taken over by the Edmonton Brick Company (1905–14) after his premature death in an accident in 1905. Occasionally brick fragments emerge from the fairways from time to time. In 1922, the city purchased J. B. Little's (of the Edmonton Brick Company) portion of the Groat flats, which had been Sandison's brickyard, and expanded the golf course to fourteen holes in 1927 and eighteen holes in 1928. A further expansion in the 1950s made it a 27-hole course; however, those gains were lost once the construction began on the Groat Bridge and its access roads.

Government Hill Park & Groat Ravine

Location: Convergence of the River Valley trail system & the Groat Ravine, north of the North Saskatchewan River

Date(s): 1990

Government Hill Park has always been a good recreational area, but it was not officially declared a park until the river valley trail system was developed along River Road and the McKinnon ravine. It now boasts picnic sites, access to running and bicycle trails in the summer, and cross-country skiing trails and tobogganing runs in the winter. "Monkey trails" (narrow dirt tracks cut through the brush by agile and generally young hikers and bicycle riders) lead up the ravine onto the grounds of Government House and the Provincial Museum of Alberta, though they should be avoided on wet days.

The old climbing tree lies north of the parking lot.

At the turn of the century, when James Carruthers, the developer of Glenora, donated the Groat Ravine to the city for parkland, a network of promenades, boardwalks, and picnic sites were laid out along the base of the ravine. There were also horse trails that linked up to other ravines. The flats area in front of the ravines was extensively used until the 1930s for gardens, and evidence of several Chinese market gardens which supplied fresh produce to shops in Oliver and downtown can be seen in the number of perennials still growing along the sides of the valley.

Another interesting specimen is the large tree with a twisted trunk near the parking lot for the Government Hill Park. It is a laurel leaf willow, approximately 50 years old. Its trunk was probably twisted by generations of children climbing on it, or perhaps it was weakened by something else that thus created this wonderfully easy climbing tree.

Archeological sites have been excavated in the valleys where the small creek emerged from the ravine. River floods would have buried most of the artifacts. The terrace up to Government House has not been extensively studied, despite the presence of the Provincial Museum of Alberta staff on site, but it might be a camping and tool-making site.

The Groat Bridge opened in 1955, following the Cloverbar Bridge in 1952. The project became a battleground for roads versus parks people, since it removed a large and popular park from a fairly exclusive neighborhood. As a result, special care was taken during the construction as a sort of compromise. To limit destruction of foliage as much as possible, the sewer in the ravine was tunneled in from mineshaft-like holes dug every three blocks, then tunneled from the south and from the north to meet underground in the middle. The road through Groat Ravine was similarly constructed in a method meant to destroy as few trees as possible, taking many curves despite calls to straighten it and speed traffic.

On the south side, environmental impact was less than expected since the Mayfair area was a gravel pit at the time. The road from the south side down into the Mayfair gravel pit was simply extended to the river's edge. The area actually benefited, since the landscaping there created Emily Murphy Park, the Mayfield Golf Club and Mayfair Park (named for Edmonton's famous bush pilot Wilfred "Wop" May), now known as William Hawrelak Park (after the infamous mayor).

Ezio Farone Park

Location: 110th Street & 97th Avenue, via Fortway Drive or
   steps
Date(s): 1992
Route: Return to the Glenora Club, and climb Fortway
   Drive, which dates back to the 1870s. Either take the

stairs (halfway up the drive) to Ezio Farone Park, or continue up the drive to the Legislature grounds. On the stairs, stop to catch your breath at the level of the LRT tracks and you will be able to see the old railway bed of the Edmonton Yukon and Pacific Railway, which snaked along the side of the valley and came out before the Groat Ravine to head north to 106th Avenue.

This park provides a welcome green space to residents of nearby highrises.

Ezio Farone Park was named in memory of a ten-year member of the Edmonton Police Service who was shot and killed while on duty in 1990. He was 33 years old. The crime was truly a shock to the city and to the police force, since no officers in Edmonton had been killed on duty for over 70 years. Farone had stopped a car suspected of containing bank robbers.

The 1.7-hectare park also contains plaques honoring the two other officers of the Edmonton Police Service who were earlier killed in the line of duty. Constable Frank Beevers was killed in 1918 while apprehending a murder suspect, and Constable William Leslie Nixon was likewise killed in 1919.

The Edmonton police force raised $500,000 from its members and within the community to build and maintain the park, a fundraising process which took about two years. Part of the money raised was to commission a $65,000 work of art for the park. The 300-kilogram bronze sculpture of Constable Farone kneeling to assist a child was designed and sculpted by Danek Mozdzenski, a local artist who was also responsible for the Heritage Trail busts. The official opening of the park and unveiling of the sculpture took place in May 1992.

The park itself was the site of archeological excavations, and many historic trade materials have been excavated here. This was a good site for camping—well-drained and flat with a sunny southern exposure and a panoramic view of the river valley, unlike the southern side of river which has steep sides, a northern exposure, and limited drainage as well as being heavily treed. First Nations peoples came here for many years. The excavations for the Legislature Building parking lot unearthed bison bones over 10,000 years old.

As you return to the Legislature Building across 109th Street, notice to the north the Grandin LRT station. The riverbank rises in a series of terraced flats from the south to the north. The old fort location is below the terrace on which the Legislature sits. The station sits on the cusp of a higher terrace above the Legislature.

Route: Proceed into the Legislature grounds to complete the tour circuit.

Jasper East Block Tour

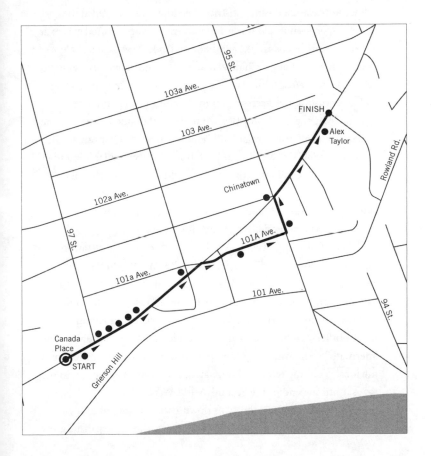

Between the Gibson Block and Canada Place, once the site of the Alberta Hotel, lies the oldest remnant of Edmonton's first commercial district. When the bulk of the Northwest Territories was transferred to central Canada's control in 1869, the Hudson's Bay Company had reserved a large portion of land for itself around its post as part of the agreement with the Dominion government.

Once individuals began to lay claim to land outside the fort for homesteading or commercial endeavors, they had to claim outside the area reserved by the Hudson's Bay Company. In Edmonton, the reserve ran from the river northward up the bank to the present-day 111th Avenue, from 101st Street on the east to 121st Street in the west. Edmonton's earliest business district, therefore, was centered at the corner of Jasper Avenue and down Namayo Avenue, or what today is 97th Street. The early 1900s saw the area boom as banks, livery stables, saloons, hotels, office buildings, Chinese restaurants, and laundries began to appear. Homes arose to the east of this area, as well as churches, schools, and other institutions necessary for the building of a community.

In 1912, the Hudson's Bay Company subdivided and sold the remainder of its substantial land holdings west of 101st Street. This flooded the market, which had been booming, with a large number of desirable lots and immediately lowered the price for all real estate in the city. Edmonton's original center of commerce gradually deteriorated as businesses moved westward, leaving behind what had started out as a potentially thriving city center.

The following years would see further devastation in Edmonton's commercial prospects with the First World War drawing away large numbers of working men and large amounts of capital. The concentration on the war effort reduced resources for building and caused the export of a great deal of produce and labour which would otherwise have been used to build up the community. The aftermath of the war was a long period of economic recession, and the local economy remained stagnated, with a short exception in the 1920s, until the end of the Second World War.

The eastern part of the city's downtown was caught in the inertia of the period. Even when Edmonton's economy began to grow again in the 1950s, spurred by oil discovery and technology improvements, the growth happened westward. The Jasper East Block remained stagnant and in some cases seriously deteriorated. Pre-1914 business block architecture predominated, and the area was not judged suitable for progressive business activities. For the cause of heritage preservation, this was a good thing; however, in more recent years business and building owners, for the most part, wished to change the outlook of the community.

Eventually, there was movement into the area bordering on 97th Street. First the Convention Centre and then Canada Place were built on sites of former landmark buildings, and the thought occurred to planners and heritage preservationists that decay might not be the only threat to the district. The Downtown Development Corporation devised a three-year project around 2000, dubbed the "Jasper East Village Project," in hopes of restoring the area by preserving the buildings in their original context and bringing the district back to some of its former glory.

Canada Place & the Alberta Hotel site

Address: 9700 Jasper Avenue
Style: (Alberta Hotel in photo) Queen Anne Style
Architect: James E. Wise
Date: 1902
Route: Start at Canada Place—it is a public building so it may be seen from the interior as well. There is a food court on the lower floor and a pedway crosses under Jasper Avenue to the Convention Centre.

The Alberta Hotel pictured here was actually the second hotel of that name built on the same site at 9732 Jasper Avenue. The original hotel was built in 1895, but by 1902 the owners thought a larger and more elegant hotel might compete more readily with the Strathcona Hotel and lure visitors into Edmonton. This building was built around its smaller predecessor in order not to lose too much business.

The Alberta Hotel was an Edmonton landmark and the destination of many famous and important city visitors.
CITY OF EDMONTON ARCHIVES EA 33-126

The hotel was a substantial building of red brick and Calgary sandstone. The circular tower overlooked the town's most prominent corner, and was topped with a conical roof and a patriotic flagpole. Full of modern conveniences, the hotel had its own electrical generator, a roof garden, and other amenities. When Sir Wilfrid Laurier came to declare Alberta as a province in 1905, the Alberta Hotel was the logical place for him to stay while celebrating.

In 1985, the federal government obtained this piece of land in a swap with the city to consolidate its offices in the downtown. This resulting sixteen-storey, pink-tinted building was completed in 1986 with 100-meter-high skylights, fountains, and glassed-in elevators overlooking the huge open atrium and lobby. The 72,000 square meters of space houses about 3,000 federal employees. The building has won several architectural awards.

Shaw Conference Centre

Address: 9797 Jasper Avenue
Style: Post Modern
Architect: unknown
Date: 1983
Route: Cross to the south side of Jasper Avenue. The Convention Centre can be best viewed from the east side—however you may want to enter the building and ride the escalators to the bottom before returning to Jasper Avenue and the tour.

Though you enter the Shaw Conference Centre on Jasper Avenue near 97th Street, the majority of the building is underground, or actually, down the hill. Edmonton Tourism occupies the top of the building, and the convention and conference rooms are located along a series of escalators which take you down closer to the river valley floor. Since the ceiling is glass, you can enjoy incredible views on the way down.

The center offers 13,935 square meters of meeting and exhibition space (though they are always looking to expand) on four levels. It is also the headquarters of the Culinary Team Canada, which has won three gold medals at the Culinary Olympics.

The Shaw Conference Centre marks the border between the old and new downtown areas and also integrates the top of the bank with the flats below.

The shape of the Conference Centre is reminiscent of the Edmonton Incline Railway, a hydraulic hoist erected in 1908 to convey coal and other goods up 61 meters to the top of the hill. The railway was actually located closer to the 101st Street and was only in operation about five years. Donald Ross, Alex Taylor, and other businessmen were partners in the endeavor, which was the idea of Joe Hostyn, who thought to save horses the steep climb up McDougall Hill and hoped that carters might give them a ride. Not many did, unless their horses were really tired or the road was excessively muddy. The charge was five cents a passenger and fifteen cents a wagon, round trip. Some people thought it was a good idea, though it never did make a fortune.

Unfortunately, as soon as the High Level Bridge crossed the North Saskatchewan in 1913 and brought the wagons across without the need to go down- or uphill, the Incline Railway was out of business. The machinery was dismantled and hauled away.

Goodridge Block

Address: 9696 Jasper Avenue
Style: Edwardian Commercial
Architect: Robert Percy Barnes
Date: 1912
Route: Proceed east along Jasper to the corner of 97th
    Street.

A simple utilitarian office and commercial building the Goodridge Block was a desirable address in Edmonton's early days.

Leonard Goodridge took over the title to the property from his mother and developed the building along with the Gem Theatre. He later sold the properties, but continued to manage and operate the Jasper House Hotel. Construction of the Goodridge Block began in 1911, with designs by London-born architect Robert Percy Barnes. The first commercial businesses in the Goodridge Block included a clothing store, a liquor store, a barbershop, and a poolroom. The upper floors were used as offices.

Next, the building was sold to Samuel Peter Wilson and his partner named Welsh. They started a dry goods and hardware store named for the partners, W. W. Sales. From 1930 to 1942, when Wilson retired, the store was a popular venue. The store's manager, Alex Ainslie, and his brothers then took over, renaming it W.W. Arcade, which became *the* place for hardware until 1991. The building was then made part of the Downtown Development plan and rejuvenated into the apartments and restaurant known as the Hardware Grill.

Until 2004, the City Market is found behind the Goodridge Block. This is not the first site of the market, which was very itinerant for many years. The city put the property on the market in 2003, looking for an interested developer and the market is looking for a new site. The market originally began in the heart of downtown, where the Stanley Milner Library stands today, it moved to its current location in 1965. In between, other locations have hosted the market, but mostly it has resisted moving away from the core. The "Rice Street Market" opened in December 1900, and for sixteen years operated outdoors. Market vendors sold poultry products, coal, firewood, and hay.

The market continued to prosper until 1964, when the city decided to close it. Public outcry prevented a closure, and the market moved to its current location on 101A Avenue. The market's commemorated its 100th anniversary in 2000, and Katherine Merritt wrote its history.

Jasper House Hotel / Hub Hotel

Address: 9692 Jasper Avenue
Style: Utilitarian
Architect: unknown
Date: 1882
Route: Proceed east to view the next building.

James Goodridge, the owner of the first three buildings east of 97th Street on the north side of Jasper Avenue, built the Jasper House Hotel in 1882. Although described in some literature as the city's first brick building, in reality the eastern part—which is the oldest—was merely the first building in Edmonton to be faced in brick. The western addition, put on in 1884, was solid brick. The building's early history suggests that it was a hangout for hunters and trappers—more a boarding house which also provided food than a hotel in the early days, although it did soon after feature a saloon.

The stagecoach stopped and started from this welcoming hotel.

In 1883, the Jasper House Hotel became the starting and stopping place for Ad McPherson's and Jim Coleman's bi-monthly stagecoach trip to Calgary. The stagecoach only traveled from Edmonton every two weeks because the trip to Calgary took five days in good weather, and longer in bad. The second week was used for the return trip, and the horses needed a day of rest in between. This uncovered stagecoach was more of a freight wagon; passengers went along for the ride. The fare was $25 one way, though you could take 100 pounds (about 45 kg.) of freight with you.

This building, the Hub Hotel, is an important city landmark as it was one of the first and longest-standing original hotels in Edmonton.

James Goodridge was born in Ontario in 1852. He came to Edmonton to join his brother Henry, who had come out in 1876, and worked at a nearby boarding house while he was constructing the Jasper House Hotel in 1882. When he added on in 1884, he was doing well enough to hire a mason to lay the brick. The one thing that made the Jasper House flourish was apparently the cooking, and the hotel early provided catering to major functions such as formal dinners like the one for Lieutenant Governor Dewdney in 1884.

After James died in 1900, his son Leonard took over most of his father's properties. The Jasper House was renovated in 1907 and in 1912. Its name was changed in 1920 to the Empress Hotel. After another major retrofit in 1940, the Empress became the Hub Hotel.

Gem Theatre

Address: 9682 Jasper Avenue
Style: Utilitarian
Architect: Magoon & MacDonald
Date: 1914
Route: Proceed east to view the next building.

This little Gem reflected the progress of the modern theatre in its heyday.

This was another of James Goodridge's properties, and it later passed on to his son Leonard. The Gem Theatre was one of Edmonton's earliest moving picture show houses. As one of Edmonton's smallest and cheapest movie theaters, it held only 490 seats. The Gem operated continuously for almost 50 years. The interior was originally decorated with lavish plaster relief in both the lobby and the theater. Two other theaters, the Dreamland and the Portola, were built nearby in 1912 and 1914 respectively, and the area soon became known as the city's first theater district.

After the Gem Theatre closed in the 1970s, it was converted into a rock club called the Gem Ballroom. Its life as a theater was not over, and in 1979 it changed owners once again. This time it was renovated and reopened as the Star Theatre.

It is hoped that the Star will benefit from the Downtown Development program and reemerge in a new incarnation soon.

Ernest Brown Block & Brighton Block

Address: 9670 Jasper Avenue
Style: Edwardian Commercial
Architect: James Henderson
Date: 1911–12
Route: Proceed east to view the next building.

The Ernest Brown Block was the headquarters for Ernest Brown's photographic studio, office, workshop, and retail store. The building was built in two parts as finances allowed, but it has architectural symmetry in the upper floors, although the street-level shop fronts have been divided and altered considerably. Initially a studio sat on the western part of the site, which belonged first to Bourne and May, and then to Charles Mather before passing to Ernest Brown. The eastern half was built in 1911 while Brown continued to work in the frame studio.

Once the first section was complete, Brown moved in while the old studio was torn down and the second part completed in 1912. The ground floor housed other businesses including a printing and stationery store and a men's clothing store. The second floor was the marble and oak studio, which was designed to capture as much natural light as possible to aid the exposure of the glass plate negatives Brown used in his work. His enlargement department and picture framing factory were located in the basement, while the upper floors were leased as offices and apartments.

This important building held a great deal of the city's history documented in photographs.

Brown was into a number of projects, but like many who had overextended themselves during the boom years up to 1913, the depression and the First World War caused him considerable financial worries. In 1924, Brown's creditors seized the property. Dominion Life Assurance and then Credit Foncier owned the building until 1950, when Harry Zurin purchased it. At some point its name was changed to the Brighton Block. It underwent renovations as part of the Downtown Development Corporation's renewal plan. It remains one of Edmonton's few illustrious pre–World War I commercial buildings.

Ernest Brown was born in Newcastle, England, and apprenticed as a photographer. He learned to paint portraits in oils (including anatomy) and the required chemistry for developing negatives. He immigrated to Toronto in 1902, then came to Edmonton to work with photographer Charles Mather, who was to travel in the north for a year. He brought his wife and family to Edmonton in 1903. He worked as Mather's assistant from 1904 and purchased his collection of negatives documenting the growth of the Canadian northwest. He took on many community projects, including organizing the first fundraising "tag-day" for the local hospital in 1906.

When his creditors seized his building and assets in 1924, they evicted him and his 50,000 negatives. Brown went to Vegreville to run another studio, but also became involved in pro-labour advocacy for the unemployed. He published a "radical" newspaper called "the Glowworm–a little light in the dark" and organized a hunger march to lobby Mayor Blatchford to start a relief kitchen.

Back in Edmonton in 1929 to help a photographer friend, Gladys Reeves, with her studio, in 1933 Brown opened the first historical museum here. "The Birth of Canada's West Exhibit" ran until 1939. His collection, grown to 150,000 negatives, was sold to the province in 1947 and housed in the Provincial Archives. He was in the midst of writing a history of the West when he died in 1951.

Pendennis Hotel / Lodge Hotel
Address: 9660 Jasper Avenue
Style: Utilitarian
Architect: Unknown
Date: 1904
Route: Proceed east to view the next building.
The Pendennis Hotel opened in the summer of 1904. It was a frame building which was originally a boarding house. The front and sides were faced with pressed metal with a false stone finish. The hotel had bedrooms on the second and third floors, and was equipped with a parlor, bar, office, and large and small dining rooms. It was well known for its excellent cuisine.

The designer wanted to link this building to its neighbor, an important feature in establishing a context for a community or commercial district.

Nathan Bell, who also ran a hotel in Dawson City, purchased the Pendennis in 1905. He added a new wing in 1912, adding fifteen rooms to the 44-room hotel. The dining room increased to hold seating for 48. Like many neighboring businesses, the Pendennis was a profitable venture until the economic recession after World War I. Its business was destroyed during Prohibition. Both factors eventually led to its foreclosure.

In 1945, it was converted into a rooming house with a new name: the Kenmo Lodge. Later the name was shortened to the Lodge Hotel. Along with its neighbor the Brown/Brighton Block, it received a façade restoration in 2001, including the cornice on the front.

Gibson Block or the Flatiron Building

Address: 9608 Jasper Avenue
Style: Flatiron
Architect: A. W. Cowley
Date: 1914

Route: Proceed east to 96th Street to view the next building. Check with the Church Street tour for information
on the St. Barbara's Church and the Chinese United
Church along 96th Street.

*Always a landmark because of its unique shape, the Flatiron building has
become the centre for many lives in the inner city.*

Designed for William Gibson, a land speculator from Ontario, the
flatiron building was destined to become a landmark. Gibson, who
also invested in the Highlands and other Magrath and Holgate holdings and a farm in the Cloverbar area, purchased two lots along
Jasper Avenue for one dollar in 1913. The lots were so cheap because
they formed a hard to sell pie shape lot due to the intersection of two
roads. Gibson and the architect, A. W. Cowley, were probably familiar with the flatiron style of building which was becoming popular in
large cities throughout North America, where rising property values
made even odd-shaped lots valuable.

Gibson intended this to be an office building to take advantage
of the booming economy and its central location within the business

district of Edmonton. He actually started with a three-storey plan, but workers on site were instructed to add another floor as they went along. The completed building cost about $40,000.

However, by the end of 1913, the economy in Edmonton had faltered, and it was soon deemed appropriate to convert the offices to apartments—except for the main floor, which retained its commercial orientation. The main-floor tenants in 1913 were a hardware store, a café, and a jewelry store, with Turkish baths in the basement. (The baths were popular with people of eastern European origin.) The baths remained in continuous operation from 1914 to the mid-1980s.

The upper floors originally housed offices belonging to a doctor, a musician, an electrical contractor, and a teacher. These offices eventually became apartments. Unfortunately, there were only two bathrooms per floor, which made for interesting arrangements in the mornings. A year after it was built, Gibson sold his flatiron building for three times its construction cost. The new owners were Germans involved in investing for foreign clients and immigration schemes. They moved in and tried changing the name to the Schubert and Wenzel Block for a time, but that name never stuck. The building continued to be called the Gibson Block.

Interesting architectural features include the heavy cornice below the roof line, the around-the-corner display window, the use of special "prism glass" bricks in a frieze above the windows, and the wooden doors in recesses topped with an arched fanlight. Those in turn are topped by wooden reproductions of keystones.

By the mid-1980s, an out-of-town company had purchased the building, which was seriously deteriorated. Because of its unique shape and prominent location, public support for its rehabilitation was high. The mayor, Jan Reimer, got involved to solve the Gibson Block problem, and in 1994, after a $3-million restoration project undertaken by the Edmonton City Centre Church Corporation (a nonprofit social service agency) with the assistance of architect Barry Johns and all levels of government, the building was reopened as the Women's Emergency Accommodation Centre and designated as a municipal and provincial historical resource in 1993.

Fort Garry–Fort Edmonton Trail & Petro-Canada Park

Address: 95th Street & Jasper Avenue

Date: 2000

Route: Proceed east to the triangular piece of parkland at 95th Street called the Petro Canada Park.

This little park is a welcome bit of green and a reminder of the downtown's historic legacy.

The Fort Garry–Fort Edmonton Trail was one of the names used to identify the primary land transportation route from Winnipeg through the prairies to Edmonton. Other names included the Carleton Trail, the Victoria Trail, and the Saskatchewan Trail, depending on the traveler's point of origin and chosen destination.

Stretching 1,400 kilometers, the trail became a vital link between the east and west, and served as the testing ground for many a missionary, policeman, and settler.

During the 1840s, the trail was used by Métis freighters hauling loads in Red River carts. One driver could control four or five carts. The oxen of the following carts were attached to the back corner of the cart in front, allowing the carts to spread fan-shaped across the prairie. In wet weather the wooden wheels of the carts dug deep ruts, five and six across the trail as the left wheel of the second and subsequent carts rode in the right track of the cart ahead. Evidence of those ruts can still be seen across farmers' fields in some parts of northern Saskatchewan.

Explorers, missionaries, and surveyors looking for routes for trade, railways, and new converts would follow in the ruts made by those carts. Later, in 1874, the North-West Mounted Police would use various parts of the trail to reach outposts in Saskatchewan and northern Alberta. Eventually homesteaders and settlers would embark over the trail with all their worldly possessions. Many would mire in sloughs and gullies along the way, some would turn back, but most would soldier on and make the West their new home.

Before the advent of the railways out to the West in the 1890s, and even afterward for those who could not afford the freight or fare of the trains or river steamers, the trail was the best way to reach Edmonton. Innovators such as Frank Oliver, newspaper publisher, and Edward Looby, blacksmith, pulled the equipment needed for their trades over the prairies in carts along the Fort Garry–Fort Edmonton Trail.

The trail passed this way along the north side of the river and headed down the slope to reach the early site of Fort Edmonton in the Rossdale flats. Later, when the fort moved up to the tableland above, the trail was altered to follow the riverbank, although the downhill section continued to provide access to the ford, and later, to Walter's ferry, across the river.

The Petro-Canada Park and the plaque from the Historic Sites and Monuments Board of Canada were unveiled in 2000 to commemorate this longstanding embodiment of the history of the

Canadian West. The land, formerly the site of a gas station, was donated by Petro-Canada.

From here you have a view of Riverdale, formerly known as the Fraser flats for the owner of the lumber mill built there. Little's brick-yard was also here, now the site of a large housing development. On the other side of the river is Cloverdale, or Gallagher's flats. During 1897 and 1898, prospectors on their way to the Klondike set up tents on these flatlands. Now you can see the pyramids of the Muttart Conservatory and, on the hill beside Connor's Road, the silhouette of the dove of peace erected in 1989 in honor of the papal visit to this city.

North-West Mounted Police Barracks

Address: 9530–101A Avenue
Style: Fortress
Architect: Roland Lines
Date: 1912–13
Route: Follow 101A Avenue eastward to view the barracks.

Best seen from the north side the various additions to the RCMP headquarters show the growth of the force's influence in the city.

In 1909, after 22 years in Fort Saskatchewan, the Mounted Police relocated to Edmonton. This barracks was constructed three to four years later at a cost of $70,000; it contained a jail with cells for both male and female prisoners. There were also living quarters for single men, and recreational rooms. Married officers lived on the grounds in row houses, which have since been demolished.

This barracks housed the headquarters of the "G" division. Over the years there have been many additions and renovations done to the building, some of which can be seen because of the various colors of materials used.

The style is traditional English fortified architecture with battlements and square turrets, which were popular in military buildings across Canada. The barracks represented the physical presence of the Mounted Police in Edmonton, and their building emphasized the strength and security they brought to the community.

Hecla Block

Address: 10141–95th Street
Style: Edwardian Classical
Architect: Hardie & Maitland
Date: 1914
Route: Follow east along 101A Avenue to view the next building.
This building was constructed by an Icelandic settler, John Johnson, who arrived in Canada from Iceland in 1876 to escape from political and environmental threats (there were lots of volcanic eruptions). Hecla is the name of an Icelandic volcano.

Distinguishing features include the keystones and simulated arches over the windows, the curved entrance canopy, the pressed metal cornice, and the stone trim defining the corners and the upper-storey courses.

Despite being in a difficult neighborhood and having been all but destroyed in a 1994 fire, the Hecla Block has been rehabilitated and its façade restored. Architect David Murray created fourteen new suites for homes and/or offices.

The Hecla block points to the successes discovered in their new land by many of Edmonton's immigrant population.

The oldest Jewish synagogue, Beth Israel, was built on the northwest corner of 101th Avenue and 95th Street in 1912. Then, Edmonton's small Jewish community was centered around this area and headed by Abe Cristall, the first Jewish immigrant to settle in Edmonton. The congregation worshiped here until 1953, when the community and the synagogue moved farther west to 119th Street and 102nd Avenue.

Edmonton Auto Spring Works
Address: 9502–102nd Avenue
Style: Utilitarian
Architect: Unknown
Date: 1923
Route: Go north on 95th Avenue to Jasper Avenue to view the Edmonton Auto Spring Works.

The McCoy family started in Edmonton in 1914 when H. D. McCoy opened a horseshoeing establishment on Jasper Avenue and 104th

Street. Like many blacksmiths he found himself in the position of having to make a change as the new mode of transportation, the horseless carriage, arrived in Edmonton in increasing numbers. Soon after the end of World War I, businesses and then private individuals switched from horses to cars.

This building seems a bit old fashioned, however, it continues to carry out its business as it reminds us from whence it came.

Sensing the need to service the new vehicles, the McCoys opened the Edmonton Auto Spring Works in 1923, specializing in repairing the metallic parts of cars, especially the springs.

The "boom town" front on this low-slung building gives it a more commanding presence on the street and harkens back to earlier frontier buildings like livery stables and blacksmith shops. The building form is moderne in style, long and low, and covered in stucco, which helps to give a streamlined appearance.

Alex Taylor School

Address: 9321 Jasper Avenue
Style: Greek classical revival
Architect: Roland Lines
Date: 1907
Route: Proceed east along Jasper Avenue past the Chinese and Vietnamese restaurants to the School on 93rd Street.

Always a community centre, this old school continues to serve the community in new ways.

Before being decommissioned in 1999, Alex Taylor School was Edmonton's longest-serving school. Built in 1907, it was one of several schools erected in that year to help educate the children of Edmonton's growing population. Initially three storeys high with eight rooms, this school was built of red brick with sandstone trim. Classical details include the geometric arch over the doorway, the serpentine roofline on the side gables, and the brick pilasters at the corners with pointed arches on top.

It was named for Alexander Taylor, pioneer telegraph operator, school board chairman, and businessman. Taylor was one of the longest-serving school board trustees, and the naming was a well-deserved honor.

The history of the Alex Taylor Elementary School paralleled that of the inner-city neighborhood in which it was built. As new immigrants moved to the city, usually starting in the Boyle-McCauley neighborhood, the ethnic makeup of the students and the languages spoken in the school changed. The first immigrants were eastern and northern Europeans, followed by Asians and Mediterranean Europeans.

Although threatened with closure in the 1970s, a new multicultural program fostered by principal Steve Ramsanker revived the school and made it a community center. The cement-block gymnasium was added in 1973 as student numbers increased and the assembly room / gymnasium on the top storey proved inadequate for their needs.

By the late 1990s, however, the school was failing structurally and the Edmonton Public School Board opted to decommission it and sell it. The Edmonton City Centre Church Corporation purchased it with assistance from a private foundation.

Now the building has a new life as a community center. It houses the offices of the Edmonton City Centre Church Corporation, which runs many social services programs including the nutritious snack and hot lunch programs in schools, the Kids in the Hall Bistro, Crossroads, and Women's Emergency Accommodation Program. Other partner organizations, such as Big Brothers and Big Sisters of Edmonton and Area, the Alberta Council of Women's Shelters, and the Success by Six program, share space in the old schoolhouse.

Chinatown

Address: 102nd Avenue to Jasper Avenue between 95th Street and 97th Street

Date: pre–World War I

Route: Return west along Jasper Avenue—the new, replacement Chinatown runs north from Jasper Avenue.

Be sure to ensure good luck by placing a ball in the lion's mouth.

Edmonton has at least three Chinatowns, but the one bordered by the Harbin Gate is a replacement to the original concentration of residences and businesses established by the first, primarily male, Chinese immigrants who came following railroad construction during the 1890s in the southern part of the province. Restricted from bringing in family members by immigration legislation in 1923, the Chinese population in Edmonton grew extremely slowly until the 1950s.

Gradually clan and benevolent organizations were formed, and as the Chinese entrepreneurs prospered they moved northwestward, establishing other congregations of population and retail establishments there.

Downtown development in the 1970s jeopardized the continuance of Chinatown in its original location. Working with city planners, the community affected a move to this location. As part of the relocation, a ceremonial entryway was built by Edmonton's sister city in Asia: Harbin. Edmonton was twinned with Harbin, a major rail center in the northern Chinese province of Manchuria, which harbored White Russians after the Russian Revolution in 1917–21. Some of those refugees had come to Canada after World War II.

Harbin has an Edmonton Road leading to its main airport. Edmonton's Chinatown gate was constructed in Harbin, taken apart, and shipped here in 1987 to be reassembled by a team of carpenters and craftsmen from Harbin. It is said to be good luck to roll a ball into the lion's mouth.

The Chinatown that remains in this area consists of mostly elderly people and new immigrants. The formal institutions which serve them, seniors' residences and societies, retain facilities in this area, and some commercial and retail spaces continue to operate here. Other developments have included a newer "China town" or little Vietnam to the north along 97th Street. Recently a Chinese market was established at the West Edmonton Mall.

French Heritage Tour

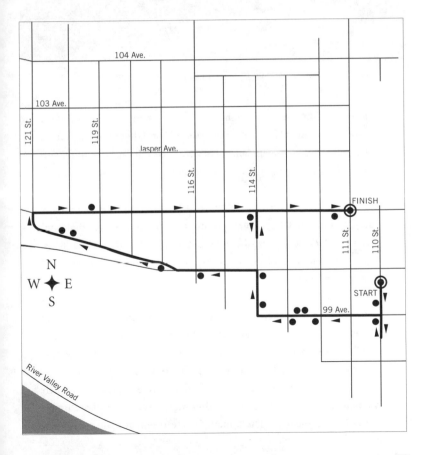

The Victoria Promenade through West Oliver combines modern art with heritage interpretation.

From Edmonton's beginnings as a western fur trade outpost, one of the common languages in and around Fort Edmonton was French. Other predominant languages were Cree and Gaelic, with English spoken by a small minority among the more educated officers. Many of the workers, traders, and trappers were Métis or of Scottish origin.

With the merger of the Montreal-based North West Company and the Hudson's Bay Company, even more French-Canadian and Métis traders came into the area. Between 1885 and the late 1890s, French-Canadian and French Métis people formed the majority of Edmonton's population.

When settlement began to expand beyond the walls of Fort Edmonton, the French were able to take up land along with the British settlers. The original organization of the land claims followed the French-Canadian river-lot system—long strips of land perpendicular to the river's edge—rather than the American grid system.

The other determining factor in the role played by French Canadians in the early history of Edmonton was the arrival of Roman Catholic missionaries. These men, Oblate priests for the most part, were welcomed by the fort's officers and men not only for the spiritual services they provided, but also because of their influence with the First Nations people. Certain priests, like Father Lacombe, Father Legal (later bishop), and Father Grandin (also a bishop), achieved legendary status for their ability to find peaceful and productive solutions to conflicts which arose between the two communities. The Oblates were instrumental in bringing health care and education to the area through their contacts with the Grey Nuns and other French Catholic orders of sisters who established hospitals, maternity homes, and schools in Edmonton and surrounding areas.

Within their parameters as spiritual leaders, the priests also managed to encourage further immigration of French Canadians into the province, to support the preservation of the French language and culture, and to settle large groups of Métis people into productive communities surrounding Edmonton. Fathers Lacombe and Morin started French immigrant groups at St. Paul, Fahler, Lac La Biche, and Bonneville. Between 1891 and 1899, the church attracted approximately 2,500 settlers from Quebec and France to bolster the francophone population in Alberta.

The arrival of the railway in 1891 brought other settlers into the community, and it began to reduce the French influence. Many immigrants from Ontario had grown up during the conflicts over language rights that arose from the aftermath of Confederation. Issues raised by the creation of Manitoba, and the land and language rights of the Métis there, influenced those who were beginning to think of establishing self-government in the western territories. While the French community still remained an important group in the city until the 1920s, their culture and language were often under pressure.

The French community in Edmonton had their own newspaper, *Le Courier de L'Ouest,* and followed their own calendar of religious and cultural holidays. The francophones were mostly congregated in the area around their institutions, the General and Misericordia hospitals, the parish of St. Joachim's, the Oblates headquarters, and the Grandin School, all in the community west of 109th Street between the river and 104th Avenue.

Over the years the French community objected to anglophone attempts to restrict the French language in hospitals, schools, and public institutions. Although many members of Edmonton's French community held elected office on city council and school boards as well as on boards of the business community before World War I, after the war they found their position in Edmonton society had slipped. By 1916, Edmonton's population numbered about 500,000 people, but only 25,000 were French.

St. Joachim's Roman Catholic Church

Address: 9920–110th Street
Style: French Gothic revival
Architect: Franz Deggendorfer
Date: 1899

The earliest Catholic missionaries came to Fort Edmonton in 1838, and they continued to visit from St. Albert and Lac Ste. Anne, where they had their missions, until 1859. The first Roman Catholic presence was established in Fort Edmonton in 1854, when a small chapel called St. Joachim's, after the father of the Virgin Mary, was built at factor J. W. Christie's request. They had their own resident priest in 1959.

By 1876, the situation had changed somewhat. Richard Hardisty, a Methodist married to a daughter of rival missionary George McDougall, requested that the Oblates leave the fort. Malcolm Groat, who had already claimed land outside to the west of the post's reserve and was married to Christie's daughter Margaret, donated about 3.5 hectares to the Catholics, and they rebuilt a smaller St. Joachim's there.

The church was served by priests from St. Albert until 1883, when first Father Scollen and then Fathers Henri Grandin and Lisee came to take charge. The threat of the Riel Rebellion in 1885 convinced the bishop, Vital Grandin, that the church should be closer to the community around the fort. He purchased lots around 110th Street, close to the river, and had St. Joachim's rebuilt in 1886. The lumber from the dismantled church was used to build a convent for

Many typical gothic features, from spires to front door arches, adorn this historic French Catholic church.

the Faithful Companions of Jesus who came to start a school in 1888 when the Catholic school board was formed.

Father Grandin left the parish in 1889 and was replaced temporarily by Valentine Vegreville, and then in 1890 by Father Leon Fourquet. The parish grew rapidly, and the bishop acknowledged its importance in 1894 when he appointed Father Lacombe and later added Alphonse Lemarchand to assist him. They built a presbytery (house for the priests) and planned a larger church. After only two years of soliciting monies from the parish, they were able to begin construction in 1898.

The fourth St. Joachim's was framed in wood and faced in red brick. It cost approximately $16,000. The church held 400 seats and was designed in typical French-Canadian architectural style with three towers and prominent arches over the doors and windows. It has a galvanized steel roof. The interior had considerable carved wood, and marble and plaster altars.

The parish grew over the years and was divided on several occasions to form new churches. St. Anthony's and the francophone parish of Immaculate Conception were created in 1901; St. Joseph's parish (which was created in embryo form in 1913) emerged in 1925. St. Joachim's became a purely francophone parish. In 1952, Ste. Anne's formed in the West End of the city.

The building was altered in 1912 when the old sacristy was demolished and a new vestry with confessionals and a basement was added to the west side. Further alterations were completed in 1923, finishing the walls in cedar to match the earlier finish in the nave, and in 1938, enlarging the basement for a hall. Anticipating further expansions, the church purchased more lots to the west and north in 1955.

The parish celebrated its 100th anniversary in 1959. In 1978, the building was designated a provincial historical resource. A new rectory was built to the north side in 1980.

Oblate Provincial House

Address: 9916–110th Street
Style: Unknown
Architect: Unknown
Date: 1935
Route: Continue southward to the next building.

This building has a variety of understated classical detailing from the dentils on the cornice to the rounded arched windows and the main floor course in contrasting stone.

This building replaced an earlier rectory for the Oblates stationed in Edmonton that had been expanded to provide space for the education of students training for the priesthood. When that function was transferred to Saskatchewan, the land was sold to the archdiocese. The archdiocese in turn gave this land to the order on the condition that they also house the clergy from St. Joachim's. Since the Oblates were instrumental in establishing the parish, this was probably no hardship.

Although the land was given to the Oblates in 1927, the house was not built until 1935. It is a three-storey, simple, classically influenced brick building with little decoration. There is a cupola on the roof, octagonal in shape. The doorway is topped with a pedimented arch, and the lower floor windows are arched with accented keystones. The cornice is nicely detailed, and a stone band delineates the first floor from the second.

This is the last remaining building of a once considerable block of Catholic institutions, including the rectory and convent of the Faithful Companions of Jesus, a teaching order of nuns who came to Edmonton in 1888. There was also a Jesuit seminary behind the church and a rectory to the north. Most of those buildings were demolished in the 1970s.

Grandin School
Address: 9844–110th Street
Style: Classical Revival
Architect: unknown
Date: 1915
Route: Continue south on 110th Street.

Grandin School is housed in an elegant and tastefully decorated brick building.

The first French Catholic school was located in the convent of the Faithful Companions of Jesus when it was completed in 1888. To begin with, two nuns taught approximately 60 students, but the community and the demand grew rapidly. Bishop Vital Grandin donated six lots to the Catholic School Board (Separate School District #7 St Joachim's—previously students had been educated within the public school district), and another five lots were purchased in 1914.

The three-storey schoolhouse was completed within a year, and it opened for a September school start. The sisters taught elementary and junior high students in both French and English. The old convent school next door was used for the junior high classes.

The style is eclectic, part renaissance revival and part classical Greek, although the appearance is symmetrical and simple. The building is solid brick. There is an arched entrance topped with a balcony. Stone contrasts the red brick for lintels and sills around the windows, and provides a continuous band above the basement and the upper-storey windows. Raised brick is used for decorative detailing between storeys and in pilasters beside the entry. Modern innovations like pipes in the walls to carry messages in sealed vacuum tubes were incorporated to enhance communications between the administration and teachers. Originally the school had ten classrooms, each with their own cloakroom. There were separate boys' and girls' entrances at the front and back.

By the 1920s, the school was overflowing, and portable classrooms, dubbed "chicken coops," were built in back. A gymnasium and assembly hall were added in 1953 and twelve more classrooms in 1962, when an increase in provincial grants was given to separate schools. By 1967, the nuns were unable to continue to provide teachers and the board replaced them with lay teachers.

Note: Between 98th and 99th avenues on 111th Street was the former location of the Misericordia Hospital. After the hospital moved to its west-end location in 1969, the remaining buildings were torn down in 1972. The Sisters of the Misericorde came to Edmonton in 1900 to start a home for the unfortunate and orphans, and a maternity hospital. This was to supplement the work of the Grey Nuns who operated the General Hospital on 111th Street at Jasper Avenue.

The Mountafield

Address: 9850–112th Street
Style: French Empire Revival
Architect: V. E. Wize
Date: 1905
Route: Continue west on 99th Avenue.

Many of the residences built in Oliver echoed the French traditions of the neighborhood, despite the Anglo origins of the owners.

Although the neighborhood had definite French roots, it soon became a popular location for the established members of Edmonton society of whichever origin.

This house was one of the earliest built in the neighborhood, and it has definite French-Canadian style. It was built, however, for an Englishman named Henry Mountafield. He was an educated gentleman with a decided wanderlust which took him from London to Japan in the 1880s, and then turned into gold lust in 1897 when he came to Canada and headed for the Yukon. After five years there, Mountafield ventured into more traditional occupations in Edmonton, serving as the city auditor in 1905. He also invested in real estate and was soon able to afford this lovely mansion.

Mountafield enlisted and served with the 19th Alberta Dragoons during World War I, but returned to Edmonton to live out his life until 1938. He married and had nine children. The Mountafields were supporters of cricket in Edmonton and occasionally distinguished themselves in the game.

Distinctive features of the house include the mansard roof and the pedimented gable containing the fanlight window on the second storey. The porch is supported by four spindle columns. The decorative woodwork on the gable is elaborate.

Duplexes

Address: 99th Avenue between 112th to 113th streets
Style: frame construction
Architect: unknown
Date: ca. 1907
Route: Continue west along 99th Avenue—viewing the duplexes on the north side of the street.

Several semidetached houses were built along the north side of 99th Avenue in this period, when Edmonton's population soared after the turn of the century and before the First World War. These two-storey brick houses feature mirror-imaged bow windows rising to pedimented gables with fanlights and porches before the parallel entrances, topped by second-storey balconies. Probably built by the same builder using variations on a single plan, they were suitable housing for young professionals or civil servants at the time.

Less-distinguished row-housing was built for the working class farther north in the Oliver community. These, however, represent an earlier period and style of building.

The rapid growth of the community, and the sometimes more humble circumstances of the inhabitants meant that sharing a structure was more viable than building a single family dwelling.

The Kirkhaven

Address: 11229–99th Avenue
Style: Edwardian
Architect: Unknown
Date: 1907
Route: Continue westward on 99th Avenue turning to view the south side residences.

This was one of the earliest buildings in the neighborhood, and it contains typical features of the most popular style of the day. The wood frame structure was sided with clapboard, and the windows bore shutters. Gables in the roof brought light to the upper floor of the two-storey building.

Originally this house closely resembled its neighbor, and several other houses in the neighborhood, but the building was altered considerably in the 1940s when it was converted into suites. Such conversions were common during the years of the Second World War when incursions of Americans building the Alcan projects (which included the Alaska Highway, the Northwest Stage Route and the pipeline) and working in aviation came to the city.

Large houses were sometimes converted to serve the housing needs of independent single residents.

Severe housing shortages resulted, and the governments encouraged property owners to take in boarders or remodel their houses into apartments. The housing crunch continued into the 1950s as soldiers returned after the war and families started growing again. The trend was to leave the older neighborhoods to singles.

Grace Lutheran Church
Address: 9907–114th Street
Style: Prairie Church
Architect: Rule Wynn & Rule
Date: 1955
Route: Continue westward on 99th Avenue.

This simple and unadorned church fits in well with the quiet neighborhood.

The congregation of this Lutheran church started about 1923 or 1924 when professors at the Lutheran seminary questioned whether there was a need for an English-speaking church. Most Lutherans practiced in their native language, either German, Swedish, Norwegian, or Danish. A canvas of the Norwood area, where a majority of Lutherans lived, found that a possible 860 families might be better served in an English-language church. They started in a building on 93rd Street and 115th Avenue, then the congregation rented the Moravian church in Norwood.

After being offered the chapel at Howard and McBride's funeral home in 1929, they moved there until 1937. By then the congregation had grown sufficiently to consider building their own facility. The church purchased property at 107th Street and 100th Avenue, which had a house on it that could serve as a hall and parsonage. The congregation worshipped in the hall until 1950, when their growth again started them off on a search for new property.

This site, a double lot with a house, was located in 1954 and purchased for $27,300. The old church property was sold to Dominion Motors for $55,000. One of the parishioners tore down the house on this site and reused the lumber for his own home. Here, a new church and parsonage were built for $100,000 in 1955, but the city refused to allow the church to use it until a basement was added. That cost an extra $18,500 and delayed the opening by a year while the funds were found and the basement completed.

In 1963, the church purchased the neighboring lot and replaced the parsonage with a hall and education wing, which was completed in 1967.

Westminster Apartments

Address: 9955–114th Street
Style: Classical Revival
Architect: unknown
Date: 1912
Route: Continue north along 114th Street towards 100th
Avenue.

The Westminster Apartments has several classical features and is also rumoured to have a resident ghost.

Built by real-estate speculators from eastern Canada, the Westminster Apartments were a response to the high demand for housing in the city before World War I. The developer, Western Canada Properties, spent $65,000 to construct the three-storey brick apartment house with 24 suites of various sizes.

The variety enticed a varied class of tenants, mostly white-collar workers who wanted an easy commute to the offices and colleges nearby in downtown Edmonton. The one- and two-bedroom suites ranged from 56 to 112 square meters, with or without a formal dining room. The interior was furnished in hardwood, decorated with molded ceilings, and had dumbwaiters and a freight elevator to help with carrying heavy goods to the upper floors. Recently, the apartments has attracted young professionals and students. The switch to condominium ownership was begun in 2003.

Two different grades of brick were used in the original construction, the finer on the façade and utility brick at the rear. Decorative patterns in glazed tile on the façade add details around the door and corners. Bands of stone divide the second storey from the first, and corbelled bricks support the metal cornice. A Tudor-style arched transom over the entry and double oak doors gives a solid and secure aspect to the entrance.

Lemarchand Mansion

Address: 11523–100th Avenue
Style: Beaux-Arts
Architect: Alfred Marigon Calderon
Date: 1911
Route: Turn west along 100th Avenue towards 116th Street.

With ambitions to create the most luxurious apartment building in Canada, Rene Lemarchand contracted with architect A. M. Calderon to design this magnificent building. Using the finest quality materials, it took two years to build and cost approximately $150,000, though it could have been more.

The Lemarchand is the neighborhood's landmark and strongest expression of its French heritage and image.

An H-shaped configuration ensures that all suites have an exterior window. The four-storey building has a lower floor of imitation stone, made from cement, above which three brick floors are constructed. The decorative elements of the Beaux Arts style include the classical columns supporting the pediment over the entrance. The thick overhanging cornice is supported by brackets and is dentilled (has toothlike cutouts). Bands of contrasting stone emphasize the protruding portico around the entrance, and the windows of the upper storeys have elaborate voussoirs with contrasting keystones. The wrought-iron balconets add a light and decorative touch.

Knowing the city fathers were suspicious of apartment developments—in case they became like boarding houses—Lemarchand wanted a distinctive and high quality building to attract elite tenants and thus he offered elegant features such as fireplaces, stained glass, marble flooring, and oak paneling. The exterior walls were extra thick, and concrete interior walls ensured the tenants' privacy. Electric dumbwaiters, an elevator, and an onsite coal degasifier (for conversion to natural gas for cooking) were extras which made life in the Lemarchand Mansion very easy.

Rene Lemarchand was the brother of the Oblate priest Alphonse Lemarchand, who served the St. Joachim's parish for many years. He encouraged his brother to leave Paris and to resettle in Edmonton in 1905. Rene Lemarchand came to Canada with considerable resources for an immigrant and was able to establish a store selling fruit and "fancy goods" before investing in real estate. The tales of how Lemarchand made his fortune include having had an eccentric and wealthy employer who used razors only once and, upon his death, bequeathed his collection of razors to his butler, Rene who sold the expensive items and made his fortune. Other investment came from the Paris waiter's union whose members Lemarchand had befriended.

This site was on the edge of settlement when it was erected—there being little development in the west until a couple of years later when the Oliver and then Glenora neighborhoods were developed.

The building was restored in 1977 and an addition attached to the eastern side for $4.5 million. The original building was then designated a provincial historic resource.

Victoria Park Promenade

Address: 100th Avenue between 116th & 121st streets
Date: 1989
Route: Continue west across the parking lot for Grant Notley Park, then north across the street before heading west again along the Victoria Promenade.

Directly west across from the Lemarchand Manor is Grant Notley Park and the beginning of the Heritage Trail extension—the Victoria Park Promenade.

Grant Notley Park was created as part of the $15-million upgrade of the Oliver area and an extension of the Heritage Trail from downtown. Walter Grant Notley (1938–84) was an outstanding parliamentarian and leader of the New Democratic Party in Alberta from 1968 until his death in an airplane crash. Born in Didsbury, Alberta, Notley received his bachelor of arts from the University of Alberta and started work as provincial secretary of the NDP right after graduation. He was elected as the member for Peace River–Fairview in 1971 and sat as the party's only representative in the Alberta Legislative Assembly until 1982, when he was joined by Ray Martin. He was killed during a visit back to his constituency in 1984.

The Promenade affords a pleasant opportunity to see the neighborhood and the lovely river views over Victoria Park.

The Victoria Park Promenade, completed in 1990, contains modern sculptures and busts of famous residents of the Oliver area. At the 116th Street end is the large modern art installment [Oliver Convergence] by Tony Bloom, a Canmore artist. The sculpture consists of a braid of parallel steel bars containing vertical steel slats or troughs inside, which tumble water within the structure. Four steel columns to the east represent the collonade, a structure traditionally used in architecture to signal entrance into a significant place. The work, commissioned by the Oliver community, cost $58,000.

Along the walkway are busts of former Oliver residents who have made contributions to the community and the city. They include Maude Bowman, first president of the Edmonton Art Gallery; Abraham Cristall, father of the first Jewish family in Edmonton and founder of many institutions; community leader Nellie McClung; and Lucien Dubuc, the presiding judge of first Alberta case heard in French. Bilingual plaques, emphasizing the role of French Canadians in settling this area, can be read as you walk along enjoying the view of Victoria Park in the river valley below.

Lessard Residence

Address: 11936–100th Avenue
Style: Queen Anne
Architect: Unknown
Date: 1913
Route: Continue westward. Note that Harry Shaw's mansion, home of the cigar king of Alberta, was located at 11716–100th Avenue, and Abe Cristall's house was located at 11814–100th Avenue, where the Mayfield Apartment building is now.

One of the few remaining single-family dwellings on Victoria (100th) Avenue, the Lessard residence is a striking reminder of the kind of houses that once graced the top of the river valley.

Features of the Queen Anne style include the asymmetrical shape and the inclusion of the turret feature topped with a conical roof. The large gable, which admits light into the attic, makes this a two-and-a-half-storey house. The main floor is faced with brick and the windows are topped with decorative arches, but the upper floor is faced with stucco and decorative half-timber divisions.

Prosper Edmond Lessard was born in Quebec in 1873 and educated in Montreal. After becoming a bookkeeper, he arrived in Edmonton in 1898 and began to work for Gariepy and Chenier, who had dry goods stores in Edmonton and other centers in the west. Eventually Gariepy's other partners sold out to Lessard, who married Helen Gariepy in 1900. By 1909, Gariepy and Lessard had sold off most of their retail holdings and were investing in real estate. Lessard also established the French-language paper *Courier de L'Ouest* with Senator Roy and took on the position of managing director of the Western Garment Company. (Later the Great Western Garment Company, otherwise known as the GWG.) Lessard served as a trustee of the Edmonton Separate School Board, president of the St. Jean Baptiste Society, and on the executive of a number of business associations, including a term as vice president of the Edmonton Board of Trade. Made captain in 1906, Lessard was a member of the Alberta Mounted Rifles regiment for many years.

One of the few remaining grand residences along 100th Avenue, the Lessard Residence is a reminder of the style of the former community.

He was elected a member of the Legislative Assembly for Pakan (now the Smoky Lake district) in 1909 and served as a minister without portfolio in Rutherford's cabinet, but he resigned from cabinet with Rutherford over the railway scandal in 1912. He was appointed to the Senate in 1922, a position he continued to hold until his death in 1931.

Annamoe Mansion

Address: 11950–100th Avenue
Style: Classical revival
Architect: Unknown
Date: 1914
Route: Continue westward to view the next building.

This brick building was a strong presence among the residences along the river's edge.

Built like the Westminster and the Derwas apartments (around the corner on 120th Street), the Annamoe Mansion was constructed to fill the demand for middle-class living spaces close to streetcars and the downtown area where most people worked. Owner Robert

Childers Barton named the building after his hometown of Annamoe in County Wicklow, Ireland.

Given the placement of the apartment building at the edge of the river valley, it was expected that Barton should insist on lots of large windows to give his tenants the best possible views. The view of the apartment building itself was enhanced by a variety of decorative touches including the use of contrasting stone and created patterns in the brickwork, especially at the corner "turrets." The small balconies with awnings give the exterior a Mediterranean air.

Beth Shalom Synagogue
Address: 11916 Jasper Avenue
Style: Moderne-international
Architect: Rule Wynn & Rule
Date: 1951
Route: Turn north at the corner of 120th Street to Jasper
Avenue and head eastward.

The Beth Shalom congregation developed from the Beth Israel Synagogue in 1928. They met initially in the hall of the Talmud Torah School. In 1932, they formed a new synagogue congregation with a less traditional form of ritual and practice and named themselves Beth Shalom, the House of Peace. Attempts to raise funds for their own building were delayed by the onset of World War II. In the interim, their plans grew to include a community center focusing on the needs of their young people.

After the war, fundraising continued, and by 1950 the synagogue community was able to turn the sod for its new facility on Jasper Avenue, which followed the movement of the Jewish community into the West End from their traditional east-of-downtown location prior to World War I.

The new facility included a gymnasium, two auditoriums, meeting rooms, a stage, and two kitchens. Elements of the international style include an emphasis on the horizontal, such as the flat roof and the long narrow windows. The pilasters to the rectangular pediment over the entry are influenced by a classical style.

The harbinger of the changing neighborhood during the 1950s, the synagogue was symbolic of the new people coming into the west end and the newer styles of architecture being employed to house them.

St. Joseph's Basilica

Address: 10044–113th Street
Style: Gothic
Architect: Henri Labelle (Quebec) & Eugene Olekshy
   (Edmonton)
Date: 1965
Route: Continue east along Jasper Avenue.

Despite its glorious appearance today, the congregation of the Basilica of St. Joseph experienced a great deal of difficulty in building this church. The parish was created by the division between the French and English members of St. Joachim's in 1913, but they were unable to obtain their own church until 1925. An attempt was made to start building before the First World War; however, plans had to be shelved before the basement was complete.

In 1924, Archbishop John Joseph O'Leary dedicated St. Joseph's as his cathedral parish, and in 1925, a crypt church was begun with seating for 900, making it the largest in Edmonton. Further construction on the building was delayed for 35 years due to the Depression and World War II. When the church was finally able to build above the basement, the foundation was found to have cracks and other problems which required jacking it up and sinking of hundreds of piles below the building to support it.

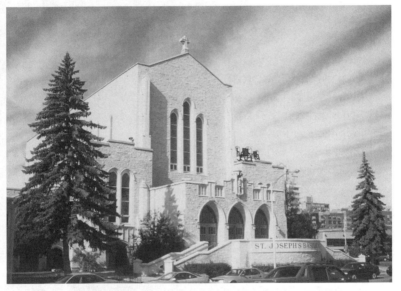

Like many great European cathedrals St. Joseph's has taken generations to build.

Construction began on the superstructure in 1961 and proceeded for two years. The interior floors are laid with ceramic tiles in patterns reminiscent of those found in European churches. The columns and walls are made of an imitation stone which dampens sounds. Providing seating for about 1,200 people, the pews are carved in oak from Quebec. The altar is Spanish marble, and there are more than sixty stained glass windows. A statue of St. Joseph the worker (also father of Jesus) is placed in a niche above the front entrance supported by a corbel. The exterior is clad in Manitoba Tyndall stone, the windows are arched in traditional Gothic fashion. The elaborate front entryway was reconstructed in 2002.

A serious case of arson in 1980 caused the church to restrict its practice of leaving the church open 24 hours a day. Pope John Paul II visited the cathedral in 1984, and it was made one of two minor basilicas in western Canada (the other is St. Boniface, in Winnipeg). The honor was bestowed as a result of the visit, but also in recognition of the pioneers and missionaries who served here.

The archbishop's house, found next door, predates the original crypt church.

General Hospital
Address: 11111 Jasper Avenue
Style: various
Architect: various
Date: 1895 - various
Route: Continue east along Jasper Avenue.

The General Hospital has evolved and changed—growing organically at times—until little of the original fabric remains—although the intentions of service to the community continues.

Although the Grey Nuns had been in Alberta for several years, mostly associated with the Oblate missions in St. Albert and Lac Ste. Anne, it was not until 1894 that five doctors in Edmonton asked them to come to Edmonton to establish a hospital for the town. The Sisters of Charity complied, but with the understanding that they would be under the rule of their own order, not the doctors, and that they would have control of admissions. The doctors agreed and the order built a hospital in 1895, staffing it with two nuns.

The first General Hospital, built facing Victoria (100th) Avenue, had 36 beds. Nursing was provided to anyone who needed it, despite inablity to pay, and care was provided in English or French. A majority of the staff were French Canadian and Catholic, but the hospital admitted both Protestant and Catholic patients in about even numbers. In 1896, the issues of French language usage within the hospital, and its policy of admitting indigent patients and requiring the doctors to care for them, caused a rift. Five doctors (all Anglophones) withdrew their services and pressured the city to establish a public "non-denominational" hospital.

The philosophy of the Grey Nuns was proven valuable to the city in 1901 when a smallpox epidemic broke out and the Public Hospital refused to treat the victims. The Grey Nuns rented a separate house and cared for all those who needed nursing. At that point the city restored some public funding to the General Hospital. A similar situation occurred during the Spanish influenza epidemic in 1918 and during the treatment of tuberculosis during the 1930s and 1940s. The General Hospital started a school of nursing in 1907; students were trained at both the General and the Misericordia hospitals.

Additions to the hospital were made in 1908 and 1928. Over the years, other expansion projects have been built over and around, replacing all of the original fabric. As advances in medical technology became available, the General was usually the first hospital in Edmonton to obtain them. Throughout its history, it was a teaching hospital for both nurses and doctors. During the 1960s, the largest part of hospital staffing was transferred to lay people, although the superior sister remained as chair of the board of directors.

The school of nursing was closed in the late 1970s, and major restructuring of the health care system was affected in the 1980s and 1990, resulting in the closing of all but the Youville wing for geriatrics in 1996 and the move of most of the hospital wards in 1998 to the new Grey Nuns Hospital in Mill Woods. With its closing the last francophone institution in the neighborhood was removed.

Top of the Valley Heritage Trail Tour

Edmonton's Heritage Trail was a joint project of the City of Edmonton and the provincial government under the jurisdiction of Historic Sites Services. The partners encouraged and sought sponsorship for many of the displays by groups such as the Rotary Club of Edmonton and others interested in the topics discussed in the galleries. The trail was developed in the late 1980s, and its first phase, running from McDougall Hill to the Legislature, was installed in the summer of 1990. This is essentially the route of this tour. The extension into Oliver is the subject of another tour. Subsequent phases of the trail will stretch the route east to the Convention Centre, then across the river along Saskatchewan Drive, and possibly down the river valley through Rossdale and even into Riverdale via Grierson Hill.

This tour covers the parts of the city that were developed before the First World War and in some cases, before the turn of the century. The piece of land between 101st Street and 109th Street was part of the Hudson's Bay reserve, but it was opened up in a piecemeal fashion as individuals convinced the local company authorities to part with lots within the reserve. In 1881, the Hudson's Bay Company subdivided some of their land west of 101st Street and south of Jasper Avenue. Edmonton, which was incorporated as a town in 1892, and then as a city in 1904, moved westward, hugging the river valley, until the reserve land was fully opened in 1912.

During the intervening years, Edmonton's population increased significantly and its ethic makeup also changed. Immigration broadened from the French and English Canadians to encompass most of the northern European nationals as well as Americans. All kinds of economic activity flourished, but the most pronounced in the days before World War I was probably land speculation and real estate sales.

The McKay Avenue district lies along what is today 99th Avenue. This was where those who made their fortunes in the heady days before 1914 built their elegant and spacious homes. Edmonton's movers and shakers built mansions on the top of the hill overlooking the river. For the most part, those have given way to downtown office towers, walk-ups, and residential high-rises. Occasionally one was missed and managed to survive; others left their mark by passing their names to their successors. The neighborhood went through some rough times in the 1980s, when it lost its sense of community, but in the 1990s, condominium development began turning the local population from renters to owners, who created the Downtown Edmonton Community Association (which included long-term tenants).

In hopes of fostering community spirit, the association has organized annual spring cleanups and worked on urban design issues with the city and on its own, including developing community gardens and park spaces, working on the preservation of remaining houses, and insisting on the integration of new units into the neighborhood image. Hopefully those small pockets of Edmonton's heritage that remain in the community will be able to resist future development pressures and will continue to remind us of our past.

Along the route, which follows the riverbank as closely as possible, you can see into the valley and the various communities below. Rossdale lies directly below the first part of the trail and offers a wealth of sources for Edmonton's history. The original Edmonton Exhibition grounds were located there, and the home of sports in Edmonton is nestled in that valley. From the fort's horseracing track to the cricket club and the baseball diamond, named for Edmonton's "Mr. Baseball," John Ducey, a variety of sports venues have been and continue to be found in the Rossdale area.

Hotel Macdonald
Address: 10065–100th Street
Style: French Renaissance revival
Architect: Ross & MacFarlane (Montreal)
Date: 1915

Probably the most loved and most photographed historic building in the city, the Hotel Macdonald has had a checkered history. The Hotel Macdonald was built over four years as a part of the Grand Trunk Pacific Development Company's cross-Canada string of hotels. The real-estate arm of the Grand Trunk Pacific Railway also used the

Both a landmark and a reminder of the West's reliance on the railways the Hotel Macdonald is still an attraction for Edmontonians and visitors alike.

same architects, Ross and MacFarlane of Montreal, to design other hotels in the chain, including the Chateau Laurier in Ottawa and the Fort Garry Hotel in Winnipeg.

The towers and dormer windows formed a simplified version of the chateau style common to railway hotels. Edmonton's version was a seven-storey French castle with turrets and gables set in a steep-pitched roof covered in copper and topped with finials. There are carved figures and faces over the entrances, arcades, and corbelled balconies off two places on the façade. The infrastructure is steel and concrete, but it is beautifully clad in Indiana limestone. Construction costs topped $2.25 million. The Hotel Macdonald was designed to impress the populace, and it has for generations.

The hotel opened in July 1915, just ten days after the biggest flood in Edmonton's history. It promised the best views of the river valley, and its only real competition came from the Grandview Hotel on the opposite corner, which was too small and too old to be much competition at all. The interior was furnished in the finest style, the ceilings oak-beamed and decorated with beautiful plaster moldings. The rotunda was paved in marble, and the lobby clock was set to Greenwich Mean Time (a legacy of the time-sensitive railway that built the hotel). The lounges in the lobby feature fine works of art, including a copy of the famous picture depicting the fathers of Confederation over a massive fireplace.

An addition to the hotel, put up in the 1950s and dubbed "The Box" for its less than creative architecture, was torn down in 1983 when the owners decided to restore the hotel, which had deteriorated during the intervening years.

The hotel was designated a provincial historical resource in 1985. Work on full restoration ceased, however, until 1990 when the building was again sold, this time to the Canadian Pacific Railway. After the new owners had returned the hotel to its 1915 state, the Hotel Macdonald reopened in 1991.

Telus (AGT) Corner

Address: 100th Street between Jasper & 100th avenues
Route: Cross 100th Street at the Jasper Avenue crosswalk
and proceed south and then west along MacDonald
Drive.

This site, central to the downtown has had a variety of buildings and functions over the years.

This corner was one of the most popular locations in the city due to its orientation on the top of the river valley by a major access to the Fort and the "downtown" of the new townsite. A number of different businesses, including the Grandview Hotel, have been situated here and many newcomers to the town erected their temporary homes (or tents) along the drive here.

In 1923, this site was chosen for Edmonton's public library. The building was designed by Magoon and MacDonald in a French Renaissance revival style, similar to that of the Hotel Macdonald across the road. Cream-colored brick and Bedford stone were used for the exterior finishes. The entrance was flanked by four large columns, which supported a large cornice. The windows were arched. Inside, more columns, these ones ionic in style, supported the roof in the reading room, which had a large skylight to bring natural light into the interior.

The Carnegie Foundation had given the city a significant donation to help establish the library. By 1964, however, city officials had decided that the building was too small, and they began to plan for a larger facility in the civic center area. The city sold the land and the library to Alberta Government Telephones, which demolished the classical building for its new tower.

For many years the AGT Tower was the tallest building in downtown. Gradually, larger and taller buildings have risen around it. Since 1983, the building was known as the nesting place for Arrow, a female peregrine falcon. In cooperation with the Raptor Centre in Wainwright, a closed-circuit camera was set up so Edmontonians could watch the hatching and fledging of several generations of birds which still nest there.

The small building on the corner (10020–100th Street) was originally the second home of the Edmonton Club, the city's oldest private club. Established in 1899 as a gentleman's club, it resisted admitting women as members until two years before its demise. Originally the club's building was in Rossdale, but the membership moved up to the top of the hill in 1906 and built a two-storey clubhouse. Later they added a third storey by changing the roof to a mansard shape. The upper room was used for billiards. The interior was lavishly decorated with oak paneling, and the club always had a superb dining room.

When the land and buildings on the corner were sold to AGT, the clubhouse was demolished and AGT leased the club this building, opened in 1971. Due to falling member numbers and the lack of fitness and sports facilities, the club disbanded in 1994.

In 1958 the Alberta Government made the provincial telephone company an arms length organization known as the Alberta Government Telephone Commission. In 1990 a reorganization formed Telus, which became the parent company for AGT and began to acquire other companies including Ed Tel (the previously municipal telephone company) in 1995 and it merged with BC Tel in 1999.

Alberta College

Address: 10050 MacDonald Drive

Date: 1903

Route: Continue traveling westward on the south side of the drive to read the McDougall Gallery displays and to see the next site.

A symbol of the importance of education to the early residents of Edmonton, Alberta College has also changed with the times.

Alberta College was established in 1903 by a group of citizens concerned about advanced education in the town. It was founded before either the City of Edmonton or the Province of Alberta, and is the oldest secondary educational facility in the province.

George McDougall, a Methodist missionary, donated the land behind the mission on top of the 101st Street hill, and a wood frame, three-storey building was erected to serve the original 67 students in three departments: academics, commerce, and music.

The new college campus, built in the 1980s, retained only the arch off 101st Street as a symbol of the earlier building and included the Muttart Hall, a state-of-the-art concert auditorium which is the equal of the Winspear Centre in acoustics, if not in size. In 2002, Alberta College amalgamated with Grant MacEwan College. It continues to offer Conservatory of Music programs as well as academic upgrading, English as a second language, and business outreach.

McDougall United Church

Address: 10086–101st Street
Style: Italianate
Architect: H. A. Magoon
Date: 1910

The site of the first building outside of Fort Edmonton, the tradition of the (missionary) McDougalls remains in this place.
City of Edmonton Archives EA 10-372

The presence of Methodists in Alberta was first felt in 1840 when Robert Rundle reached Fort Edmonton. He was an itinerant missionary, however, and traveled throughout the province seeking new converts. Another missionary, Peter Campbell, stopped in Edmonton in the 1860s, but it was to be another ten years before Edmonton had a resident Methodist.

George McDougall established a school, in 1871, to teach English to the children of Hudson's Bay Company employees, as the most prominent languages then were French, Gaelic, and Cree. The original Methodist mission house, the first building constructed outside the palisades of Fort Edmonton, was built in 1872, and the following year a log church was consecrated. Services were conducted in English and Cree. The McDougalls were a family of Methodist missionaries; George and his son John started missions to the native peoples in Pakan, northeast of Edmonton, and in Morley, west of Calgary. After the smallpox epidemic of 1870, in which several of the McDougall women and children died, the survivors moved to Edmonton briefly before resettling in Morley.

The second Methodist church was built in 1892, this one larger to accommodate the growing congregation. Even that proved inadequate, and a third, the brick McDougall Church, was built in 1910 and dedicated in honor of George McDougall. That church cost $90,000 to construct and provided seating for 1,200. The little mission church was left beside its bigger sister for many years, serving as a museum for the history of the Methodist mission. It was moved to Fort Edmonton Park's 1885 Street in 1978 to serve as a reminder of its role in the city's history. A small Methodist cemetery existed between the two churches for a few years, but it was removed to the Edmonton Cemetery about 1924 for reasons of public health and to free the land for development.

The larger church, which became part of the United Church of Canada during the union of 1925, assisted the congregation through participating in a number of community events which have been important in the life of this church. McDougall Church was the first home of the Edmonton Symphony Orchestra and the Edmonton Opera. The first music festival (since the Kiwanis Music Festival) was held at McDougall, and Alberta College, which has a fine music program, was initiated from McDougall Church.

The concrete and brick structure of the McDougall United Church is 38 meters long by 25 meters wide. The nave (central part of the church) rises unobstructed to the high ceiling, and there are two asymmetrical towers at the front of the church, the taller one being a bell tower. The central pediment has an open bed through which an arched window with a contrasting keystone protrudes. This gable is echoed on the rear face.

In 1954, an addition at the rear of the building and alterations to the entrance modernized the structure, but it remained basically intact. The building is an eclectic mixture of styles, having some Gothic features mixed with classical and Italianate influences.

Edmonton Journal Building

Address: 10006–101st Street
Style: Post Modern
Architect: unknown
Date: 2001

The Journal Building represents much of the history of communications in this community.

The *Edmonton Evening Journal* was first published in 1903 as a kind of Conservative antidote to the "Liberal rantings" of the *Edmonton Bulletin* editorials churned out by the publisher Frank Oliver.

For a while the *Journal* offices were located underneath the second phase of the Tegler Building, on 101st Street and 102nd Avenue north of Jasper Avenue. The *Journal* had a lease, and the paper was not about to move until its new building on 100th Avenue and 101st Street was completed. Tegler wanted to expand his building north to the corner, so he built over the small building that the *Edmonton Evening Journal* was renting, and when they moved out he demolished the building and built down to the street level. There were several papers in circulation in those days, but they gradually died out.

The new *Edmonton Journal* Building was completed in 1921, designed by William Blakey in an Edwardian "freestyle". In 1922, the city's first radio station was set up in the *Edmonton Journal* Building. The manager of the CJCA station, Dick Rice, set up the equipment in a corner of the newsroom and began to broadcast. The antenna was strung from two poles on the roof. The station was there until 1928, when it moved out to the Yellowhead highway near Oliver on the way to Fort Saskatchewan.

When the *Edmonton Bulletin* stopped publishing in 1951, the *Edmonton Journal* became the only newspaper in town until 1978 when the *Edmonton Sun* started publishing a morning paper. The Journal added an addition to the west in 1952 and a new press building in 1955. Further growth in the paper and new technology made the construction of a separate $35 million production plant called "Eastgate" a necessity in 1980. A new $15 million office complex was erected on the old company parking lot beginning in 1988 and opening in 1991.

This Post Modern building was erected on the site of the *Journal*'s earlier headquarters in time for the 100th anniversary of the newspaper in 2003. A small portion of the original building's wall is "preserved" inside this building as a token to the heritage preservation movement's unsuccessful attempt to save the old Journal Building.

Salvation Army Citadel

Address: 10030–102nd Street
Style: Fortress
Architect: George McDonald
Date: 1925
Route: Continue west to 102nd Street. At the intersection of 100th Avenue and 101st Street is a small triangular park called the Veterans' Park, which housed the cenotaph until 1980 when it was moved to city hall.

The building is a three-storey "fortress" with a central tower flanked by two slender towers linked by a series of vertical brick piers. The brown clinker brick is contrasted with various colored bricks to form patterns which are accented with tiles on the façade. The flat roof is bordered by a gabled parapet at each corner. Recessed panels hold the windows on either sides of the towers, and the entry is recessed and arched. An interesting off-center brick balcony is found halfway up the right tower.

This small military-inspired temple was the home to the Salvation Army in Edmonton between 1925 and 1964. It was called the Citadel and cost $39,000 to construct. Charles Rich, the Salvation Army superintendent for western Canada, officially opened the building, which operated as both a church and a headquarters for the army's social outreach programs. In 1964, the church relocated to 108th Street.

The Citadel was then bought for $100,000 by Joe Shocter for an amateur theater group. After years of producing shows on Broadway, Shocter was convinced to try promoting drama in Edmonton. The Citadel Theatre Company renovated the building into an intimate 227-seat theater in 1965 and occupied it until 1976. The first production was *Who's Afraid of Virginia Wolfe*, and audiences found the experience of being so close to the stage exhilarating. After the Citadel Theatre moved into its new building downtown, the old Citadel was converted first into a restaurant, then a disco. In 1978, Frank Cairo remodeled the building into the Marvel Beauty School.

This building was not only the centre of an evangelical spiritual movement in early Edmonton, but also lent its name to one of the city's theatrical movements.

By the mid-1980s, the building had again become home to rock and roll nightclubs, and most recently raves have been held in its hallowed halls.

All Saints Anglican Cathedral

Address: 10035–103rd Street
Style: Moderne
Architect: William Blakey
Date: 1956
Route: Turn south and then west to follow 100th Avenue toward 103rd Street.

The Anglican presence in Edmonton reaches back to the days of Fort Edmonton around 1875; however, Canon Newton, the English church's missioner, was never as successful at recruiting or getting along with the fort's officers are were the Methodists and the Roman Catholics. Newton was never allowed a chapel inside the fort grounds and had to make do with land donated by Malcolm Groat and lumber donated by a few reluctant Anglicans.

Despite its poor start in the community, the parish of All Saints grew from a relatively small gathering of souls to a significant presence in the downtown, thanks in part to the rector of 1903, Henry Allan Gray, who was subsequently elected the first bishop of the Edmonton diocese in 1914. Another factor which may have led to the growth in the parish was the musical leadership provided by Vernon Barford, who served as organist and choirmaster for over 40 years. His role in the city's musical history is legendary.

All Saints Church (later cathedral) had several buildings in and around this area before finally settling on 103rd Street in 1927. The first church on this site was destroyed in a fire, and the congregation worshiped in the church hall for many years, through the Depression and World War II, until they could raise enough money to build a replacement. They finally did manage to build a crypt church in 1950. Plans were made to raise a traditional Gothic church over the crypt; however, many problems, from weaknesses in the

Like many downtown churches this building is quite recently built although it remains on the site of previous versions.

original foundation to lack of consensus among the congregation to weak fundraising, delayed the project for years.

Finally, in 1955, with new plans from William Blakey and the ability to borrow the necessary funds, a new foundation was laid in September and construction begun. The new cathedral was dedicated in May 1956. One of the first tasks was to inter in the south wall of the sanctuary the ashes of their beloved dean, Grant Sparling, who had succumbed to a heart attack after the previous Easter service.

The new cathedral cost over $280,000 and left the parish in debt for many years. However, the acoustics in the building, the generous donation of an excellent organ by Dr. Harvie Hebb in 1959, and the direction of H. Hugh Bancroft as choirmaster and organist allowed the cathedral's musical legacy to continue.

As early as 1965, the cathedral was discussing plans to redevelop the parish hall site; however, the timing was not good until the 1970s, when the need for housing for senior citizens became critical and the Alberta Mortgage and Housing Corporation was assisting a number of groups to build. The Cathedral Close was built to provide low-cost housing for seniors; initially, space for the cathedral offices and meeting rooms was provided on the second floor.

Eventually the management of the close was severed from the church, and in the 1990s the atrium between the cathedral and the close was developed, giving the church its own office space, Sunday school facilities, kitchen, and hall space. In 2000, the offices of the diocesan synod moved into the atrium as well.

Foster McGarvey Funeral Home
Address: 10008–103rd Street
Style: Moderne
Architect: Rule Wynn & Rule
Date: ca. 1950
Route: Return to 100th Avenue and face west across 103rd Street.

The conversion of an old house into an office or commercial facility was a common practice in the downtown area.

This building is situated on the site of Dr. Edward Ainslie Braithwaite's home. Braithwaite was a member of the North-West Mounted Police and was with the force in 1884, coming out west in time to see the Riel Rebellion. He served as the force's medical officer and remained on the force until 1931, making him one of the longest-serving officers in the history of the Mounted Police. While he was stationed in Edmonton, he became the city's first medical health officer and its first coroner. When Alberta was made a province, he took the title of the first provincial coroner as well.

Braithwaite built his large Victorian mansion on this corner, near the mansions of Frank Oliver and John A. McDougall, the merchant. There were extensive grounds around the house and outbuildings, which included two stables and a carriage house. Other prominent Edmontonians lived along Victoria Avenue in similar style. Braithwaite had been a member of the Masonic order since 1893, and when the Masons desired to move from their small quarters on 102nd Street near Jasper Avenue, he donated part of his grounds (to the west of his house) for their temple.

After Braithwaite's death in 1931, the building was purchased by Foster McGarvey for use as a funeral home. Eventually the building required significant alterations and modernizations, and around 1950 the old Braithwaite house found itself incorporated into a whole new structure designed by Rule Wynn and Rule. The roof of the former residence is just barely visible atop the new structure.

Oliver Building

Address: 10225–100th Avenue
Style: International-Moderne
Architect: McKernan & Bouey
Date: 1958
Route: Turn to the south to view the sites of the Oliver and the McDougall residences.

This office building maintains the name of the family who originally built on this property.

The Oliver Building sits on the site of the former Frank Oliver residence. Oliver was the editor of the *Edmonton Bulletin,* the town's first newspaper, which was published from 1881 to 1951.

The residence was a three storey brick mansion built in 1905. The Olivers did not live long in their new home, since Frank Oliver was elected Member of Parliament for Edmonton and the family moved to Ottawa almost as soon as the house was completed. He was minister of the interior in Laurier's government (after Clifford Sifton). As such, he drew the boundaries of the constituencies in the new province of Alberta (which may have helped elect a Liberal government in the province) and ensured that Edmonton was declared the provincial capital. In the interim, he loaned the house to the provincial government as the site of the first Government House (the residence of the Lieutenant Governor).

The Olivers returned to live in the house from 1916 to 1944. After they vacated the house, the most famous tenant in 1940s was the Canadian military, which was headquartered here to supervise the Alcan Highway project to Alaska.

In the late 1950s, the residence was sold to the federal government, and in 1957 construction of the Oliver Building began. It would be used by the federal Department of Public Works for the district as well as by the Central Mortgage and Housing Corporation in Alberta.

The building has two storeys above grade and two basements built down the hill, below grade. It was designed so that the government could later add two more storeys if required. The building was framed in reinforced concrete, and the walls finished in brick stone and pre-cast concrete panels faced with terrazzo. Hollow aluminum sections hold the windows in place, but they can be opened for fresh breezes coming off the river. The cost of the finished building was approximately $565,000. Although it was completed by the fall of 1958, a federal labor dispute delayed the official opening until 1959.

In 2002, architects Manasc and Isaac bought the building, and after four months of renovations, the almost 1,400 square meters of space was retrofitted for an architectural studio and office, and an industrial design consulting company called d-lab.

Hilltop House / McDougall House II

Address: 9910–103rd Street
Style: Foursquare
Architect: David Hardie
Date: 1912
Route: Proceed slightly down the 103rd Street hill beside the Oliver Building to view Hilltop House on the west side of the street.

One of the last remaining residential mansions in downtown and a reminder of the wealthy (commercial) McDougall family.

Hilltop House was the home of John C. McDougall, though the land originally belonged to his father, John A. McDougall, who lived in a modest house on this site until his mansion directly to the north, on the corner of 103rd Street and Victoria (100th) Avenue, was completed.

John A. McDougall arrived in Edmonton in 1879 and began to trade with the native people in competition with the Hudson's Bay Company. He was quite successful, eventually establishing his own shop on Jasper Avenue and soon partnering with Richard Secord in other commercial and real estate ventures. He was elected mayor of

Edmonton and served a term as a provincial MLA. John C. McDougall was born in 1883.

This land was purchased from the Hudson's Bay Company in 1891, and the first McDougall mansion (9936–103rd Street) was completed in 1900. The mansion had expansive lawns and gardens with stables and a tennis court on the grounds. The McDougall family lived there until 1946 when the house was acquired by the Independent Order of Daughters of the Empire as a home for orphaned children of veterans. In 1968, the YWCA acquired the house for a women's rehabilitation center. It was demolished to make way for the new YWCA in 1973, which has now become condominiums.

Hilltop House was constructed for young John in 1912, and unlike the first home, it managed to survive the various developments that have surrounded the house by high-rises. In 1920, an addition to the rear of the house added a billiard room and a bedroom above. John C. worked at his father's and Richard Secord's company, serving as an administrator and accountant. He was married and had two children, John F. and Eleanor.

After John's death in 1952, his widow sold the property to the provincial government. It was used as a drug treatment center and later as a home for battered women. Vacant during the late 1980s, the house was renovated to serve as offices for a variety of government commissions. Few changes were made to the fabric of the house, which included a number of built-in cabinets. The house is listed on the "B" list of the municipal Registry of Historic Resources, but it is still in danger of being demolished unless a sympathetic owner designates it as a historical resource.

The house was listed for sale in 2003 at $989,000.

Central Masonic Temple

Address: 10318–100th Avenue
Style: English Gothic revival
Architect: William Blakey
Date: 1931

Route: Return up the hill and continue westward along
100th Avenue until you are across from the Masonic
Temple.

*At one time, everyone who was anyone was a Mason and this building was the
centre of the community's social life.*

The Masonic Lodge No. 7 was formed in 1893 out of the Grand Lodge
in Winnipeg. The first master was A. W. Sutter, and a building on
102nd Street was used for gatherings. The mandate of the society,
which members insisted was not a secret order, was to improve
humankind through works of charity and fellowship among members. The Masons were often prominent businessmen in the community, and their networks were used to improve the community. Very
few institutions were started without the Masons' involvement, and
they often were prominent in the opening ceremonies for public and
religious buildings where they ritually laid the cornerstone.

The cornerstone for their own building, the Central Masonic
Temple, was laid in 1930 after years of subscriptions had created a
building fund of approximately $200,000. The land was purchased
from Dr. E. A. Braitewaite, one of the founding members of the lodge.

The intention was to provide lodge rooms for all units of Masons in city and a center for cultural activities for the community.

In the basement was a large banquet hall; on the main floor, an assembly hall and ballroom which the members hoped the community would use. The upper floor housed a dozen rooms reserved for other lodges in the city looking for facilities. The architect, William Blakey, was also a lodge member (Ivanhoe lodge), and he included emblems of masonry in his design.

Distinguishing features of the English Gothic style include the impressions of piers and buttresses worked into the brick, the archway niche around the entrance, and the central tower. The materials were, for the most part, derived from local sources, with locally made brick, steel, and concrete. The contrasting "stone" used for the door dressings, windows and quoins (contrasting corner pieces) was actually artificial stone called "ashlar."

Grand entrances were created by the use of oak doors (with separate doors for the public and for lodge members) covered with bronze lockplates and topped by transom lights with oak tracery. The six niches on the exterior façade were intended for statues. The interior foyer was paved in terrazzo, and the 500-seat auditorium it led to became the center of community cultural life before World War II. It was the largest venue for concerts, balls, dances, and Royal Conservatory of Music examinations.

In 2001, the Masons started renting out the hall again for public functions.

Gariepy House

Address: 9947–104th Street
Style: Second empire
Architect: P. Anderson (contractor)
Date: 1902
Route: Continue west to the corner of 104th Street.

Gariepy House is one of few remaining structures from the period before Edmonton was incorporated as a city. The mansion supports a mansard roof, with through-the-eaves (or dormer) windows, a corner turret with circular dormers, and niches for religious statuary. These are suggestive of the original owner's French origins, although the style was out of fashion by the turn of the century. The small wooden cornice is supported by wooden brackets, and the stone string course divides the upper and lower floors.

The Gariepy House was another important residence of an influential Edmonton businessman found in the downtown residential community.

Joseph Hormisdas Gariepy (1852–1927) came to Edmonton from Montreal in 1893 and opened a grocery store. He expanded his business to Morinville and later partnered with Lessard, who became his son-in-law in 1900. He was so successful in his mercantile and real estate dealings that he became a major entrepreneur and a leading citizen in Edmonton.

Gariepy was president of Fort MacKay Oil and Asphalt, an early oil exploration company, and twice president of the local Board of Trade, as well as holding a variety of public offices, including alderman and school board trustee. Two of his sons would also be elected city aldermen.

Gariepy built this brick mansion in 1902 in an area of significant houses for the well-established businessmen of Edmonton, such as McDougall, Secord, and Dr. MacKay. The house was purchased in 1923 by J. A. McDougall (a real estate dealer and developer) and resold the following year to the Sisters of Providence of St. Vincent de Paul (General Hospital) for use as a convent. They added the east wing in 1926 (as large as the original house) and called it Rosary Hall. The addition maintained many of the architectural and decorative features.

The original wraparound verandah was removed at some point, although many of the house's other distinctive features have been preserved.

McKay Avenue School

Address: 10425–99th Avenue
Style: Romanesque
Architect: H. D. Johnson
Date: 1904
Route: Turn south on 104th Street toward 99th Avenue and there turn west again.

The oldest remaining brick school and the first school built in Edmonton share this site and function as the School Board's museum and archives.

The school was named for the avenue on which it was built, and the avenue was named for one of its early residents, the prominent pioneer doctor W. M. MacKay. The name was incorrectly carved on a school nameplate, and subsequent attempts to have the misspelling corrected have been disallowed.

Dr. William Morrison MacKay joined the Hudson's Bay Company in 1864 and served as company doctor until 1898. He worked primarily in the Peace and Athabasca districts; once he skated from Grouard to Edmonton (approximately 250 kilometres) to provide medical care to a sick patient. Fort MacKay and MacKay Lake were both named in his honor. He was much respected as a doctor, and he served as the first president of the Northern Alberta Medical Association.

After his retirement he built his home across the street from the school at the corner of 105th Street and 99th Avenue, and lived there until his death in 1916. Originally 99th Avenue was called MacKay Avenue.

McKay Avenue School is the oldest brick school in the city. Built with red stretcher bond brick and sandstone, the building has engaged columns and a round Romanesque arch above the main entrance, which was typical of schools in this period. The windows on the upper floors have rounded arches, while the main-storey windows have heavy contrasting lintels of stone. The cost of construction was $44,000. The original school consisted of only the western section, but in 1912 an addition of four rooms was added to the east.

The peak enrollment occurred in 1916 when 456 students were registered. Famous alumnae of McKay Avenue School include actor Leslie Nielsen and bush pilot Wop May.

In the absence of appropriate space before the building of the Legislature, the Government of Alberta used the upper assembly room for the first two sessions of the Legislative Assembly in 1906 and 1907. After many years the school's enrolment declined during the 1970s as the surrounding community changed from residential to high-rise. The school was closed in 1983 and restored by the Edmonton Public School Board, with help from the other levels of government, for use as the school board's archives and museum. The building was rededicated by Governor General Jeanne Sauve during her visit to the city in 1986.

1881 School House

Address: 10425–99th Avenue
Date: 1881
Route: Walk around to the west side of the school to view the 1881 School House in Dick Mather Memorial Park.

A visit to the 1881 school house shows just how far education has come in the past 120 plus years.

In 1880, various citizens in Edmonton applied to form a school district and began to plan for a school for the community's children.

The following year, after a community-wide subscription for funds and materials, the 1881 School House was constructed. It was a 7-by-9-meter, planed wood structure, insulated with sawdust and heated with a woodstove. The school trustees were Malcolm Groat, Matthew McCauley, and William Rowland. They had an $800 budget, of which $500 was earmarked for the teacher's salary.

This was the first official school in Alberta (before Alberta was even made a province and before the town of Edmonton was incorporated.) The school district was finally organized in 1885 as Protestant Public School District No. 7. The organization could then levy taxes on property and possessions to support the school.

James Harris was the first teacher. From an initial 28 children, student numbers grew to 83 in 1889. An additional classroom was added in that year for $1,550; the original school was tendered at $968. The first female teacher, Lillian Osborne, was hired in 1889, but she was paid $400 less per year than the male teacher.

After this schoolhouse was replaced, it was sold and moved to the river valley for use as a residence. It almost floated away during the flood of 1915, but some quick-thinking soul secured it to nearby trees with cable and it was saved. Once the Edmonton Public School Board Museum was established, the old schoolhouse was brought back to the original site and restored as a living museum.

Note: The Secord Mansion, built in 1907, was originally called the Chateau Rochelle and located at 9842–105th Street. Richard Secord was the partner of John McDougall, the 1904 Conservative representative for Edmonton on the Northwest Territorial Council in Regina and one of the early teachers at the 1881 School House. In 1951, the city purchased the Secord Mansion for the Edmonton Art Gallery, and it was used in that capacity until 1967. The building was demolished in 1968 to make way for the Secord Apartments.

First Presbyterian Church
Address: 10025–105th Street
Style: Gothic revival
Architect: Wilson & Herrald
Date: 1911
Route: Leave the park and turn north on 105th Street, returning to 100th Avenue.

The third First Presbyterian Church is an impressive Gothic structure which carries the weight of the religious tradition it houses.

Presbyterians began meeting together in 1881, and they built their first wooden church at 99th Avenue and 104th Street in 1882. When they outgrew the first First Presbyterian Church building, they built another larger church of brick at 103rd Street and Jasper Avenue. That one was outgrown within a decade, and plans were made for a larger facility. The cornerstone of the third First Presbyterian Church was laid in 1911 on 105th Street, and the building was officially opened in 1912 by Rev. David G. McQueen, the pastor from 1883 to 1930.

McQueen was also the first moderator of the Alberta synod and the first national leader of Presbyterians who did not join with the United Church in 1925. The third church was the largest and most costly (double the estimate of $85,000) of Presbyterian churches in city. It has seating for 1,200 souls. The large and numerous Gothic arched windows increase the light inside church and "lightened" its imposing exterior presence.

The building was declared a provincial historical resource in 1978.

The Arlington

Address: 10524–100th Avenue
Style: Classical influences
Architect: Unknown
Date: 1909
Route: Continue west along 100th Avenue.

A "syndicate of local capitalists" responded to the local housing shortage caused by the booming economy and rise in population which occurred before the First World War, and they built this apartment block along Victoria Avenue. The five-storey apartment building was marketed to young professionals and white-collar workers.

The simple exterior, which was clad in red brick laid over a steel frame, exhibited classical detailing. Modern construction techniques and a large labor force were employed to speed the construction, and it was estimated that the building went up at a rate averaging one floor per week. The construction cost was approximately $130,000.

The Arlington still serves the housing needs of the young professionals and students it was built to attract.

Distinctive features include the symmetrical construction around the central doorway, the dentilled cornice (toothlike notches under the overhang), and the "keystone" detailing in the center of windows and the arched entryway. The continuous sills under the windows and the bands or string courses separating the floors were other classical details. The suites were luxurious compared to most apartments constructed during this period and certainly when compared to rooming houses farther east of downtown. The apartments had central heating, gas stoves, private bathrooms, a central passenger elevator, and built-in furniture like Murphy beds, dining tables, desks, buffets, and bookcases. There were 40 suites of three to six rooms, which in 1910 rented for about $30 per month.

Crown Land Timber & Registry Office

Address: 10523–100th Avenue
Style: Utilitarian
Architect: Government of Canada
Date: 1893
Route: Turn to look to the south side of 100th Avenue.

This unique building has a military and social history few downtown buildings can rival.

This building is probably the oldest existing land titles office in Alberta. Under its "modern" stucco finish lie 45 centimeter-thick brick walls. It was roofed with galvanized iron. There are one and a half storeys to the building, topped by a hipped gable roof with a hipped dormer.

This building was constructed the year after the federal government tried to move the land registry office to the south side of the river, nearer to the then terminus of the Calgary and Edmonton Railway. Edmontonians, already frustrated that the railway company did not cross the river into their town but opted to start in the competing town of Strathcona, reacted negatively to another move that might jeopardize their prosperity. An angry mob led by Mayor Matt McCauley detained the wagons loaded with files and furniture and forced the government to reverse that decision.

The building was occupied for office space by the 19th Alberta Dragoons from World War I until the 1930s and renamed the Victoria Armouries. The Edmonton Fusiliers took it over until the end of World War II. Next the 19th Armoured Car Division occupied it for a few years. It was called Victoria Armouries for 30 years, and then used for office and laboratories of provincial government's department of health.

The building was designated a provincial historical resource in 1977.

Federal Building

Address: 9820–107th Street
Style: Art deco
Architect: Department of Public Works, Government of
   Canada
Date: 1955
Route: Continue along 100th Avenue to 107th Street, turn
   south to 99th Avenue, and continue west until you
   come to the Federal Building.

Plans for the Federal Building were drawn in 1930, but the economy and other distractions kept the Canadian government from constructing this building for over twenty years. Once the economy in Edmonton and elsewhere had recovered, the government was interested in reviving its plan to centralize all federal departments working in Alberta.

Finally constructed in 1955, the Federal Building was one of only a few art deco buildings in Edmonton. Its art deco details are, however, quite muted, perhaps because by the time the building was built, the style was falling out of favor. The exterior decoration is found only on the upper part of façade. The important element in this building is its size and its massing on the site. The lines are simple and crisp. Only the metal ornament that surrounds the main entry and interior decoration of the entrance foyer strongly suggest the art deco style.

The Federal Building needs a strong supporter and developer to ensure this building can again fulfill its potential as a viable part of the downtown community.

Despite its promise, the Federal Building was never a success. Its antiquated facilities soon put it out of favor with employees, and structural materials, such as asbestos, and its massive size render it a difficult building to rehabilitate for an alternative use. The Federal Building has been abandoned for several years, and several attempts at restoration and adaptation have failed.

Bowker Building

Address: 9833–109th Street
Style: Beaux-Arts
Architect: Cecil Burgess
Date: 1955
Route: Return to 99th Avenue and continue west until 108th Street, where you will see the rear of the Bowker Building and the Legislative Assembly building. Proceed around to 109th Street to see the façade of the Bowker Building, or study the building from the rear.

Few office buildings could match the elegance and presence of the Bowker building.

Although designed in 1931, just a year after the Federal Building was conceived, the Bowker Building was also not constructed until 1955. The two buildings could not be more different in conception. The Bowker Building's architect, Cecil Burgess, was the resident architect of the University of Alberta and a professor there. His concern was to create a context for the Legislature Building by creating other neighboring buildings of similar architectural style and massing.

Despite being on the cusp of a new progressive postwar building program, Burgess was aiming for a historical allusion to create a classical precinct for the government center of Alberta. He designed a classical revival building in the style of the École des Beaux-Arts with some moderate art deco detailing.

The building has been known by variety of names, including the Federal Building, and it has housed a variety of provincial departments.

The building is clad in Manitoba limestone, which is harder than the sandstone used in the Legislature and hence more useful for detailed carving. Decorative crests placed in the pediment include the head of a First Nations man and the Alberta coat of arms. The building is ringed by Corinthian columns. A mansard roof covered in copper has aged with a lovely patina. The building cost about $1 million to build, and in 1980 it was totally refitted and renovated, including adding a sixth floor which blends well with the exterior.

The best view is from the east side, not 109th Street.

Legislature Building of Alberta

Address: 109th Street & 98th Avenue
Style: Beaux-Arts, with classical revival and Edwardian influences
Architect: A. M. Jeffers & Richard P. Blakey, Government of Alberta
Date: 1907–13
Route: Return to 108th Street and go south into the Legislature grounds past the reflecting pool.

The symbol of the Alberta people and their government, the Legislative Assembly building and grounds are part of the capital city's downtown community.

Designed to link the newly established capital city with more ancient and established government structures, the classical style employed for the Alberta Legislature Building is similar to three other prairie legislatures. Alberta became a province in 1905, and the location of the capital city was decided the following year. Until the new Legislature was complete in 1913, the fledgling government met in the Thistle curling rink and at McKay Avenue School.

Alberta's Legislative Assembly sits on the site of the last Fort Edmonton. The remaining buildings of the fort were used by the Hudson's Bay Company for storage and by the City of Edmonton for its telephone company until 1914. The last buildings were finally dismantled in the summer of 1915.

Early photographs of the construction of the Legislature Building and the High Level Bridge show the clerks' quarters and some storage sheds on the lower grounds of the Legislature. The site was chosen partly for its association with the mercantile authority wielded by the Hudson's Bay Company in the northwest since the late 1700s. Symbolically the transfer of the site to the new provincial government reflected the change in authority.

The building was constructed of a steel frame and covered in sandstone from the Glenbow quarry near Calgary and another in Ohio. The Beaux-Arts style emphasized symmetry, which is reflected in the paired columns around the entrances. The plan is a T-shape stretching to the river in the south. Offices flank the sides of the circular rotunda under the dome at the intersection of the "T," and the assembly is to the rear at the top of the grand open staircase.

Interior finishes include marbles brought to the site from Italy, Pennsylvania, and Quebec for floors, walls, and staircases; granite columns; stained glass windows; mahogany paneling; and massive oak doors. The smooth-walled classical elevations on the exterior rise above a rusticated stone foundation. The formal entry has a columned portico. The dome and cupola are framed in steel and covered in terracotta, which was an unusual choice at the time. The building took six years to finish and cost approximately $4 million to construct and furnish.

Route: You may continue into the Legislature for a tour of the building. Explore the extensive pedway system under the Legislature grounds and visit the interpretive center there. Several cafeterias can be found on the precincts, or dining establishments can be found along 109th Street, 100th Avenue, and Jasper Avenue as you return to the starting point of this tour.

Church Street Tour

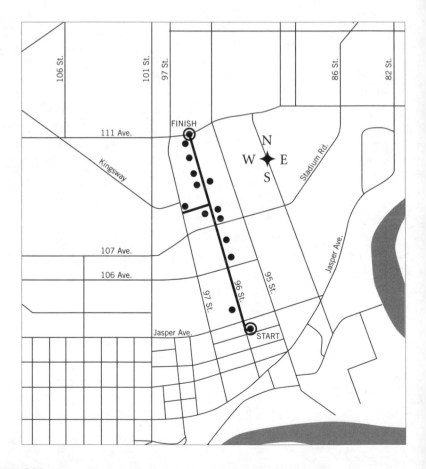

The first involvement of white Europeans in the Edmonton area came with the construction of fur trading posts in the river valley. Gradually they drew other kinds of people into the area to interact with the native population and to service the growing numbers of Europeans settling around Fort Edmonton. Missionaries, farmers, and ranchers, as well as merchants, slowly came into the area to make a new life.

When the Government of Canada acquired the lands in the Northwest Territories in 1869, it hoped that immigrants would fill the lands and make it both profitable and secure for the national commonwealth. Although the Canadians purchased the land, part of the deal was that the Hudson's Bay Company retain a "reserve" of land around their posts to protect their future financial interests. (The railway companies received similar land grants around the rail lines which they could sell to immigrants.)

At Edmonton the Hudson's Bay Company chose land directly north of the trading post site (just south of the present Legislature Building), from the river to about 111th Avenue and from 101st Street to 121st Street. This caused a bit of a problem for new residents of Edmonton, who wanted to build near the center of activity. In the 1880s, the "town" grew up east of 101st Street—with the exception of a few Hudson's Bay Company employees who managed to secure lots closer to the fort along the edge of the upper riverbank. The company did eventually allow individuals to build west along the riverbank, and the roadways of 100th and Jasper Avenues were sketched out with use.

When Edmonton incorporated as a town in 1892, the center of town was 97th Street, where the first fire hall and the town council's chambers and offices shared space. The area that developed around this core contained businesses (commercial and industrial) as well as residential housing—mostly for the working classes. The Rat Creek, which flowed to the river, passed to the north of the neighborhood and provided water and sewerage for the industries that lined the ravine. The town dumping grounds were just north of the creek's outflow into the river valley.

As soon as people began settling in and around the downtown area, missionaries and clergymen came to serve their spiritual needs as others moved in to serve their secular and physical needs. For many years, because settler numbers were small and many of them were barely surviving in this new land, there was little money for building churches and paying the clergy. The faithful relied on itinerant ministers and missionaries who were funded by European church organizations. Eventually, however, as numbers grew and financial situations improved, the call for places of worship took precedence over other concerns in the community.

Because this neighborhood was convenient to new immigrants and workers, the establishment of churches here began early and continued for decades. Over time, as the origins of the immigrants changed the ethnic and linguistic nature of the neighborhood, new churches were added and others were altered to suit the needs of the newcomers. The history of the churches on Church Street is dynamic and rich.

The Boyle-McCauley Area

The area in which Church Street is located is named for John Robert Boyle and Matthew McCauley, early businessmen and political activists in Edmonton. The neighborhood stretches south to north from 105th Avenue to Norwood (111th) Avenue, and east to west from 82nd Street to 101st Street. In 1912, the streetcar began running down 97th Street from Jasper Avenue before turning east at 106th Avenue. This further encouraged development and boosted the prosperity of businesses along the route.

The expansion of the streetcar line to the northeast to service the new community of Highlands also offered workers who resided here (such as miners and meat packers) access to the industrial development occurring in that direction.

John Robert Boyle (1871–1936) came from Ontario farming stock, but went to work to provide himself more education than his family could offer. He came to Edmonton as a teacher until he could enter law school. He was admitted to the Alberta Bar in 1899, and in

1904 he served the new city of Edmonton as an alderman. When the Province of Alberta was created in 1905, Boyle ran as a Liberal for the seat of Sturgeon in the new Legislative Assembly. He would be elected five times to the Legislature and eventually serve as the Liberal party leader. In 1918, he was elevated to cabinet as the minister of education, and then as attorney general until 1926.

When Boyle retired from politics, he was appointed to the Supreme Court of Alberta. Both a street and a neighborhood in Edmonton, and the nearby village of Boyle, are named for him.

Matthew McCauley (1850–1930) was born in Ontario to an Irish father and a Scottish mother. At 21 years of age, he moved to Fort Garry and worked as a laborer before starting a hackney carriage (taxicab) business. In 1874, he married his first wife, Annie, and they had eight children. In 1879, the McCauleys moved west. They farmed near Fort Saskatchewan for two years before setting up a cartage business and butcher shop in Edmonton.

McCauley was involved in numerous political and social causes in Edmonton, including founding the Norwood Residents' Grievance Committee to counter the adverse effects of the fumes from the Burns Company (an abattoir) and other disturbing smells from the city's incinerator at the dump. He also served as director and president (1890–95) of the Edmonton Cemetery Company, president of Edmonton District Agricultural Association (which operated the Exhibition) for sixteen years, and first chair of the school board beginning in 1881 and serving for nineteen years. McCauley was Edmonton's first mayor after its incorporation as a town in 1892, and he negotiated a charter for a street railway.

When his first wife died, McCauley married another Annie and sired another four children. In 1896, he was elected to the Legislative Assembly of the Northwest Territories (before Alberta was made a province in 1905). After his term ended, he ranched at Beaver Lake from 1901 until returning to Edmonton in 1905 to run for Legislature of the new province of Alberta.

He again retired after a term, and in 1911 became warden of first federal penitentiary in Alberta, which was located near this neighborhood. McCauley again retired, this time to the Okanagan until his 75th birthday, then homesteaded in the Peace River country until his death at age 80.

St. Barbara's Russian Orthodox Cathedral

Address: 10105–96th Street
Style: Byzantine
Architect: Unknown
Date: 1957

Although appearing small in area, the high ceilings and especially the dome of this church give the interior a great feeling of spaciousness and height.

Russian Orthodox missionaries came to North America via Alaska as early as 1794 to serve the traders and the native people there. From Alaska, they spread along the coast to California, and eventually, in 1897, two missionaries from California came to Alberta and the Rabbit Hill and Wostok settlements of Russian and Ukrainian immigrants.

About 1900 or 1902, Father Jacob Kurchinsky came to Edmonton and started a house church which belonged to Slavic immigrants. Late in 1902, he bought this site on Syndicate Avenue and Grierson Street (100th Avenue and 96th Street), converting a house into a chapel. His congregation was made up of Galacians, Bukovinians, Trans-carpathians, and other immigrants from the Austro-Hungarian Empire.

After Father Kurchinsky returned to Russia, around 1907, he was replaced by Father Skibinsky, who agreed to build a new church on the site. It would be designed in traditional Byzantine style, formed in a cross with a high cupola covered with galvanized metal perched on the four corners of the nave. It was a wooden framed structure, with a dome 10 meters in diameter and almost as high, topped with a three-barred cross. It was completed in 1908, consecrated, and named for St. Barbara, who was martyred in North Africa in 200 AD. A fragment of one of her bones is kept in a reliquary in the church.

In 1912–13, the parish built a house for the minister on the site beside the church, which was later dubbed "the Institute" and used to accommodate rural students attending school in Edmonton. The parish built a hall in 1914 under the church on a new foundation. Fluctuations in immigration caused by the two world wars and the Depression meant that the church membership stayed relatively small until the 1950s.

By 1956–58, however, the church had grown both in member-ship and importance, and in 1959 the wooden structure was torn down, to be rebuilt in cement and brick. The original cross was saved (installed in the church cemetery near Nisku in 1979) along with the original iconostasis, which was carved in red cedar (unpainted and unique in Canada) in accordance with Russian traditions. St. Barbara's was dedicated, and it became the cathedral for the Russian Orthodox churches in Edmonton.

In 1979, the parish received a historical board plaque for the 75th anniversary of St. Barbara's. The bell tower to the south of the build-ing (in front of the seniors housing complex) was dedicated in 1993 as a tribute to Father John Margatich, who was St. Barbara's minister for 35 years.

Chinese United Church
Address: 10152–96th Street
Style: Unknown
Architect: Unknown
Date: 1953

Both in style and in use of materials this church fits with our image of a Chinatown structure.

Missionary work among the Chinese in Edmonton started with the work of two missionaries, the Reverend Mar Shong and Mr. C. P. Leung, who had been working in the Chinese community in east-central Edmonton before 1933. Edmonton did not really have much of a Chinatown until after 1911. Before 1900, fewer than twenty Chinese men lived in the city. Unlike Calgary, which was more accessible to Chinese immigrants because of the early arrival of the Canadian Pacific Railway and the Chinese laborers used to build it, the few Chinese in Edmonton were scattered until just before the First World War.

In 1911, Edmonton's Chinese population had increased to 154, of which only four were women, so natural growth was all but impossible for the community. Immigration restrictions from the 1920s to the 1940s aimed at limiting Asian immigration caused the numbers to decline, and the prevailing social attitudes among European residents in the city did not encourage wide-scale settlement. By the 1930s, however, 300 to 400 Chinese people were living in Edmonton, mostly congregated for living and commercial purposes in the area east of 97th Street and 101A Avenue.

Methodists and Presbyterian missionaries often approached Chinese men with the opportunity of learning English as a method of introducing them to Christianity. Since learning English was a desirable goal, they were able to convert a few of these men, but the numbers of new Christians remained small. Many found that the Chinese clan associations or other clubs were better able to meet their needs for friendship and assistance.

About 1933, the Reverend Fong Dicknanas started a Chinese-language parish using temporary worship space in houses or whatever was offered. In 1947, the United Church of Canada bought two lots on 96th Street for the parish to build a frame and stucco house church.

The congregation built the new church and converted the house behind it into low-cost housing for seniors. The community was very concerned about their single, elderly male members, since few had family in the country. The Boyle Street area in which the church was located had deteriorated into slum housing, and most Chinese workers and businessmen had moved into more prosperous neighborhoods. New immigrants still came into this neighborhood until they got a foothold in Edmonton.

By 1970, the congregation numbered about 130 members, and the church offered English classes and ran Chinese films and educational activities.

The 1970s brought a threat to Chinatown in terms of the eastward-creeping development of the city's downtown, and deteriorating conditions in the inner city. Several projects to consolidate government offices and widen roads were delayed until city planners could implement a plan and process to relocate and "save" Chinatown. Eventually, the move was only a matter of a few blocks, with new facilities, such as the Chinese Elders' Mansion (1977) and the Harbin Gate, being provided to highlight the special nature of the community, and other businesses and residential facilities taking advantage of the opportunities to start fresh.

The old Chinatown was essentially demolished, most of it beneath the development of the new Canada Place, and by the mid-1980s a replacement Chinatown had been constructed, as planned, to the northeast of the old site.

During the interim, when the fate of old Chinatown was subject to debate and planning processes, many Chinese merchants and restaurant owners took matters into their own hands. They relocated away from both the old Chinatown and the replacement Chinatown, emerging in clusters of strip malls farther north on 97th Street and creating a new ethnic shopping area, parallel to other ethnic community areas such as Little Italy and later Little Vietnam.

Here the emphasis is on family shopping for both the Chinese and Vietnamese people as well as other non-oriental people.

Family Worship Centre

Address: 10605–96th Street
Style: French Gothic revival
Architect: Unknown
Date: 1913
Route: As you proceed north to the next stop on the tour, you will pass sites where churches once were, but which have now been replaced by other facilities. If you have a vehicle, you may wish to return to it and travel the intervening blocks by car. This is an inner-city neighborhood, and there are several social service agencies along the route, some of whose clientele will be coming and going on the street.
10341–96th Street was the site of the original Bissell Memorial United Church until the 1950s. Today the Bissell Centre, a social service agency, is located on the site.

10362–96th Street was in 1914 the church of St. Mark's of the First Born, about which not much is known.
10542–96th Street housed the Community Service Mission in the 1940s.

Although an old style the use of the lighter colours and trim give this renovated building a sense of a new start.

This church was built before World War I as the Grace Methodist Church. It flourished until the union of Methodist, Presbyterian, and Congregational denominations in 1925, when it was apparently considered surplus to United Church needs. It remained vacant until the late 1930s, when it became St. John's Ukrainian Greek Orthodox Church. It remained part of the Eastern Rite churches until early in the 1950s.

By 1954, it had changed its stripes again and become the Second Christian Reformed Church, an offshoot of the successful First Christian Reformed Church (see attraction no. 12 on the Church Street Tour).

Late in the 1980s, the Christian Reformed parish no longer needed this church, and it became the Family Worship Centre (which is affiliated with the Pentecostal church). Significant alterations and additions to the building occurred then.

Although altered considerably since its original construction, the structure has retained a few of its distinguishing features. The corner tower and steeple has simplified turrets on the four corners, typical of this Gothic revival style. The roof is steep-pitched, and the small extension on the south side is reminiscent of a buttress support for the structure. The hall added to the north somewhat distorts the symmetrical feeling that the church should project. Similarly, the windows are square rather than arched.

Other churches once in this block included:

10628–96th Street—a Ruthenian Presbyterian church in 1914, which was renamed in the 1930s as the Ukrainian Presbyterian Church. In 1940, it became the Ukrainian Labour Temple, an ethnic workers' cooperative society which was restricted during the Second World War.

10632–96th Street—the hall for the Presbyterian Church in the 1930s, but in 1940 it briefly became a separate Church of the Nazarene.

Mustard Seed Street Church / formerly Central Baptist Church

Address: 10639–96th Street
Style: Gothic revival
Architect: Unknown
Date: 1912

In 1898, a group of seventeen German domestic servants were gathered together by Rev. Abraham Hagen, a visiting Baptist minister from Vancouver, for a service in the Baptist tradition. From his early organizational attempts, the First German Baptist Church was begun the following year. The parish rented the Indian Methodist Chapel (at 101st Street and 100th Avenue, thereafter the *Edmonton Journal* site) for the first few years before buying two lots on Isabella (97th) Street and Namayo (104th) Avenue.

This impressive building was created by the massing of the two perpendicular gables around the square bell tower and hexagonal spire.

In 1901, they built a church which was enlarged twice in subsequent years as the church membership grew. In 1902, the congregation was accepted as part of the North-Western Conference of German Baptist Churches of North America. Later this church became a full-fledged member of the Northern Conference of German Baptist Churches of Canada.

When streetcars began running up 97th Street in 1912, church members found the noise not conducive to worship. They sold out and built a brick building on 96th Street at 106A Avenue which cost $44,000. The old missionary Hagen came back to dedicate the church and placed a history of the congregation in the cornerstone. John E. Knechtel was the new pastor to 181 members.

Between the world wars, the parish sponsored a German-language gospel radio program in an attempt to reach the many Germans who had left the city during the First World War. World War I, the Depression, and World War II caused the German population in Edmonton considerable difficulty. Many people lost jobs, were separated from family, and forced to work in camps. Those who remained experienced harassment and prejudice. The church was vandalized, and several members moved to English churches to distance themselves from things German. Between 1924 and 1926, the attitudes toward Germans caused by the war had significantly reduced the church membership. They had no pastor, and the church suffered.

By 1938, there was some recovery, and the church helped to establish the Christian Training Institute to encourage new ministers. In 1940, the name was changed to the Central Baptist Church, and by 1943, services were offered in English. A new electric organ was acquired.

In 1948, the congregation undertook a remodeling program costing $6,000. By 1950, with the influx of immigrants after the war, membership had grown to 535. New churches were spawned: in 1951, the south-side McKernan Baptist Church was formed; in 1954, Emmanuel; and then in 1956, German Zion on the south side. By 1957, Central Baptist started looking around and raising funds for a new location. It purchased lots on 76th Avenue and 106th Street, in Capilano, in 1958; more lots were purchased in 1961 in North Edmonton.

The church amalgamated with Lauderdale Baptist Church and created the new Namayo Park Baptist Church in 1963. Those remaining at Central Baptist decided to relocate in 1967 to 94th Avenue and 95th Street.

This church remained empty for several years before being purchased in 1973 for $126,000 by the Friars Steakhouse Company. The parsonage at 10860–96th Street was also sold. The former church building then served as the site of Danny Hooper's Stockyards Night Club before again being abandoned until 1993, when it was acquired to serve as the home of the Mustard Seed Street Ministry's church.

More a social service agency, although it does offer Sunday services, the Mustard Seed serves 5,000 hot meals a month, offers a soup kitchen four times a week, and supplies Sunday brunches after services provided by churches of many denominations around the Edmonton area. The Mustard Seed movement is North America–wide and is loosely affiliated with the Baptist Church. The other churches that contribute to the food programs here also provide aid when disaster threatens, such as a flood from a broken pipe in late 1990s and the failing roof in 1999.

Agencies such as the Inner City Advocacy Network operate from the church, and they run the annual "Meet the Street" walk, an all-night event to raise awareness of the issues of poverty and homelessness.

St John's Lutheran Church

Address: 10759–96th Street
Style: Asymmetrical Modern
Architect: Unknown
Date: 1971
Route: Continue northward along 96th Avenue crossing 107th Avenue carefully with the pedestrian light. This is a very busy crossing at times.

The modern interpretation of the steep cast roof allows for the high ceilings expected in a church on a fairly small downtown lot.

Initially this church was known as St. Johannes First German Evangelical Lutheran Congregation. The pastor from the Trinity Lutheran parish on the south side of the river, Gustave Poensgen, decided about 1900 that the Germans on the north side should have access to services. Initially German immigrants had settled south of the river, especially around the Ellerslie area.

Many eventually moved into Strathcona, and some ventured across the river into Edmonton to take advantage of some of the industrial jobs offered there. There was no bridge at that time between Strathcona and Edmonton, though the river could be crossed using ferry services; however, those were often disrupted by weather, ice, and spring floods.

The building of the Low Level Bridge in 1900 eased that situation, and Poensgen was able to cross easily, so the hall of Gariepy and Lessard at Jasper Avenue and 100th Street (on the northwest corner) was rented for church services. By September 1904, German Lutherans on the north side had built and dedicated a new frame church at 103rd Avenue and 96th Street, paying $500 for the land and $950 for the 8-by-11-by-5-meter building with a small foyer at the front.

During 1905, there were discussions among the various Lutheran communities about union. St. John's (Evangelical Lutheran) and St. Peter's (of the Missouri Synod) attempted to merge their two parishes for six months before an irreconcilable rift occurred. There are still three different Lutheran Synods represented on this street.

In 1906, a new church was built at 108th Avenue for a cost of $1,800. It was enlarged in 1910 to add seating for up to 220, a new basement for the Sunday school, and a steeple. (James E. Wize designed the additions to create a 29-by-11.5-meter building at a cost of $7,000.) For the first time, the evening services were conducted in English. One of the parishioners donated a real pipe organ.

In 1913, the congregation built a parsonage which would be used until 1955 as the house for the ministers, then for the following five years as an extra Sunday school class. The wars and the Depression, however, seriously affected the parishioners' ability to support the church, as many lost jobs or moved away. The congregation managed to stay open with support from the Board of American Missions, but their debt grew. Anti-German sentiment resulted in a name change to its English equivalent, and after 1939 English services were held more regularly.

After World War II, the immigration of Germans began to increase again, and by 1946 St. John's was again self-supporting and on the way to paying off its debt. After 1947, the church began a program to "catch up" on repairs, including replacing the pipe organ with an electric one. A Latvian congregation also shared the facility. In 1954, they purchased the next lot and planned for a new hall for Sunday school and an auditorium. Construction began only in 1960 with significant volunteer labor to keep the construction costs to $43,000. The building was dedicated in 1961 and soon paid off.

By 1971, a larger church was required again. The present building with 350 seats was erected at a cost of $150,000 and dedicated by May 1972. Fundraising for the completed church was accomplished by 1977. This church also hosted a Chinese congregation for several years.

St. Josaphat's Ukrainian Catholic (Ruthenian) Cathedral

Address: 10825–97th Street
Style: Prairie cathedral
Architect: Philip Ruh
Date: 1939
Route: Take a detour from 96th Street, turning west on
108th Avenue toward 97th Street.

An earlier church was built on the same site in 1904, but it soon proved to be too small. In 1939, this church was constructed of brown brick with imported marble, wrought iron, and gold inlay, with copper on the domes. The church is built in the shape of the cross with seven domes representing the seven gifts of the Holy Spirit. There was controversy during its construction. During World War II, building materials were at a premium to assist the war effort, and some considered this an extravagant use of metal during the restrictions of the war. As well, since the copper reflected light, it was thought to impede aviation at the nearby air field.

This is one of Edmonton's architectural gems, as well as a cultural icon and community landmark.

Because the majority of the work on the building was accomplished with volunteer labor, the $250,000 estimated cost for completion was significantly reduced. The church seats 500, so it is not the largest Eastern rite church in Edmonton. About 1943, it became the headquarters of the western eparchy (diocese) of the Ukrainian Catholic (Eastern rite) Church. In 1948, St. Josaphat's became the cathedral, and the bishop's palace was built nearby for $50,000.

A commission was given to Julian Bucmaniuk (and his son) in 1950 to paint frescos on ceiling and walls, and to design the iconostas, the special screen between the congregations seating and the altar. Julian Bucmaniuk (1885–1955) was a Ukrainian artist who trained in major European centers of the arts (Paris, Florence, Rome) and immigrated to Canada in 1950. He worked on the project until his death in 1955, after which the work on the iconostas was finished by two students, Parasia Iwanea and Deacon Ivan Denysenko.

St. Joseph's was designated an Alberta historic site in 1984, not because of its age, but because of the architecture and interior details. It is the best example in Alberta of the prairie cathedral style developed by Rev. Philip Ruh, and it has the most ornate and unique frescoes. Philip Ruh (1883–1962) was a Belgian who came to Canada from Germany in 1911 to be a missionary in northern Alberta. He was also a self-taught architect before being ordained, and while here in Canada he designed some 30 Canadian churches, including the monastery in Mundare and a church in Leduc. One of his Ukrainian churches from Smoky Lake was dismantled and shipped to the Museum of Civilization in Hull, Quebec, for reconstruction within the museum.

The church follows a typical transcept design (a Greek cross with seven domes) with the sanctuary at the east end. There are cornices on part of the façade. Ruh employed a number of different architectural styles, including pseudo-classical or American colonial features in the front columns, Roman-style octagonal copper cupolas and drums for supporting the larger domes, and a Renaissance style for the decorative cupolas. The largest dome, representing Christ, the head of the Church, is open into the church below.

The interior is richly decorated with frescos in a Baroque style with neo-Byzantine influences. The frescoes were created in the traditional manner in a medium of egg tempera (milk, eggs, linseed oil, and tempera powder). The original plaster applied by the volunteer builders was too smooth to hold a fresco, so it had to be chipped off by hand and reapplied. (Stories abound of the broken hearts that caused.) The ceiling fresco is called *God the Creator,* and Saint Josaphat is pictured over the sanctuary.

There are also special stained glass windows, the best of which celebrates the life of Sister Josaphata Hordashevka, the founder of Sister Servants of Mary Immaculate, an order which cared for disadvantaged children in the Ukraine.

Immaculate Conception Roman Catholic Church / Mary Queen of the Martyrs (Viet)
Address: 10830–96th Street
Style: French Gothic revival
Architect: Unknown
Date: 1903
Route: Return east to 96th Street to continue the tour northward.

Father Thibaut, a missionary at Lac Ste. Anne, came to dedicate this new French-language Catholic church in 1903 which cost $10,000 to build. The exterior of the church was brick on a brick foundation.

The interior was painted light blue with an arched ceiling, and the woodwork was oiled fir. The French Gothic revival style can be seen in the prevalence of buttresses at the corners and the sides of the building, which support and emphasize its vertical aspects. The high spire and decorative features such as the statue above the door similarly draw the eye upward. The rose window in the tower, the arched Gothic windows, the small pinnacles around the tower, and the steep-pitched roof are all classical features of this architectural style. Decorative elements, such as the white dentilled molding below the eaves and the cutwork in the tower cornices, lighten the effect of the structure's massing.

There is an organ loft at the rear of the church and a statue of the Virgin was placed over the altar as well as on the exterior in an arched recess typical of this style. Initially about 200 francophone families were members of the parish.

Over the years the church has been remodeled at least three times. At some point the brick was covered in stucco. In 1983, in response to the Vatican's encouragement, a partial immersion tank was installed along the north wall for baptism. Hollywood actor and singer Robert Goulet was baptized here in the 1950s, and he trained in the church choir.

By 1990s, the numbers attending this church had dropped to between 60 and 70, and the church was threatened with closure. Many francophone families had moved to other neighborhoods,

Typical of the gothic style, the intention is to draw the eye upward towards the heavens.

especially around the Bonnie Doone area around Le Cité and Faculté St. Jean on the south side of the river. In 2000, the parish was amalgamated with St. Thomas Aquinas Church in Bonnie Doone after it had been without its own priest for a decade. The final French-language mass was held in January 2001. Its most recent change has been the amalgamation with Mary Queen of the Martyrs (a Vietnamese-language parish previously on 108th Avenue and 109th Street).

The property to the north of the church is also owned by the Catholic Church and now serves as offices. A shrine to the Virgin Mary can be seen to the south of the church.

Sacred Heart / First Peoples' Roman Catholic Church

Address: 10821–96th Street
Style: French Gothic revival
Architect: Hardie & Maitland
Date: 1913
Route: Turn to face the east side of the street for the next
   building.

This Gothic revival–style church opened on December 25, 1913, to serve English Catholics in the eastern part of the city. The construction cost was $50,000 for the church and $8,000 for the rectory beside it. The congregation raised over a quarter of that amount in the first year of operations.

Originally the church seated 1,000 in the nave and also contained a U-shaped gallery around three sides—part of which was called the Sisters' Gallery. The two buildings are joined and share a heating system which is powered by a large furnace in the basement of the rectory and fed into the church through underground pipes. The Reverend Maxim Pilon directed the parish initially.

The church measures 19 by 28 meters and contains such Gothic details as a central pointed arch above the front door and windows, rose windows, and two towers, the tallest of which is 40 meters. At the time of construction, it was the tallest tower in the city. The redbrick

This is a highly decorated version of the same style as the last stop.

walls are buttressed and contain stained glass windows with decorative detailing to emphasize the Gothic style. In 1928, a pipe organ was purchased for $8,000.

In 1909, the first four room brick Kinnistino Street (96th Street) School, which is located across the street south of the Immaculate Conception Church, was opened. In 1907 an old parish hall was pulled across town from Oliver to serve as a temporary structure for the school. In 1911 the school size was doubled by adding a second storey. It was renamed after the Sacred Heart of Jesus in 1918.

In 1966, a fire set by an 8-year-old boy caused $200,000 worth of damage to the interior, leaving only a shell of the church building. The following year, extensive renovations replaced the interior details, except for the U-shaped gallery (which was replaced only across the back), and in light of Vatican II innovations to include the congregation more in services, placed the altar in the center of the church. The organ was rebuilt.

During the 1990s, the church also hosted a Spanish mass and a Croatian congregation, as well as aboriginal groups. The church members operated a food bank depot and offered an annual Christmas dinner to the poor. In the last five years, it has become the First People's Church and now contains examples of native spiritual art and artifacts.

Ansgar Lutheran Church

Address: 10857–96th Street
Style: Danish church
Architect: Holn Moller
Date: 1939
Route: Turn to the north to view the next building.

Danish immigrants first came to the Edmonton area from the midwest American states, mostly Nebraska, around 1903, although Danish immigration numbers remained minimal until after the First World War, when people began arriving directly from Europe as well as via the United States.

Note the step like detail over the entrance and the gable ends of the church.

In 1929, a wealthy Dane named S. P. Sorenson launched a settlement scheme through the Canadian National Railway to bring Danes into central Alberta in block settlements. He brought over 300 families and settled them near Innisfail at Dickson. Like most block settlement schemes, this one was not completely successful. Not all the settlers stayed on their assigned farms; many moved to cities like Edmonton in search of work and prosperity.

In 1930, a congregation of Danes started worshipping in the Norwegian church at 84th Street and 109th Avenue. There was also a Swedish church at 107th Street and 99th Avenue. In the 1930s, this area attracted northern European settlers since it offered work in industries with which they were familiar. By 1939, the Danes were numerous enough to build a new church for themselves for $5,000. It is a frame and stucco structure built according to plans drawn by an architect from Copenhagen, Holn Moller, and overseen by local architect W. G. Blakey (who also has several churches to his credit, including the Anglican curches of Christ Church and All Saints Cathedral, and Highlands United Church). The step design over the entrance and at the side of the gable roof is typical of Danish architecture. The church seats 150 people. The parsonage at 9554–108A Street was built at the same time. The Reverend Emil Nommesen served the parish initially.

In 1945, Ansgar celebrated its fifteenth anniversary with approximately 400 Danish members. A second wave of Danish immigration after World War II saw the numbers increase again during the 1950s. English services were introduced for the second generation, who had been educated in the Alberta school system and saw integration as a key to their success.

By 1978, the first generation were sensing the loss of their culture, and with the support of the government's multiculturalism programs and assistance from Alberta Housing, the "Over 60" group built a seniors home with a Scandinavian flavor, called the Ansgar Villa. They also began a research project on the history of Danish settlement in Alberta. In 1985, the church began to offer language classes and ethnic activities, and to alternate the sermons in English and Danish. For some people, the church has become a vehicle to preserving the Danish language and culture.

St. Stephen the Martyr Anglican Church
Address: 10909–96th Street
Style: Prairie Church Architecture
Architect: Unknown
Date: 1914
Route: Continue north along 96th Street.

The Anglican Church has been a firmly established entity in Edmonton since the nineteenth century; originally centered around All Saints Church, west of the downtown area, near the river valley on Hudson's Bay Company reserve lands. In June 1905, the rector of All Saints Anglican Church, Henry Allen Gray, held a meeting of parishioners in the eastern part of the parish to see if they would be willing to start a mission church there. All Saints Church purchased two lots on Kinistino and 15th Street (the former address of this site) from Robert Belcher of the North-West Mounted Police, who had been transferred to Lethbridge. Architect R. Percy Barnes drew up plans for a church to be called St. Paul's. Individual contributions were collected from all those who attended the meeting, but the total proved inadequate, so the grand plans had to be cut back.

This is a simplified version of a prairie church architectural style, with details and trim like half-timbering to give it an "English" air.

By August 1905, a 10-by-15-meter frame church had been built with $500 loaned from All Saints for furnishings, and an organ was donated. The minister was promised $150 per year as a stipend. H. H. Wilkenson was hired, but he did not prove a popular choice; attendance soon fell and financial difficulties ensued. Wilkenson left for Fort Saskatchewan in 1908, and H. H. Summers became the new, more popular vicar until 1911. The congregation and Sunday school grew, but not enough to counter the earlier debt. A new rector, George Howcroft, built a rectory for himself soon after his arrival in 1912, and talk began about enlarging the church. By 1914, the congregation had borrowed heavily to build a new church of brick. Unfortunately, the war brought hardships to many families and debts went unpaid, interest accumulated, and the minister was often not paid. In 1918, the lands were listed by the city for tax sales.

Howcroft returned to England in 1920, and the diocese began to discuss merging St. Paul's with St. Andrew's, another Anglican church which had been built in the interim at Jasper Avenue and 93rd Street. The diocese thought to redistribute the parishes in the east end "with a view to having fewer and stronger parishes." By September 1922, the parish was over $5,000 in debt. Overwhelmed, they decided that amalgamation was the only hope. The vestry turned the church keys over to the diocesan executive, which moved to amalgamate under the name of St. Stephen's.

The merged congregation called F. C. Cornish from Gleichen as their new minister. The Beulah Tabernacle purchased the old St. Andrew's, but even with the sale, outstanding debts from both parishes remained and several St. Andrew's members refused to join St Stephen's. The style of worship practiced at St. Paul's and St. Stephen's was "high church," or Anglo-Catholic (incorporating full sacramental teaching and the idea of the church as a divine society). It took several years to pay off the bond holders of St. Andrew's.

In 1927, an English philanthropist, S. Attenborough, offered to pay off all outstanding debts and mortgages of St. Stephen's on the condition that the parish sign an undertaking never to mortgage any of its property again. Despite what some considered the poor placement of the church in the parish (too far north, and surrounded by French Roman Catholics), the church continued. Because of its worship style, it was never too popular in the city. It received a new organ from Bishop A. E. Burgett (the second Anglican bishop in Edmonton) in 1930 and a bell in 1933.

During the 1950s, the church was involved in some mission work, but it has never really prospered enough to emerge from the community, and since the 1980s, it has frequently been threatened with closure. Since it offers a special style of worship for Anglicans, those who appreciate it are quite loyal. In the 1990s, the church became more involved in community issues and began using the rectory as a treatment and recovery center for persons with addictions.

St. Stephen the Martyr Church is a simple structure with stucco and half-timbering decorative features on the exterior. It is brick over a cement foundation with an entrance foyer typical of prairie church architecture. The hipped roof has minimal decorative features on the windows and eaves. The interior is rectangular with two side chapels opening into the central nave area. Interesting details in this church include its collection of relics and icons, which contribute to its liturgical style.

There is little or no information available on the Holy Trinity Russian Greek Orthodox Church at 10902–96th Street, except that it was originally used for another church and the onion dome was added when it was converted to Holy Trinity.

First Christian Reformed Church
Address: 10952–96th Street
Style: Post Modern
Architect: Unknown
Date: 1948
Route: Continue north along 96th Street.

Christian Reformed churches have an unadorned exterior and lack the decorative or stained glass windows of many other churches.

Prior to the First World War, immigration to western Canada from the Netherlands underwent a brief period of growth. Like the Danes and Germans, the Dutch were offered a number of organized colonization schemes to form group settlements, such as the one at Neerlandia. Many immigrants, however, came to the city and stayed there. Initially, churchgoers met for worship in a tent on Canadian Pacific Railway station land at Jasper Avenue and 109th Street under the direction of the Reverend Mr. DeKoekkoek.

By 1913, there were enough members to build a First Dutch Reformed Church at 93rd Street and 105th Avenue. During the war, however, membership declined. At the end of the war in 1918, the remnants were officially organized into a congregation with 18 adults and 23 children. By 1925, Dutch immigration was growing again and congregation numbers increased. In 1927, they held their first English-language service. The larger number of congregation members forced consideration of enlarging the church.

Land for a new church was purchased in 1948 near 110th Avenue and 96th Street. A simple steep-roofed, rectangular church was built for $32,000. Again the congregation grew, and by 1951 they were considering starting a second congregation. As an alternative, a split-off group used MacDonald Baptist Church, then the Masonic Hall, then the auditorium at Alberta College. By 1953, they were looking to build but didn't have the funds. They decided instead to buy the old Ukrainian Orthodox church on 106th Avenue and 96th Street (see attraction no. 3 on the Church Street Tour), which was renovated by the 1,000 members and dedicated in 1954. This church building was remodeled in 1960.

By 1955, the First Christian Reformed Church was planning for a third congregation to form. They used the old Jewish synagogue at 95th Street and 101st Avenue, then bought old Central United church at 99th Street and 106th Avenue. Eventually, they sold that site to the Hope Mission. A fourth congregation was formed in Beverly (Maranatha), a fifth on the south side (Braemar), and a sixth at Ottewell.

St. Peter's Lutheran Church

Address: 9606–110th Avenue
Style: Gothic revival
Architect: Unknown
Date: 1928

Note the similar features of the gothic style (arched windows and doors) and the steeples like other churches found on this street.

The Missouri Synod of the Lutheran Church in North American first began its missionary work in the Edmonton area in 1894 when Missioner Eggers of Great Falls, Montana, held German services for settlers at the Fire Hall No. 1 (at 96th Street and 101st Avenue). The main Lutheran presence was established at Stony Plain between 1894 and 1897. Their pastor, Emil Eberhardt, held services in Edmonton and the Mill Creek area from time to time.

By 1904, there were enough congregants to call Walter Lussby to Edmonton to organize St. Peter's. They built a small structure on Nelson (107th) Avenue and 3rd (103rd) Street. As the group grew, in 1911 they were able to purchase three lots on the corner of Kinistino (96th) Street and Wilson (110th) Avenue for $4,000. There they built a temporary structure for another $2,000 They sold the former church building, and the Missouri Synod gave them a grant of $5,000, which allowed them to also start a school. H. W. L. Schultz came to be their pastor.

Between 1914 and 1922, Rev. Alfred Rehwinkel was pastor, and with the congregation's support he founded Concordia College as a seminary to train Lutheran ministers and to educate their children. They were forced to close the school during the war because of anti-German sentiment and the restrictions on German-language use. In 1919, Rehwinkel was joined by John C. Mueller, who oversaw the building of the new church. During the construction period, members worshiped in the Ukrainian Catholic National Hall (9520–109th Avenue; later a Seventh Day Adventist church).

The church was completed in 1928 under August Mueller, who served until 1960. Later, a parish hall replaced the old school, which had also served as a hospice for German immigrants. During the Depression, the church offered soup kitchens for those afflicted by job loss and poverty. They also sponsored a radio show on CFRN called "The Lutheran Hour."

By the 1950s, membership had reached 500 with new immigration, and St. Peter's was able to purchase a pipe organ. In 1960, the church welcomed its first Canadian-born pastor, Norman Threinen, who had been educated locally at Concordia College. The church was extensively renovated in 1968 for the 60th anniversary. In the 1970s, the church started enacting a live nativity scene at Christmas time. Involvement in the community continued, and in the 1990s, they contributed regularly to the food bank and sponsored "The Rock," an inner-city assistance society that offered a somewhat controversial community breakfast to area residents and the poor.

Mui Kwok Buddhist Temple
Address: 11036–96th Street
Style: Prairie church
Architect: Unknown
Date: ca. 1914

The simple structure of the prairie church architecture is adaptable for a number of uses.

This church was originally built as a Church of Christ (Disciples) house of worship around the beginning of World War I. It is a simple rectangular structure with rounded arched windows and an entry foyer in front. Called the Central Church of Christ and in existence until 1960, it left few records of itself.

The site was vacant during the 1960s, but in the 1970s the building became a Ukrainian Seventh Day Adventist church. (An earlier Seventh Day Adventist church had been located at 10902–96th Street until 1951.) Later the ethnic makeup of the community was reflected in a name change to the Korean Seventh Day Adventist Church.

It was again left vacant in the 1990s and has recently been reincarnated as a Buddhist temple.

Other Buddhist temples in the area include:

Chin Yin Temple (Chinese) at 10853–98th Street

Truc Lam Monastery (Thai) at 97th Street and 113th Avenue.

Downtown Core Tour

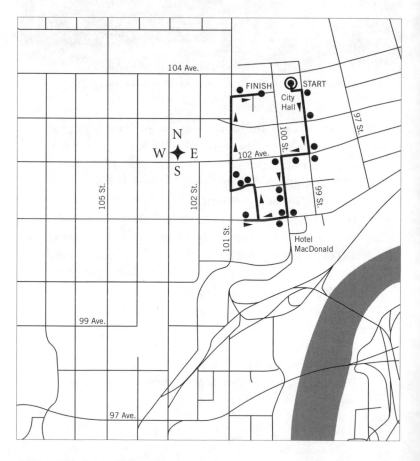

Jasper Avenue was the center of activity even in 1921—looking west from 99th Street.
CITY OF EDMONTON ARCHIVES EA 160-18

Edmonton's civic center is really the creation of the post–oil age in Alberta. Although earlier attempts had been made at creating a central municipal center for the city, economic and political events conspired to keep the dream at bay. Edmonton's growth was never according to any particular plan, and it suffered through a series of booms and busts that hampered the building of momentum in its development.

Initially the center of commercial activity in Edmonton evolved to the east of the Hudson's Bay reserve, around the 97th Street and Jasper Avenue intersection. This development was interrupted in 1881 when the Hudson's Bay Company subdivided some of its reserved lands south of Jasper Avenue and west of 101st Street, leading to a gradual shift southwest for residential development and some commercial activities.

The drift became an avalanche in 1912 when the remainder of the reserve was put on the market at the same time that other speculative land developments were occurring to the east and west of the Edmonton core, and the city was in the midst of amalgamating with its former southern rival, Strathcona. Suddenly there was a variety of commercial centers and competing areas calling for development dollars. This period of intensive land speculation and investment gave way in 1913 as the overloaded economy began to fail and was forced into recession and depression during and in the wake of the First World War.

Recovery after the war was extremely slow and followed by the 1930s, when the country and the world suffered through the Great Depression. Only after the Second World War and the discovery of oil did Edmonton really begin to grow and rebuild. Prior to then, the governmental and cultural facilities in Edmonton were mostly pre–World War I or early 1920s neoclassical structures, such as the Carnegie Library, the Federal Post Office, the Court House, and the Civic Block (all now demolished and mostly forgotten).

With the return of optimism caused by the burgeoning oil economy and new ideas circulating about town planning which arose out of the reconstruction era after World War II, civic authorities began to think about building a unified civic center that would represent the new age of progress and prosperity Edmonton was entering.

Webb and Knapp, Canada's biggest real estate company at the time, was invited to become involved in developing a planning proposal for a civic center in the late 1950s. The consultants enthusiastically produced, at their own expense, a model for a civic center which, although it did not prescribe architectural details, did focus on encouraging the development of buildings with a moderne and international style focus.

It suggested that the types of buildings in a planned civic center would include municipal government offices and service providers, cultural facilities, commercial and professional office buildings (at a recommended height of three storeys), at least one high-rise hotel, a recreation center, and a coliseum. They also recommended a special "northern development pavilion to showcase the city's connection with the north."

Studies were undertaken by the Alberta Association of Architects and the Downtown Design Committee. The planned objectives were:

to enhance City Hall with a fine Civic Park, lending beauty and dignity to the center of Edmonton; to house governmental and cultural agencies on sites suited to their growing needs, their purpose and their importance to the community; to strengthen the existing downtown retail activity and encourage its expansion; to realize the full potential for commercial development within a framework of ordered growth; to create a dynamic urban centre, giving form to the city and a richer life to its citizens.

Although the plan was adopted in principle in 1962, it was never followed through. Remnants of the ideas generated, however, did influence those who decided on the placement and design of various buildings that are found now in the city's center.

By 1962, several downtown core buildings had already been erected. City hall, the 1957 version, replaced the former Civic Block as the seat of the city council chambers. This was a thoroughly moderne building complete with an abstract sculpture of Canada geese rising from the water of the fountain in front of the building, which was instantly dubbed "the spaghetti tree" and reviled by the majority of the citizens. As part of the Civic Block's retrofit as the new police headquarters, it was clad in shiny metal siding to streamline and modernize it.

Other buildings which began to replace the pre–World War I institutions around the central park (which would become Sir Winston Churchill Square) took on aspects of the "in" architectural styles of the time. The city's centennial project for 1967 was to replace Carnegie Library with a streamlined tower balanced on a pedestal reminiscent of the Bauhaus functional buildings erected in postwar Europe.

While the progressive plan was not carried out in full, the pieces that were constructed in this period are individually representative of the dream civic center originally presented. Unfortunately, individual components of the various interpretations of the style did not make a cohesive civic center, and today, when the style is not widely appreciated, the downtown seems more stark and unwelcoming than an embodiment of the spirit of progress.

Recent additions and replacements for individual parts of the downtown core—the new city hall, the Winspear Centre, alterations to the Stanley Milner Library and Edmonton Centre complex—have injected a new design element into the mix. The downtown of Edmonton is again in a period of transition. It will be interesting to see what survives and how the parts will contribute to a new whole.

City Hall

Address: 1 Sir Winston Churchill Square
Style: Eclectic
Architect: Gene Dub
Date: 1991

Like the moderne style of many of the Sir Winston Churchill Square buildings, the emphasis here is on the horizontal line of the building, except for the vertical pillars, the clock tower and the striking asymmetrical pyramids on the roof.

This is the fourth city hall. It replaced a 1957 city hall designed by Hugh Seton (Dewar, Stevenson and Stanley) and constructed for $3.5

million during the mayoral term of Bill Hawrelak. Another former city hall, the Civic Block was demolished to make way for the Winspear Centre.

Tenders for a new city hall were sent out in 1990 on an original plan which had cones over the central portion of the building. Early focus groups among the citizens of Edmonton forced the removal of the cones, which were replaced by pyramids. During all the design stages, the costs of the new city hall kept escalating, which resulted in more design changes to achieve cost cutting. An entire wing was removed, and the clock tower and reflecting pools were restricted to optional components subject to funding.

The building finally went ahead, and was at least $10 million over the initial budget estimates by the time it was completed. The clock tower and skating rink were saved due to the generosity of private donors, including Dr. Dick Rice who provided a major donation for the clock. A contest was even held to name it. "The Friendship Tower" was the winning entry. Despite all the squabbling and headaches, at the end of construction the consensus was that the new building was more visitor-friendly than the last city hall and perhaps more of a landmark. Certainly the City Room—the space in front of the grand staircase and under the large pyramid—is an excellent public space for gatherings and ceremonies.

The new city hall is faced with Manitoba Tyndall stone and topped with a nine-storey-high pyramid. The interior contains hanging glass walls, terrazzo flooring, and a showpiece council chamber with movable walls for audiovisual presentations. The fountain and reflecting pool in the front courtyard are converted for ice-skating in winter and changing facilities are provided inside.

Tours of the city hall's interior can be taken at various times during weekdays. Inquire at the desk inside the central entrance.

Behind the city hall, you can see the CN Tower, the former home of the CNR station, and beside it to the east the Sir Alexander Mackenzie Building, the 1966 post office tower.

City hall sits atop the LTR system and is attached to the system of pedways and overpasses that link the majority of the downtown buildings. It faces Sir Winston Churchill Square, which was named for the British Prime Minister and which contains a statue of the famous politician and orator, donated by the Sir Winston Churchill Society of Edmonton. The square was completely redesigned and made over for the city's 100th anniversary in 2004.

Other buildings around the square are mostly retail spaces and cultural facilities. Before the late 1950s and 1960s, when most of these buildings were constructed, the civic center looked much different. There were several residential homes on the side streets around the Civic Block, which was on the east side of what is now Churchill Square. On the west side was the 1911 Greek, classically influenced courthouse, which housed the supreme and district courts of Alberta until 1972.

The land was sold to Woodwards department store, which demolished the courthouse for Edmonton Centre (now remade into part of the City Centre retail complex). The city market lay on the south side of the square, and behind the market's mostly low-lying buildings was the federal post office. Commercial buildings were at most three storeys high and had large display windows at street level.

Edmonton Art Gallery

Address: 2 Sir Winston Churchill Square
Style: International
Architect: Donald G. Bittdorf
Date: 1969
Route: Head to the southeast corner of the city hall block.

The Edmonton Art Gallery on Sir Winston Churchill Square is actually the fifth home of the city's collection of art since the Museum of the Art Association began in 1923. It is, however, the first of those buildings which was actually designed as an art gallery. Previously the Museum of Art's collections have been housed in the Hotel Macdonald, Secord House, the Civic Block, and the civic library.

The strong and stark lines of the Edmonton Art Gallery provoke strong opinions of its design among Edmontonians.

In the mid-1960s, after the Edmonton Art Gallery board had been discussing for years how to raise the money required for construction of a gallery, they were given a large memorial donation by Edith Condell, in honor of her son, on condition that they construct a building before the end of 1969 or lose the money to the University of Alberta. Given the pressure to perform, the city was convinced to donate the land, and the construction of the Arthur Blow Memorial Gallery was completed on time.

The award-winning design of local architect Donald Bittdorf is of a simple rectangular form set on a platform raised above the street. The interior is furnished in natural materials, including fine woodwork and furniture within spacious galleries. The central foyer contains a sculptured staircase leading to the second-floor galleries. A large auditorium and meeting rooms are found on the lower level. The gallery was enlarged in 1977, but in the 1990s it began to suffer for not being modern or large enough, and without the appropriate environmental equipment or enough gallery space to accept larger exhibitions which travel from other galleries.

Talk has already begun and fundraising started to replace this gallery.

Francis Winspear Centre for Music

Address: 4 Sir Winston Churchill Square
Style: unknown
Architect: Cohos Evamy Partners
Date: 1997
Route: Proceed south past Chancery Hall toward 102nd
Avenue.

Like the Citadel beside it the Winspear Concert Hall uses windows and an open floor plan in the lobby area to draw the public into the building to experience the treasure of the concert hall within.

The Francis Winspear Centre for Music replaced the Civic Block, once Edmonton's city hall and a former police headquarters as well. The Civic Block had been built in 1913 with Edwardian styling and a brick and terra cotta exterior. Though intended for only temporary use as a city hall before conversion to offices, it was used by the city until 1957 and then covered with metal sheeting and glass to update it. It housed several municipal offices and the Edmonton Museum of Art collection (which later moved to Secord House). Interior detailing included marble staircases and balustrades.

The Winspear Centre was designed to replicate the acoustics of the classic European concert halls of the late nineteenth century found in Vienna and Amsterdam. The acoustical designers were Artec Consultants of New York. The shoebox-shaped hall consists of an 1,800-plus-seat main concert hall and rehearsal space.

Dr. Francis Winspear (1903-1997) donated $6 million to the capital campaign, which was at the time the largest private donation given to a performing arts organization in Canada. He had been a strong supporter of the arts in Edmonton, both personally and through his private foundation as well a contributing to the School of Business at the University of Alberta, his alma mater. A founding member of both the Edmonton Symphony Society and the Edmonton Opera Society his commitment to the music community in Edmonton was well known. The federal and provincial governments each provided $15 million, and the city leased the land to the Edmonton Concert Hall Foundation for 90 years at $1 per year—which was equivalent to a $6-million contribution.

Very quickly the concert hall became known for its excellent acoustical qualities. The next exciting acquisition for the hall was the Davis concert organ, which was launched in September 2002. The generous donation of Dr. Stuart Davis was made in memory of his wife, Winona, because of her love of music. Together the organ and the concert hall contribute greatly to culture in Edmonton, and with the art gallery and the Citadel Theatre form part of what is being called the Edmonton Arts District downtown.

Citadel Theatre

Address: 9828–101A Avenue
Style: Post Modern
Architect: Barton Myers (Toronto) & R. L. Wilkin
    (Edmonton)
Date: 1976
Route: Continue south to the corner of 101 A Avenue.

The drama of the building's occupants is as much on display to those outside through the Citadel's windows as are the dramatic presentations made to the audience inside the five theatres in the complex.

The Citadel Theatre was the first professional theater organization in Edmonton that has become a prominent regional theater in Canada. The company started in 1965 in the old Salvation Army Citadel on 102nd Street and took its name from that building. Joseph Shoctor, the Citadel's producer and managing director, was the son of a Russian Jew who immigrated to Canada in 1913. Educated at the University of Alberta, Joe Shoctor became a lawyer and a theater promoter who acted as much as he produced.

When the time came to expand the Citadel out of the small venue, Joseph Shocter and artistic director John Neville were instrumental in the design and construction of the new facility. The project began with a fundraising goal of $2.5 million, to which the three levels of government contributed, including a 50-year lease at $1 per year. As well, a major donation came from Dr. Dick Rice.

The building is constructed of structural steel, glass, and Medicine Hat brick. The original configuration included three theaters—the Shoctor (main stage), the Rice, and the Zeidler halls—

plus a restaurant and lobby. The main theater had 675 seats, the farthest only 21 meters away from the stage. It opened to rave reviews in November 1975.

A $10-million addition and renovation in 1984 added the Lee Pavillion and two more theaters, the 656-seat McLab Theatre, and a 150-seat Tucker Amphitheatre, making the Citadel now the home to five unique theaters. The Foote Theatre School, production facilities, and multipurpose classrooms are also contained in the facility. The Lee Pavillion, integrated with the city's pedway system, is an indoor garden which was created with a grant from the private Clifford E. Lee Foundation.

Stanley Milner Library

Address: 7 Sir Winston Churchill Square
Style: International Moderne
Architect: Dr. A. O. Minsos, Rensaa Minsos & Associates
(Edmonton)
Date: 1967
Route: Turn to the west along 101A Avenue to reach the
Stanley Milner Library.

Following the belief of Andrew Carnegie, the American philanthropist, that literacy built better citizens and would create a better world, the American Carnegie Foundation provided money to North American towns and cities on a per capita basis for the construction of public libraries. After several years of arguing about the size of Edmonton's population (and hence the size of the grant) in 1923 a compromise was accepted by the Edmonton City Council which allowed the largest Carnegie library in North America to date to be built on the North Saskatchewan riverbank at the corner of 101st Street and Macdonald Drive. It served Edmontonians for over forty years as the primary library.

By 1960, the growth in collections and the number of people using it had rendered the library inadequate in the eyes of the authorities. The land was sold to the Alberta Government

Telephones company in 1966, and the classical building was demolished to make way for AGT's new office center.

Perched atop its pedestal, the library tower serves as a beacon for those seeking knowledge and culture.

Plans for a new library were started in 1961, but took several years to come to fruition. The site chosen for the new library was across from the city hall, which was where the city market had been for many years. It was essentially an open-air market with occasional large open sheds which gave purchasers access to the produce.

Prior to settling at the Churchill Square site, the market had moved a number of times, including to Rice Street. An abortive attempt by the city to move the market away from the city center was conducted in 1914 when the city built facilities at the corner of 101st Street and 107th Avenue. For the most part, the market producers simply refused to go there, remaining in temporary shelters at the old site. In 1964, however, the market was successfully relocated to 10165–97th Street, making way for the new library on the square. The timing was right to make the building the city's centennial project for 1967—hence the original name: the Centennial Library.

Construction of the six-storey, 20,160-square-meter building began in 1965 although the process was beset by numerous problems, including the resignation of the associate architects, Richards, Berretti and Jellinek. The building is designed as a tower placed upright on a flat pedestal. In keeping with European architect Le Corbusier's tenet of the building as a machine, the library was conceived as a market where people came to "shop" for books. The main floor was designed to resemble a retail department store with separate areas which all filtered into the checkout area.

The construction process was an example of modernist construction techniques—cheap and fast to produce a flexible facility. The wall panels were made of pre-cast brick, lighting came in the form of a continuous luminous ceiling, and metal pan forms were used to pour concrete floors which made the structure lighter. The interior space was designed to be flexible with portable shelves and wall dividers. The construction costs came in at just over $3.7 million with another $500,000 for furnishings.

The building was officially opened and dedicated by Princess Alexandra of Kent in May 1967. The lower three floors were dedicated to the library, and the upper floors were used for city offices until such time as the library needed to expand. There was an 800-car parking garage below the building.

Rensaa and Minsos were important Edmonton architects whose firm was established in 1948. They were the designers of the Edmonton International Airport, the Westmount Shopping Mart (Edmonton's first shopping mall), Ross Shepherd Composite High School, Winnifred Stewart School, and the School of Nursing Residence at the Royal Alexandra Hospital.

A major $6-million, 930-square-meter renovation to the library was undertaken in 2000, adding an atrium in front of the entranceway and an attached café to the west side. The children's books section was moved upstairs to the east side of the entrance, and a display gallery opened in the atrium. The heritage collection was amalgamated into its own reading room on the second floor.

In 1996, the library was renamed after Stanley Milner. He had served as the chair of library board from 1963 to 1968 and was a driving force behind the building's initial construction. Milner received the Alberta Order of Excellence in 1995, and he served as alderman, deputy mayor, and chair of University of Alberta board of governors. He was associated with Chieftain Developments, Wardair, and other airlines.

Churchill Wire Centre

Address: 10003–103rd Avenue
Style: Moderne
Architect: Max Dewar, City of Edmonton
Date: 1945–47
Route: Continue west to the corner of 101st A Avenue and 100th Street.

The low slung building again contrasts the horizontal building structure and materials with vertical detailing of the windows and the columns between them.

This is the last of the historic buildings on Sir Winston Churchill Square. It was the home of Edmonton's first municipally owned telephone company. It replaced the original company building built on site in 1907, and added to in 1921.

Moderne building details include the black granite base topped with the white terrazzo finish. There is a regular rhythm of windows: two together, then a pilaster followed by two windows together. The cornice is stylized rather than attached to the building, as in classically influenced buildings, and has dentils. The chevron motif in the spandrels (the flattened, fluted pilasters that flank the corner entry), the stainless steel detailing, and use of glass block are also features of a moderne building.

Note the carving above the entry. The figure standing on a globe, holding lightning bolts aloft, represents long-distance communication with electricity.

McLeod Building

Address: 10136–100th Street
Style: Chicago commercial
Architect: John K. Dow (Spokane)
Date: 1915
Route: Head south on 100th Street.

The McLeod Building was financed by Kenny McLeod, an early resident of Edmonton with many business interests. He came to Edmonton in 1881 and worked as a contractor before branching into other business fields. He built scows for the government troops during the Riel Rebellion, and he worked at a sash and door factory. His mother and sisters soon joined him, and one sister, Helen McLeod, became the first newspaperwoman, writing for the *Edmonton Post* and the *Evening Journal*. Eventually he made some money in real estate and retired to Vancouver in 1908.

He returned to Edmonton in 1910, ready to farm at the western edge of the city. He hired an American architect to build his signature building in Edmonton; the man had built an identical building in Spokane. For 40 years, the McLeod Building was the tallest in Edmonton. It's said that McLeod

The steady rhythm of the windows and the even spacing of the columns make this building attractive and eye-pleasing despite its size and massing on the corner site. Note the clock tower on the opposite corner, the last remnant of the downtown post office.

determined his building's height by allotting one floor for each of his children.

This nine-storey, steel and brick building is detailed with Edwardian classicalism. Note the balconet over the entry, the window keystones, and the colored tiles used for decoration. The entablature at the top of the building, under the heavy overhanging cornice, is dripping with heavy modillions. The Chicago commercial style stresses the vertical aspect of the building and gives an impression of massing or presence on the site. There is also a typical division of the building into three parts, separating the ground storey from the intermediate one, and again a division of the top floor with a cornice.

The Post Office Clock that stands on the corner of 100th Street and 101st A Avenue is the last remnant of the 1910 federal government building that was sited there. The post office was a larger version of the Strathcona builing which remains today. The lot and building were purchased by the city in 1967 and sold five years later to Leamar Developments for construction of the Plaza Hotel. The post office was demolished, and the clock tower dismantled for future reconstruction. The city, however, used the stone for a memorial garden monument, and the modern tower was installed in 1978 outside the Westin Hotel, thanks to the gift of an anonymous donor.

Canada Permanent Building
Address: 10150–100th Street
Style: Edwardian baroque
Architect: Roland Lines
Date: 1910
Route: Proceed southward along 100th Street.
The Canada Permanent Company of Toronto occupied this building from 1910 to 1961 and leased extra space to other companies.

It is a three-storey rectangular building constructed with a reinforced concrete frame. The building was faced with red brick and stone, and divided into three bays on the front façade, decorated with lots of classical detailing. A stone balustrade at the crown of the flat

Easy to miss amidst its taller neighbours this building is a treasure trove of classical detailing and symbols.

roof gives it extra height. The central date stone sits in the middle of the balustrade, framed in a swag garland topped by urns. Below that a broken pediment rises from the heavy cornice, which divides the top floor from the lower two-thirds of the building. The pediment is supported by pilasters with ionic capitals (with curled tops).

Edwardian baroque was a very popular style, especially for banks at the turn of the twentieth century in Britain and the British Empire, as it was felt that the classical detailing projected a reputable image. In 1975, the bank was converted to a restaurant.

Imperial Bank

Address: 9990 Jasper Avenue
Style: Neoclassical
Architect: A. J. Everett, Imperial Bank, with Rule Wynn & Rule
Date: 1952
Route: Proceed south to Jasper Avenue. Turn east to look across the street.

Despite its modern appearance this building incorporates many of the classical symbols and much of the classical style in more traditionally built banks.

The history of the Imperial Bank of Canada began in Edmonton in 1891 when G. F. R. Kirkpatrick arrived on the second train into Edmonton, which pulled into the Calgary and Edmonton Railway station in Strathcona. Kirkpatrick would serve as the bank manager in Edmonton for 45 years. He also took a term as the City of Edmonton's treasurer in 1904. He came to open the first bank in Edmonton, which began in an upstairs room of a wooden building on 102nd Avenue, north of 100th Street.

Over 70 years in the city, the bank built and occupied three buildings on or near this site, one of which was a temporary Quonset hut erected across the street while this building was under construction. In 1961, the Imperial Bank merged with the Canadian Bank of Commerce to become the Canadian Imperial Bank of Commerce (CIBC). The bank remained here until 2000, when the branch was closed and merged with the 101st Street and Jasper branch, also housed in a historic building.

The bank's second location was a neoclassical-style, three-storey "temple" with huge marble columns, built in 1907–08 on the corner of McDougall (101st) Street and Jasper Avenue. Johnson and Barnes designed that one (and the Goodridge Block). It was demolished in 1950 to make way for a four-storey CIBC.

The bank erected the Quonset hut on grounds of the Hotel Macdonald and went to a great deal of trouble to assure clients that the building, and their money, were secure. Difficulties ensued once the second bank building was torn down. Wartime shortages meant that there was too little structural steel, and construction was halted once the building had a basement and a ground floor. Deciding that was enough to start with, the bank opened that branch in July 1952. Construction resumed the following year, but the bank decided to increase the building size to seven storeys. It was completed in 1954 at a cost of $950,000.

The exterior was decorated with bas relief carvings. Metal spandrels between windows were shaped into the bank's logo, and the quoins and pilasters stylized as bands of rectangles. The material is Indiana limestone. Inside, contrasting light and dark marble were used, and three photographic murals by local artist Alfred Blythe were displayed on the east wall.

Look across the avenue to view the Frank Oliver Memorial Park, which was opened in August 1964.

Oliver (1853–1933) was the publisher of Edmonton's first newspaper, the *Bulletin,* issued on December 6, 1880. His office building is now part of the Walter Museum site in Kinsmen Park; it contains his chair and part of the printing press brought to Edmonton in 1873 from Ontario by Red River cart. Oliver served on the Northwest Territorial Council in 1883 and in the House of Commons from 1896; he fought for self-government of the territories. Between 1905 and 1911, he was minister of the interior and encouraged greater immigration to the West.

Empire Building

Address: 10080 Jasper Avenue
Style: Renaissance revival
Architect: Unknown
Date: 1905
Route: Move further west along Jasper Avenue to the
Empire Building.

This Empire Building is an eleven-storey office building with a gray façade. The lobby has been described as small and welcoming with its logos on the doors and a curved steel ceiling. It replaced the original Empire building, which was torn down in 1962. The original Empire Block was built in 1905 by McDougall and Secord for the offices of their financial businesses and to be leased to others. Liggetts Owl Drugstore operated on the main floor for many years.

The building was severely damaged by fire in 1942, but it was renovated and reoccupied within three months. McDougall and Secord also owned the second Empire Building; they were simply keeping up with the times.

Compare the Jasper Avenue streetscape with what can been seen today. The Empire Block, ca. 1900

CITY OF EDMONTON ARCHIVES EA 516-1

Union Bank Inn / North West Trust Building

Address: 10053 Jasper Avenue

Style: Edwardian

Architect: Roland W. Lines

Date: 1911

Route: Continue west along Jasper Avenue and go about a block and a half until you are at the Scotia Place—look to the south side of the avenue.

This building was also designed by Roland Lines, the architect of the Canada Permanent Building (attraction no. 8 on this tour) and the North-West Mounted Police barracks (on the Jasper East Block tour). The Union Bank Building cost $60,000 to construct in 1911 and is one of the few pre–World War I buildings left on Japser Avenue.

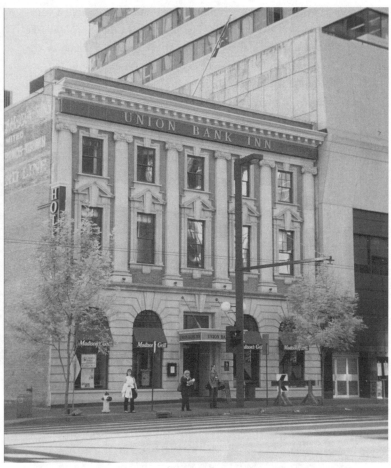

It is interesting to compare the scale of downtown buildings of today and yester-day. This was an impressive construction in pre-World War I Edmonton.

Originally this was the Union Bank's main office in Edmonton and its largest banking facility west of Winnipeg. Classical detailing includes the regularly spaced pilasters and pediments on the upper portion of the building, again representing the stability and perma-nence typical of bank buildings of the era. This building used con-trasting red and white stone to give a three-dimensional effect to the five-bay façade. The lower portion of the building is faced with banded, rusticated stone which is shaped into an exaggerated voussoir pattern over the windows. The flat roof is capped with a large entablature on which the architrave frieze bears the name of the bank "inn" below the tin cornice decorated with modillions.

The building was purchased in 1929 by James Richardson, and until 1970 commercial grain and stockbrokers' businesses occupied the building, which during this period was known as the Richardson Building. In 1970, it was owned briefly by North West Trust, and in the 1990s it was converted into a downtown executive suite bed and breakfast inn.

Kelly Ramsey Building

Address: 10040–101A Avenue & 10048–101A Avenue
Style: Chicago commercial
Architect: *Kelly,* Van Siclen; *Ramsey,* Magoon & Macdonald
Date: *Kelly,* 1915; *Ramsey,* 1927
Route: Turn north and follow Howard (100A) Street, and
then head west on 101A Avenue to face the Kelly-
Ramsey buildings.

Although owned by the same businessman and intended to complement each other, the side by side retail premises have quite distinct looks.

James Ramsey (1864–1939) was a department store owner who opened up a store in the Tegler Building (directly behind this building) soon after he arrived in Edmonton in 1911. When the store required more space, Ramsey moved into the building erected by John Kelly, a blacksmith who dabbled in real estate.

After Kelly's death, Ramsey bought the building from his widow in 1926 for $100,000, which apparently was the cost of construction eleven years earlier. He then expanded his store westward, calling it the Ramsey Building. In 1929, he sold his stock and goodwill to the T. Eaton Company, but kept the buildings, which were leased out. An astute and well-traveled businessman, Ramsey served as a city alderman for the 1915–16 term and as a Conservative MLA from 1917 to 1921. He retired after selling his store and wintered in Nassau, the Bahamas, where he died in 1939.

The provincial government bought the building for Workers' Compensation Board offices in the 1940s. Recently the buildings have been used for artists' studios with commercial and restaurant spaces on the street level.

The Kelly Ramsey Building is really two four-storey, brick and steel frame buildings that were supposed to look like each other, since the Ramsey portion was an addition to the Kelly Block. In reality their appearance and styles are quite different. The Kelly Block is done in dark brick, sporting pilasters with modern capitals at the tops and a metal cornice. The Ramsey Building has a stone façade, three-part windows, and a smaller cornice.

Moser & Ryder Building

Address: 10169–101st Street
Style: Edwardian / art deco
Architect: probably James Henderson
Date: 1910
Route: Continue around the corner on 101st Street heading north. You may want to cross over to the west side of the street for a better view of the Moser Ryder Building.

Downtown is the site of urban "progress" and the Moser Ryder building has changed over the years, which may have ensured its survival in the face of its neighbors' (like the Tegler Building on the left) destruction. Moser Ryder on the right.
CITY OF EDMONTON ARCHIVES EA10-367

This building has probably undergone the most significant facelift of any pre–World War I building in Edmonton. Originally the building was an excellent example of Edwardian classical revival, but it was completely done over in 1944 by a new owner. After being touched up in 2004, it is now a fine example of art deco–moderne style.

The Moser and Ryder Building began its life as a mixed commercial-use building. There was a warehouse in the basement, with retail space and office suites above. It has housed a grocery store, a department store, a trust company, and finally a jewelry store.

Moser and Ryder were prosperous businessmen who came to Edmonton in the early 1900s and made their fortunes in real estate. They decided to supply the need for bachelor apartments and offices in the downtown. This four-storey brick building with 1,860 square meters of space, originally divided into 53 rooms and 24 furnished office/apartments with shared baths, seemed to fit the need. Moser and Ryder retired early and lived in southern California after retirement, monitoring their holdings from afar. When their estate was sold in 1929 to a group of Calgary investors, the building's price was $200,000.

As you can see in the archival photo, the original façade of the building was elaborately decorated with classical details such as garlands along the frieze and pilasters running up the facade in parallel rows from the corners up to parapets on the roof. Then, during the Second World War, a fire caused considerable damage to the façade and the owners opted to alter it significantly during restoration.

The facelift in 1944 changed the Edwardian style to art deco and made it just the right style for the Walk-rite Style Shoppe, a women's clothier and shoe store, which remained in the building until 1974 when Johnstone Walker's women's wear moved from Jasper Avenue.

Next, the First City Trust Company purchased the building in 1986, moving out of the McLeod Building to what they called the new Bay Street of Edmonton; 101st Street had several financial companies on it. The trust company put $560,000 into building renovations. Architect Rick Wilkin wanted a contemporary look that also looked like a bank. In the interior, parts of the floors were cut out to make an atrium, and glass block was replaced with plate glass and chrome frames. These were only the latest of many changes and additions made over the years. Since most of the original façade had been destroyed earlier, restoration was not considered.

The "Bay Street" move was apparently not successful, and the trust company sold the building in 2002 to Swedish Jewellers which moved from Manulife Place, again putting in more than $2 million to acquire and renovate the Moser & Ryder Building.

Note in the archival photo the Tegler Building, next to the Moser and Ryder Building.

The Tegler was the building whose destruction started a wave of protests over the lost of heritage buildings in Edmonton. H. A. Magoon had designed the massive office and retail space, a prime example of pre–World War I commercial architecture, constructed in two stages between 1911 and 1913. Framed with reinforced concrete and clad in brick and stone with neoclassical detailing, it was a landmark building in downtown Edmonton.

Early tenants included the *Edmonton Journal*, the James Ramsey department store, and then Eatons (until its own building was ready in 1939). When the demolition permit was issued at city hall without so much as a question and the Tegler Building imploded in a glorious display of wanton destruction, citizens rose up to complain of a process which allowed them no way to save a beloved building. Reform-minded groups and heritage preservationists rallied around the Tegler Building and formed groups such as URGE (the Urban Reform Group of Edmonton) and SPARE (the Society for the Protection of Architectural Resources in Edmonton).

YMCA

Address: 10030–102A Avenue
Style: Edwardian Commercial
Architect: Unknown
Date: 1908
Route: Turn east on 102A Avenue and return toward city hall.

The YMCA was started in Edmonton by an act of the Legislature in 1907. The organization's first building, built in 1908 at the corner of May and Howard streets, opened its doors in February 1909 to approximately 470 members.

The building had a swimming pool, a gymnasium, a running track, and rooms for visitors to stay. Alexander Rutherford, the first premier of Alberta, and John A. McDougall, a prominent local businessman, helped found the association and assisted in raising over $28,000 for the building fund. By the fall of 1910, membership had topped 1,000.

In 1951, this four-storey addition, which is now the only remaining part, was made to the building, and subsequent renovations and additions have helped it continue to serve as a center for fitness and community programming.

Route: Complete the circuit of the tour by continuing westward until you reach city hall.

YMCA Building ca. 1920 *The present day YMCA is the replacement to the original building, and faces a similar fate as its predecessor depending on the actions of the city council in the fall of 2004.*

University Garneau Tour

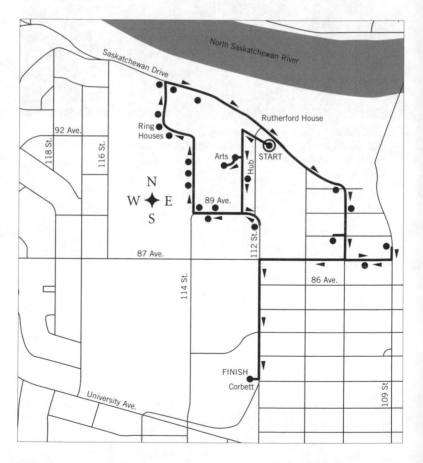

The Neighborhood of Garneau, ca. 1915
CITY OF EDMONTON ARCHIVES EA 160 -292

Established in 1906 by an act of the Alberta Legislature sponsored by Alexander Cameron Rutherford (premier, provincial treasurer, and minister of education), the University of Alberta didn't have a president or faculty or students until 1908. First the land had to be purchased by the government, which chose river lot 5 on the southern bank of the North Saskatchewan River, some 2.4 kilometers west of the town of Strathcona. It had previously been Isaac Simpson's farm and contained approximately 105 hectares of brush and scrub poplar trees which the government bought for $150,000.

Premier Rutherford recruited Henry Marshall Tory, a professor of physics from McGill University in Montreal (Rutherford's alma mater), to be the first president starting in January 1908. They shared a dream of a nondenominational, state-sponsored college in the new province. Tory was charged with determining the number of students eager to study, and with building or finding classrooms and accommodations for the students and the faculty he was to recruit. Rutherford also offered the first scholarship of $100 to the student with the highest matriculation marks.

The first four faculty members instructed in the traditional university program of liberal arts studies. William Hardy Alexander taught classics, Luther Herbert Alexander taught modern languages, English was the sphere of Edmund Kempus Broadus, and William Muir Edwards was responsible for mathematics and engineering.

Forty-five students, including the premier's son Cecil, began in temporary quarters at the Queen Alexandra School in Strathcona in the fall of 1908. They moved into the more spacious second floor of the Strathcona Collegiate in January 1909. In the meantime, plans and construction carried on at the site of the permanent campus. The university commissioned two architectural firms, Nobbs and Hyde of Montreal and Darling and Pearson of Toronto, to create a unified, dignified plan of the entire campus which could be erected as time, students, and finances allowed.

Construction of the first building in this plan, the Arts Building, was begun in the summer of 1910—but was stalled by the Railway Scandal that rocked Rutherford's government. The new political "ins" started on another building, and by 1911, Athabasca Hall became the first building to be completed, holding administrative offices, classrooms, and residences for some students, the rest being accommodated in Strathcona. The first convocation was held for those students who had started at the University of Alberta with some advanced credit, but the first graduation ceremony for those students educated completely at the University of Alberta was held in the spring of 1912.

By then the student body had grown to 175 students. The Faculty of Law was added in that year, followed by the Faculty of Applied Science (later Engineering) and a preliminary program in medicine in 1913. The other development in 1912 was the Faculty of Extension, which was created to take the knowledge and resources at the university, especially from the area of agricultural research, out into the rural community. Radio, traveling lectures, and displays at special events brought professors and ordinary people into closer contact and mutual respect.

Although severely affected by the outbreak of World War I—82 students of a class of 450 lost their lives, as well as a few professors and support staff—and the Spanish influenza epidemic that followed, the university continued to construct buildings, establish faculties, and teach students. Agriculture, home economics, dentistry, pharmacy, accountancy, and graduate studies were all initiated during the war years, and after the war a rise in the research sciences was inevitable.

The university did not suffer such a serious decline as a result of World War II, due in part to assuming of the duties of teaching and certifying teachers from the provincial Normal School and to the increase in the number of women attending the campus. Once the war was over, a veritable boom in registrations was experienced as returning soldiers took advantage of the educational opportunities.

New faculties added during this era included the increased certification of medicine graduates. Engineering, chemistry, and biochemistry grew into separate departments, and to manage all those additions, a parallel development of university administration occurred.

The academic growth, which included the development of many more degree-granting programs, began to demand a concurrent growth in the physical plant of the university. Between the late 1950s and the 1970s, expansion plans took hold. Much of the campus was dug up in the mid-1960s to accommodate the underground tunnels used for the massive electrical and heating/cooling systems, which were installed before the largest building projects were undertaken.

The administration building, clinical sciences building, the physical education center, the physics and chemistry buildings (now called CAB), the education building, the Donald Ewing Cameron library, the Henry Marshall Tory building, the biological sciences center, Lister Hall residences complex, the student's housing complex (HUB), and the married students quarters at Michener Park were all built in rapid succession.

The university received much criticism for its expansion activities, not the least of which was for the lack of architectural beauty and adherence to any kind of developmental planning for the campus as a whole. The human scale of the buildings was lost, and the lack of green space abhorred. Descriptions of the campus range from eclectic urban campus to an ugly hodge-podge of styles.

The incursions into the nearby neighborhoods and other lands held to the south around the university farm caused quite a bit of consternation and possibly the destruction of several potential historic resources. It harmed the relationship with the Garneau neighborhood, which still feels the imposing force of the university plant.

Garneau is named for the original settlers on the land, Laurent and Eleanor Garneau. Laurent was born of a French father and Ojibwa mother from Michigan who came to Canada when their son was young. The Laurent Garneaus came to Edmonton from Red River in 1874 after Red River Rebellion (1869), where Laurent had been a supporter of Riel, like many of the Red River Métis.

They homesteaded at river lot 7 (109th to 112th Streets south from Saskatchewan Drive) and built a cabin which today would be at the end of Hub Mall, with a view of Fort Edmonton on the tableland of the north bank of the river. Laurent was always welcome at the fort for his fiddle and musical talent. The Garneaus were francophone and Métis, which set them apart from many of the newcomers who came into the area with the arrival of the Calgary and Edmonton Railway in 1891. Laurent was elected to the Council of the Northwest Territories, but he was not allowed to take his seat due to his continued involvement with Riel and for his support of the Edmonton Resistance Movement in 1882. In 1885, he was imprisoned for his support of Riel.

The Garneau farm was still a significant distance from the town of Strathcona; however, the decision of the Alberta government to purchase the adjoining river lot 5 (odd-numbered lots were on the south side of river; even, on the north) changed the prospects. In 1909, Garneau subdivided the northern part of the property and sold the first three lots to Alexander Cameron Rutherford. He never became wealthy from his real estate, and Garneau left the area to assist with Father Lacombe's Métis settlement vision farther east, near St. Paul des Métis, sometime after 1900. He died there in 1921.

Father Lacombe desired to see the Métis people settled in a secure environment where they would not be subject to prejudice from Protestant and English settlers and authorities. It was his wish to reinforce both the Catholic religion and the French language by maintaining the separate settlement of the Métis people. Although the settlement scheme did attract a number of Métis they were never large enough to have the influence on local government he wished. The town name was eventually shortened to St. Paul.

Some members of the family, including Eleanor, remained behind, living in their farmhouse. Between 1910 and 1913, there was a large amount of development in the area as professors, businessmen, and professionals moved into the promising district.

Garneau has survived economic downturns better than many neighborhoods because of its proximity to the university and the government center (over the High Level Bridge). It contains a mix of faculty and civil servants, as well as businesspeople who appreciate the higher education level in their neighbors.

As with the university, the 1960s saw a boom in more moderate housing south of the campus, and the influx of new families and young professionals, as well as students and faculty with slightly more bohemian lifestyles than those found in Glenora or the Highlands, introduced businesses such as cafés and coffeehouses, bookstores, and boutiques along the major arteries around the district.

The only threat to the neighborhood came in times of university expansion. Several houses in Garneau were bulldozed in the 1970s, and community advocacy groups were fostered in those times. That threat continues today.

Rutherford House

Address: 11153 Saskatchewan Drive
Style: Jacobethan revival
Architect: Arthur Wilson & David Herrald
Date: 1911

When the Alberta government purchased land for the University of Alberta (at Education Minister Rutherford's urging), Rutherford himself bought the adjoining 0.5-hectare lot in order to be close to his dream. His dream house was a 400-square-meter mansion which cost $25,000 and took two years to complete. This was the second residence for the Rutherfords (they had sold their earlier home at 8715–104th Street), and they lived here from 1911 to 1940. Although it was conceived at a time when he was at the height of his political career, Rutherford was no longer the premier by the time his family moved into the house.

A fitting monument to the man who was responsible for the creation of a University on this spot.

The Rutherfords named their new three-storey mansion "Achnacarry," and Mrs. Mattie Rutherford and their two children, Cecil and Hazel, found they had more than enough room for living and entertaining. The house had a formal dining room and drawing room, a library which served as Rutherford's home office, a large kitchen, and four bedrooms plus a maid's suite with a separate entrance and back staircase, as well as a verandah at the back. Materials on the interior included golden oak and maple flooring and paneling. The fireplace in the library was block and replaced with an electric heater to help preserve the books from damp, dust, and soot which would have arisen from a regular fire. Despite looking like an ancient Scottish castle, the house was equipped with all the modern conveniences available in 1910, including electric lights, central heating, flush toilets, and a well-outfitted kitchen with running water.

The architectural style is Jacobethan revival, like Government House across the river. Its distinctive features include the two storeys of bay windows on either side of the front entrance, which is graced with Doric columns holding up the second-storey balcony. There are prominent Dutch gables at the sides of the house, and the roofline is crenellated, which makes it look like a small fortress or castle. The steps rise to a porch surrounded by a stone retaining wall created with stones hauled from the nearby Mill Creek.

The house used to have a semicircular carriageway off Saskatchewan Drive, making for a grand entrance to this grand house. Originally there was also a brick garage behind the building to house the Rutherford car, since Mr. Rutherford was one of the earliest owners of an automobile in Strathcona.

Although Rutherford was a strong supporter of the university, and university students were often invited to use his library to study, the university did not take very good care of the building when it came to be in its care. The Rutherfords sold the house in 1940 to the Delta Upsilon fraternity, and it was used as a residence for fraternity members until 1967. In 1966, the university wanted to demolish the building to make way for the new humanities complex. Public opinion was strongly opposed to the demolition project, and the University Women's Club raised $17,000 to save it.

Eventually the university relented and leased the building and site to Alberta Public Works, which carried out $120,000 of restorations (there were twenty years of frat parties held here) over three years. In 1973, the building was opened to the public, and it is now operated by Alberta Historic Sites Service as a museum celebrating the life and legacy of Alexander Cameron Rutherford.

Rutherford, nicknamed the "Gentleman of Strathcona," came to the new city at the end of the Calgary and Edmonton Railway line in 1895 to practice law. He became involved in a number of community projects, including politics, very soon after arriving from Ontario. He served as the secretary-treasurer of the town council when Strathcona was incorporated in 1899. He was elected to the Northwest Territorial Council in 1902 and served as deputy speaker until he became the first premier of the new province of Alberta in 1905, serving as the provincial minister of education at the same time. Rutherford was a founding member of the Historical Society of Alberta and president of that organization from 1919 until 1940. He was chancellor of the University of Alberta from 1927 to 1940. Rutherford died in 1941.

There are tours of the house museum as well as special programs offered for groups. A wonderful café and gift shop make Rutherford House a great place to return to at the end of this walking tour.

HUB International

Address: 112th Street from 89th Avenue to Saskatchewan Drive

Style: Arcade

Architect: Barton Myers & A. J. Diamond; A. L. Wilkin

Date: 1972

Route: Head to the northwest end of HUB Mall and either walk along beside it or climb upstairs into the mall to view the interior.

HUB Mall is properly named the Housing Union Building, which only partially explains its function on campus. Three levels of housing for 850 students line the east and west sides of the building. Running along the center space on the second level and the occasional mezzanine gallery are 50 commercial spaces let out to bookstores and audio sellers, food franchises (including the requisite coffee and beer venues so important for student life), and providers of typing, copying, and other services.

Initially a roadway ran under the building, along which precious parking spaces could be leased; however, that road was closed and the space closed in to house more office space and a daycare, which are accessed from the staircases that descend to ground level at regular intervals.

The HUB is a unique feature on the University of Alberta campus.

The building was one of the most innovative housing projects designed in Canada in the 1960s, an adaptation of the nineteenth-century vaulted shopping arcades found in European city centers. The acclaimed design was created by the Toronto firm of Barton Myers and A. J. Diamond, who used the services of Edmonton architect A. L. Wilkin for oversight of the building project here. The HUB is six storeys tall and some 290 meters long, with one of the largest acrylic vault domes in the world.

Arts Building
Address: 11316–89th Avenue
Style: Neoclassical
Architect: Nobbs & Hyde, with Cecil Burgess
Date: 1915
Route: From the southern end of the HUB you can see the Fine Arts Building and to the east of it, the Law Centre. Return to the center of the HUB, exit by the Rutherford Library and go north west to the Arts Building.

One can imagine a different environment on campus if all the buildings had followed the template of the Arts Building.

Opened by Lieutenant Governor George Bulyea in 1915, the Main Teaching Building, as it was then known, contained classrooms, the library, and professors' offices. The principal architect, Percy Nobbs, called his style "Elastic Free Classical," which allowed him to use the details of classical styles, yet not be tied to the conventions of any particular one.

The building has a sandstone and granite foundation. Its brick walls are trimmed with sandstone, much of which was fashioned onsite as the building was being constructed. The arch over the central main entryway, is not a traditional classical feature, is contrasted above by the pointed pediment over the window surrounded with the double ionic columns that support the upper pediment with dentils. Various carved crests representing the arts and sciences decorate the building, and some of the lintels over the windows on the main floor are decorated with the same chevron-like device found over the larger window grouping above the entry. An oriel window on the south façade (a Tudor revival feature) is found under a sundial which counts "only the sunny hours."

To the west of the Arts Building, Convocation Hall abuts as a wing of the main building. Laboratories designed with similar coloration and massing were added to the sides.

The Arts Building was one of the buildings conceived as part of the grand design for the University of Alberta drawn by the Montreal architectural firm of Nobbs and Hyde in 1912. Their scheme laid out a complete campus of classical-influenced buildings in a formal plan of which this building would be the eastern vanguard. Behind it to the west would range administrative buildings facing, and a convocation hall and the laboratories perpendicular to, a landscaped avenue leading from the southern edge of the campus to the river.

On the western side of the avenue there were to have been the student residences in three-quarters quadrangle configurations (of which Athabasca, Pembina, and Assiniboia are the only pieces realized), as well as other faculty buildings; and on the western edge of the campus, colleges around full quadrangles. Probably less than 5 percent of the buildings designed in this scheme were ever completed, due to the intervening wars, lack of available funding, and perhaps an overly ambitious plan.

A study of the Arts Building will give a sense of how differently the campus might have turned out had the historical development been different. Go inside briefly to see the interesting historical panels in the lobby.

Power Plant

Address: 113th Street & 88th Avenue (approximately)
Style: Utilitarian
Architect: Unknown
Date: 1915
Route: Skirt around the south side of the Arts Building to view the sundial and find the Power Plant.

A good example of how functional can also be attractive.

The east section of the Power Plant was constructed first. The building was constructed of red brick using high-quality brickwork, including a process of brick patterning called diapering. The detailing of urns at the roof line echoes the work on the near-by Arts Building and helped this building fit in with the original university scheme.

The building housed the boilers required to generate electricity for the university and was also used before 1920 for oil sands research conducted in the basement by Dr. Karl Clark. Both medical and engineering students had lab space here. The addition on the west side is slightly less decorative and more utilitarian.

In 1972, planning started to redesign the building for student use, and in 1978, architect Richard Wilkin adapted the building into the Graduate Student's Association Centre housing offices, meeting space, and a pub. The interior of the pub space shows exposed ducts and pipes decorated in bright colors with hardwood floors and exposed brick walls. The design for the adaptive reuse of this building maintained its historic identity as a utilitarian building, changed for a modern use. There is also a campus post office housed at the east end of the building.

Rutherford Library

Address: 112th Street & 89th Avenue
Style: Georgian revival
Architect: Rule Wynn & Rule; *addition,* Monsos, Vaitkunas & Jamieson
Date: 1951; *addition,* 1974
Route: Turn around and walk east toward the Rutherford Library.

In 1909, the university senate authorized the purchase of $5,000 worth of books. Those books and the library were housed first in Athabasca Hall, then moved in 1915 to the newly constructed Arts Building, where it remained for over 30 years. In 1948, the architectural firm of Rule Wynn and Rule was commissioned to design a new library, with the proviso that it fit in with the style and coloration of the earlier buildings on campus.

The decorative detail of the old Rutherford Library contrasts with the stark facades of many of the newer university buildings.

The architects chose to create a solid and functional building in rose-colored brick using white limestone trim to embellish the exterior with muted classical details. The corner quoins (alternating pieces of the trim intruding into the brickwork around the corners), the courses that divide the lower from the upper floors, and the horizontal and vertical alignment of the multi-paned windows suggest the Georgian style. Other classical details include the white entablature under the partitioned cornice and the pediment over the entry and upper gallery windows. The interior was finished with marble flooring and staircases, and bronze fixtures. Similar classical detailing can be found in the entryways and in the basement washrooms.

Many alterations to the interior have occurred to facilitate the growth of the library. In 1970, planning began for the expansion of the library to the north. The firm of Monsos, Vaitkunas and Jamieson came up with a design for a new building, in orange and red brick, which was joined via an atrium to the original library by 1974. The building was also linked at that time to HUB Mall via a second-level pedway.

Old St. Stephen's College

Address: 8820 – 112 Street
Style: Tudor revival, with some Gothic revival features
Architect: Magoon & MacDonald
Date: 1911
Route: Head south across 88th Avenue to Old St. Stephen's College on 112th Street.

An interesting mix of stylistic features creates an imposing educational structure.

Old St. Stephen's College was built as the southern campus for Alberta College. It was the Methodist theological college and student residence, and actually the first building occupied on campus. After the union in 1925 of most of the Methodist, Presbyterian, and Congregational churches in Canada, the college amalgamated with Robertson College of the Presbyterian Church and was renamed St. Stephen's in 1927.

Constructed with a steel frame and brick exterior, the building shows several Tudor and Gothic stylistic features. The decorative battlements around central towers and roofline and the towers themselves are reminiscent of Gothic revival features used in many educational structures of this period in the city. Note the small simulated buttresses around the towers. The towers house stairwells to higher floors. The recessed entries and the quoin-like cuts into surrounding brickwork around doors and windows, as well as the label molding over the doorway, are Tudor revival features. The grouping of the windows, especially to the sides of the entryway, is another Tudor detail.

St. Stephen's served first as a college and then, after the construction of the new, smaller college immediately to the south, as a convalescent home, a nurses residence, an army barracks, and a student residence. Eventually it was considered redundant to the university's needs, and the Alberta government took it on, renovated it in 1979, and has since used it as the home of the Historical Resources Division of Alberta Culture.

As it is a public building, you may be able to gain access to the interior reception area, at least during working hours.

St. Joseph's College

Address: 89th Avenue & 114th Street
Style: Jacobethan revival
Architect: Edward Underwood
Date: 1926
Route: Head west along 88th Avenue past the Education Building. The Education Building was constructed between 1963 and 1965 at a cost of $4 million. The Environmental Engineering Building, south of St. Stephen's, was built in 1965.

St. Joseph's College was started by the Christian Brothers in 1926 as a Catholic college associated with the University of Alberta. The Carnegie Foundation provided $100,000 toward its initial construction cost. Since 1963, it has been administered by the Basilian fathers as a nondenominational college.

Design in the shape of an "E," the building is constructed of red brick in the Jacobethan style, an offshoot of the English Tudor revival style often associated with university and governmental buildings (e.g., Government House). Typical features of this style seen here include tall, narrow windows and the cross-gabled roofline.

This college is a comfortable and attractive residence for students.

Exterior decorations characteristic of Jacobethan architecture include the detailing between the windows in the three-storey bays, while the coat of arms over the main entrance and the nine stone plaques depicting religious precepts remind viewers of the college's religious history. The main residential parts of the college are flanked by a chapel and a gymnasium wing.

Medical Sciences Building

Address: 11304–89th Avenue
Style: Neoclassical
Architect: Percy Nobbs
Date: 1921
Route: Face north and view the Medical Sciences Building.

Also known to students as the Dental Sciences Building or the Dentistry/Pharmacy Centre, the Medical Sciences Building has housed a number of students from various health care faculties over the years. The first medical studies classes were held in 1913, although the Faculty of Medicine was not created until after World War I. Pharmacy instruction began in 1914, and dentistry in 1918. The three departments were housed in this building when it opened in 1921.

The eye-pleasing symmetry of the building is topped with a unique cupola.

As part of the grand classical campus scheme of Montreal architects Nobbs and Hyde, the building has classically inspired details carried out in red-brown brick and sandstone accents. There is a central cupola atop a stone balustrade, and the façade is divided by brick pilasters (flat, attached column-like structures) which support stone entablatures. Other classical decorations include crests and urns. Additions were tacked onto the building in 1946, 1947, and 1951. In 1961, the interior rooms were enlarged and modernized.

The Medical Sciences Building also houses a Slowpoke nuclear reactor and its research lab in the basement. "Slowpoke" stands for "safe, low-power, kritical [critical] experiment."

Administration Building

Address: 11339–89th Avenue
Style: International
Architect: Hartley (Public Works)
Date: 1957
Route: Continue west towards the Administration Building.

The emphasis on the horizontal aspect of the building, which is typical of this style, is juxtaposed with the vertical detailing of the narrow insets which house the small windows.

Started the same year as the Golden Jubilee Auditorium, the Administration Building was one of only two public works projects begun in 1955. The four-storey building housed the offices of the president, the bursar, the registrar, and the provost, as well as the student advisory services and the National Employment Services when it opened in 1957. The building includes a penthouse apartment.

The building cost over $900,000 on completion, requiring about $300,000 more and a year longer in construction than anticipated. It is faced with red variegated tapestry brick, similar to the Engineering Building, with Indiana limestone details. The lobby, entry, and main-floor washrooms have terrazzo floors, and the lobby walls were finished in marble.

The Administration Building once housed seventeen temporary classrooms as well as the bookstore. It was the first building on campus to have air-conditioning and a passenger elevator. The sculpture beside the walkway to SUB is called *The Peace Dove*.

The New Students' Union Building (SUB), to the west of the dove, was built in 1967 for $6 million. It was built to hold the offices for the student's union, a bowling alley, a curling rink, bookstore, bank, cafeteria, barbershop, games room, and lounge. The Student's Union also employs about 200 part-time workers here in a variety of capacities. Architects Richards, Berretti and Jellinek also designed a central courtyard which can be viewed from within through the wide panes of glass.

An eight-storey tower holds offices, a ballroom, a radio station, and the Room at the Top (RATT). In the pedestal section are a theater, an art gallery, and a meditation room. Stuck on the south side of the building is a cast-aluminum abstract sculpture which cost $25,000. The artist, Jordi Bonet of Ste. Genevieve, Quebec, wanted to express enthusiasm and movement.

Pembina Hall

Address: 9037–116th Street
Style: Neoclassical
Architect: Cecil Burgess
Date: 1915
Route: Proceed around the east side of SUB to head north to the three residence halls.

Pembina Hall was the third student residence built in this row of classically influenced buildings. The neighboring two halls had been built to an almost identical plan drawn up by the provincial architect. By the end of 1912, however, the University of Alberta had hired its own architect. The Nobbs and Darlings campus plan, drawn by Percy Nobbs of Montreal in 1910, was given to Cecil Burgess, who had been a lecturer at McGill and an associate of Nobbs'. He had come out to Edmonton to become the university architect and was to supervise and, in some cases, provide his own designs for individual buildings within the campus plan.

Pembina Hall offers a tangible exposition of the myriad classical details used to decorate this architectural style.

This was the first structure he designed, and it harmonized with other structures already standing. It served as both a residence and a teaching center from 1915. In 1918, however, it was taken over as an emergency hospital during the Spanish influenza epidemic. Several medical students resisted the order to leave the campus in order to stay and attend their sick colleagues. At least one, the son of Henrietta Muir Edwards (one of the five women's advocates who launched the Person's Case), contracted the disease and died.

During the Second World War, between 1941 and 1945 Pembina Hall was used as a Royal Canadian Air Force training center. The university carried out significant renovations in the mid-1970s, upgrading the rooms and locating the offices of some student services here.

A detail of the central entrance to Pembina Hall shows myriad classical details, including the swan's neck pediment over the windows with the filial breaking through between the two scrolls. The window itself rests on the thick entablature supported by the ionic

A study of Pembina Hall's entry reveals a wide variety of classical details.

columns surrounding the doorway. There is quoin-like stonework cut into the brickwork around the windows and the carved crest on the façade of the crenellated parapet at the top of the building. Over the entryway is the university's motto: *Quaecumque vera* (whatsoever things are true).

Athabasca Hall

Address: 9111–116th Street
Style: Jacobethan
Architect: A. M. Jeffers
Date: 1911

Compare this with the slightly more ornate St. Joseph's College.

This was the first building actually completed on the University of Alberta campus. The Arts Building was started the year prior under the sponsorship of Premier Rutherford. Political misfortunes caused Rutherford's government scandal and forced resignations, and many of the projects associated with Rutherford were tainted as well.

The University of Alberta was one of Rutherford's pet projects, and funds to build on the foundation laid in 1910 dried up. The new government focused its attention slightly to the west and called upon the Public Works department to build a residence and faculty office building.

The plans for Athabasca Hall were drawn by A. M. Jeffers, the Public Works chief architect, who was also working on plans for the Legislature Building and Government House. There was some reference to the ideas suggested by the Nobbs and Darling campus plan; however, Jeffers was an architect of some note already and he preferred Jacobethan themes. The hall has a distinctly English look with a parapet around the roofline and stone quoining at corners. Only the battlements of the bayed "turrets" are crenellated like a castle. The U-shaped red brick structure is enclosed on three sides by a landscaped area. The stepped front gable at the roof is echoed in the stepped stone cap over the arched doorway.

Athabasca Hall housed the first classrooms on campus as well as housing student residents and their library. The faculty and the administration had offices in the building as well.

In the late 1970s, the university carried out a significant restoration of this building and documented its history and legacy. The work received a Heritage Canada award of honour in 1978 for excellence in preservation of historic properties.

Assiniboia Hall
Address: 9137–116th Street
Style: Jacobethan
Architect: A. M. Jeffers
Date: 1912
Route: Continue to the north to the next building.

Assiniboia Hall was the second building built on campus. As soon as Athabasca Hall was finished, work began on its near twin. Excavation started in the fall of 1911, and it took a whole year to complete the construction. One must remember that the tools of the construction trade at the time were much less mechanized than after the war. It took 100 men with shovels and numerous teams of horses and wagons to dig and haul away the dirt before laying the foundation. Dozens of masons cut stone on site and shaped the building as true craftsmen, not just laborers.

Assiniboia is the poor cousin in terms of decorative elements to its nearest neighbors.

Like its closest neighbor, the Assiniboia Hall has Jacobethan "bones," but it is significantly less decorated. There are crenels in the "turrets" beside the entryway, but there are no quoins around the windows or doors. The gable is simply rounded, and above the archway the entablature is plain.

Like Athabasca and Pembina, Assiniboia Hall housed lecture halls, administrative and faculty offices, and students' residences. It also received renovations in the late 1970s.

Ring Houses 1–4

Address: 1-4 Ring Road
Style: Prairie Victorian
Architect: unknown
Date: 1911–12
Route: Proceed north and skirt around the end of the
Centre for Subatomic Research and the nanotechnology
labs to reach the ring road which circles down to
Saskatchewan Drive.

*The faculty housing represented here came in a variety of housing styles popular
at the time.*

Along this lane behind the Biological Sciences Building are found four buildings constructed around 1911–12 as residences for faculty. There were at one time ten faculty houses, originally found on the "ring road" around the campus grounds, but several were demolished during the university's expansions.

Ring House 1 was the residence of the university president, the first being Henry Marshall Tory, but it was later replaced by the Saskatchewan Drive house across from the Faculty Club. This ring house was used temporarily to house women students as overflow from the Pembina Hall residence, and it now houses the Ring House Gallery.

The other Ring Houses, 2, 3, and 4, now house various university services such as the University of Alberta Press and the Early Child Development Studies offices.

A typical ranch style this house had many open-plan rooms suitable for entertaining.

The president's house, at 11515 Saskatchewan Drive, was built in 1961 for president Walter Johns after Ring House 1 was deemed obsolescent. This was built by the Department of Public Works, and many extras were cut from the original plans to keep construction on budget. In 1996–97 it was renamed the Alumni House and is now run by the University of Alberta Alumni Association as a conference center.

Route: Continue out to Saskatchewan Drive.

The Faculty Club, at 9307–116th Street, has a mandate to promote friendship, fellowship, and intellectual association among the university faculty. This building was completed in 1964 and has been expanded several times.

Biological Sciences Building
Address: 11455 Saskatchewan Drive
Style: Gothic Revival - Fortress
Architect: Department of Public Works
Date: 1969
Route: Head east along Saskatchewan Drive.

The University's Gothic Horror Building—a huge undertaking at the time of construction.

Described as a monstrosity by architect Peter Hemmingway and stoutly defended by various professors and officers of the university's Board of Governors, this building has always caused controversy. The main architectural feature of the Biological Sciences Building is its massing. The stone courses are marked on the exterior, which helps to emphasize the horizontal, but this still appears to be a huge and imposing structure.

It has also been described as "Western Canada's most expansive single building." There are 54,163 square meters of floor space in six interrelated units including a twelve-storey tower. It is estimated to have cost between $17 million and $20 million. The Biological Sciences Building was the last building on campus for which Public Works supervised the construction. It was built by several different contractors working at once, and has interlocking floors and departments. It houses the offices of the general science faculty and five departments: botany, genetics, psychology, microbiology, and zoology. It contains specialized equipment for each faculty including troparctic controlled greenhouses on the south roof which can simulate various climates.

More horror stories are told to first-year students about this building—such as getting lost in the maze of "bio sci"—than for any other building on campus.

Route: Head back east along Saskatchewan Drive—past the new Earth Sciences Building, the Henry Marshall Tory Tower, and the Tory Lecture Theatre (aka "the Tory turtle," noted for there being no perpendicular angles in the design).

Built in 1967 for $5 million, the fifteen-storey Tory Tower, with two wings of three storeys each, is larger than the Education Building. It commemorates Henry Marshall Tory, co-founder and first president of the university (1908–28). The separate but adjoining lecture wing was built by Public Works in the same year. An underground tunnel connects the two buildings, and the lecture rooms in the hall are wired for closed-circuit TV and AV aids. The Tory Buildings serve the social science fields.

Route: Return to the tour's starting place near Rutherford House, or continue with Garneau section.

Adair Park

Address: Corner of 110th Street & Saskatchewan Drive
Route: Proceed east along Saskatchewan Drive, turning south on 110th Street where the park sign is.

This park is named for Mr. and Mrs. Joseph Adair, who were generous with their time to a number of charities and causes, including the University of Alberta. Joseph Adair (1877–1960) was born in Scotland and trained as a printer. He came to Canada in 1899 and to Edmonton in 1906 to work for the *Edmonton Bulletin*. He started his own linotyping business in 1911.

Adair served on the Edmonton Public School Board, and on the library and Exhibition boards. He was alderman from 1921–24. Mrs. Adair also participated in a number of causes, and she died also in 1960.

At the base of the Adair sign and plaques in a small plaque for the Garneau family.

Warren/Burgess Residence

Address: 10958–89th Avenue
Style: Craftsman
Architect: Unknown
Date: 1911
Route: Continue south on 110th Street.

This house belonged to two different but important members of the faculty of the University of Alberta.

Percival Sidney Warren was a founding member of the U of A's geology department. He started in 1920 and taught until 1955, serving as departmental chairman from 1949 to 1955. He lived in this house from 1926 to 1940.

A peaceful site along the edge of the riverbank tells the story of the neighbour-hood and some valued University supporters.

Faculty at the University chose their homes near their work and their colleagues.

Cecil Burgess lived in the same house from 1941 to 1971. Born in Bombay in 1871 while his Scottish father worked for the British government on an archeological survey of India, Burgess was raised in Scotland and trained in architecture there. He came to Canada in 1903 when he worked as an associate with Nobbs and Hyde, architects in Montreal. In 1910, he came to Edmonton as the founding professor and only head of the Faculty of Architecture within applied sciences at the U of A. The department folded when he retired, as the university thought it would take at least two professors to replace him. After his retirement in 1940, Burgess continued to work in architecture (drawing many rural hospitals) and to lecture (on architecture and town planning) in the city. He lived to the age of 101.

At the university, Burgess was also responsible for working with the plan developed by his mentor and professor of architecture from McGill, Percy Nobbs, to supervise the construction and design of several of the university's signature buildings. Burgess had a hand in the Arts Building, the Pembina Residence, the south wing of the University Hospital, faculty housing, and buildings on the university farm. He also designed several public buildings for the provincial government as well as private and commercial buildings in Edmonton. He served as a member of the Edmonton Town Planning Council and tried to ensure the appropriate use and preservation of parkland within developments (which would be a boon to community leagues).

Within the yard of this house is the Michelet tree, an aged and unique specimen.

The house was designated a municipal heritage resource in 2002. It is a craftsman-style, circa 1911, wood-frame, timber-lap and shingle-sided house with triangular knee braces and an addition to the rear.

Emily Murphy's Residence

Address: 11011–88th Avenue
Style: Craftsman
Architect: Unknown
Date: ca. 1917
Route: Continue south on 110th Street to 88th Avenue turning west until you see the sign on the south side for the Emily Murphy house.

Transformed into rows of university housing these buildings have lost much of their original character and context over the years.

Like the majority of houses in this block, this house was built around the years of the First World War. Samuel T. Mains, the manager of North American Collieries, was the first owner. The house was designated a provincial historical resource, however, because of its association with the next owner, Emily Murphy. Mrs. Murphy and her husband, the Reverend Arthur Murphy, lived here between 1919 and 1930, when she died from complications of diabetes.

The Murphys also lived briefly in a house at the end of the block (8703–112th Street), for one year in 1917, before moving into this house.

One of the few remnants of a distinguished neighborhood, this mansion sits of the corner of the University campus.

Several similar houses were lost to this neighborhood when the university built the Faculty of Law building in 1971, including houses along 111th Street, such as Dr. Eardley Allin's house at 8808–111th Street, which was a Tudor Victorian mansion built in 1914. Besides Dr. Allin (known for founding the Allin Clinic), the house was the residence from 1920 to 1922 of George Smith, the provincial minister of education, and Dr. Frank Crang, from 1922 to 1940. It passed to the Allin family after Crang's daughter married Dr. Earley Allin. It was sold to the university in 1968 and demolished.

Garneau School

Address: 87th Avenue between 109th & 110th streets
Style: Edwardian revivial
Architect: Unknown
Date: 1923
Route: Continue along 110th Street and then turn east on 87th Avenue.

The Garneau School has an impressive entrance way reminiscent of a European castle or fortress.

The first Garneau School was built in 1913 on Laurent Garneau's land about 112th Street and 84th Avenue. It was a simple frame lumber building with four classrooms. It was soon deemed too small for the need and later served as a nurses' residence and a lecture hall for the University of Alberta. Community growth and the desire for a more permanent school drove the school board to acquire land from Bishop O'Leary (for $36,800) at 109th Street and 87th Avenue. The three-storey brick school was built in 1923 with sixteen rooms for classes, the library, and offices.

Initially, the school trustees wanted to name the new school for royalty, such as King George or the Prince of Wales. Dr. Crang was opposed to it being named for a Catholic and a "half-breed" (as he characterized Laurent Garneau). He preferred the name of a medical scientist associated with the University. Neighbors objected to changing the name of the school at all, simply because it was in new facilities. When the trustees finally voted, the vote was six to one for Garneau.

In 1941, an addition was used to accommodate the Edmonton Normal School (whose facilities had been given to the No. 4 Initial Training School for the Royal Canadian Air Force). A brick-clad frame building was also added at that time for the gymnasium and auditorium, to be shared between the junior school and the normal school. The opening address was given by William Aberhart, the minister of education. Once the teacher trainees returned to the university campus in 1958, the extra space was used for the training school for nursing aides.

Garneau School was threatened by demolition in 1967 when a south-side freeway project was debated in the city. The planned METS (Metro-Edmonton Transportation System) roadway system would have gone right through the front doors of the school in 1982. With the disruption planned for the residential neighborhood, the university expected to expand and build right up to the edge of the freeway. The project was finally rejected by the city in the late 1970s.

The junior high school program at Garneau was discontinued in 1981. Instead, the school offered elementary programs, such as the Caraway program from 1973 through the mid-1990s, and the university's Child Study Centre (an elementary school program).

The 75th reunion for Garneau graduates was held in 1998. Preston Manning (formerly head of the Alliance Party) was one of the alumni.

Garneau Theatre

Address: 8712–109th Street
Style: Moderne with art deco detailing
Architect: William Blakey
Date: 1949
Route: Continue east to 109th Street and turn north to the
Garneau Theatre.

The moderne style was meant to remind the public of the futuristic new technology expected inside the new theatre building.

When the Garneau Theatre opened its doors on a Friday night in October 1949, it was declared to be the "finest suburban moving picture house in the west." It seated 780 movie goers at five cents a seat, in a pleasant theater painted in tones of blue and maroon with silver and gold ornamentation. The seats were leather with mohair backs, and at the end of every second row were "two's company" seats for those who liked to snuggle while they watched a movie. There was also a large stage for stage productions.

Somehow the theater managed to obtain for its lobby the very furniture used by the King and Queen at the Hotel Macdonald during the Royal visit in 1939. The ushers were clad in scarlet Eton jackets with pillbox hats and blue striped trousers. Directors of the theater included some of Stathcona's leading figures, such as Dr. McIntyre, R. J. Dinning, S. E. Noble, and Frank Doncaster, among others.

The heritage value of the Garneau is very high because it has not been significantly altered from the original. High-quality materials used at the time of construction meant that little has had to be replaced. The best technology available at the time for ventilation was used, which has meant the theater never needed to be air-conditioned. The original boiler is still in operation. Features of the moderne style include the chevronlike steps on the sign over the marquee as well as the interior decoration of pillars and pilasters. A restoration in 1996 brought back much of the interior décor with vintage light fixtures and the removal of a false ceiling in the lobby. Heritage planners have called it one of best examples of moderne–art deco architecture in the province.

When the Famous Players company's lease expired in 1990, the theater owners threatened to close it if they could not find another tenant, since the "days of the single movie theatre are over." After months of hand-wringing and very little action, the Society for the Protection of Architectural Resources in Edmonton (SPARE) took on the project of saving the Garneau. The group encouraged the owners to designate the building under the Municipal Heritage Resources program in light of its architectural and historical significance as one of the earliest examples of "moderne" architecture in Edmonton and one of very few left in western Canada.

Various artistic groups took advantage of the vacant situation to book midnight showings of independent films, live performances of Fringe overruns (e.g., Three Dead Trolls in a Baggie), and benefits. In December 1991, the Magic Lantern set it up as a discount movie house—and possibly to book local bands in on other occasions. Later developers also tried to put a restaurant into the theater space over the opposition of the neighborhood. Finally, in 1996, the Garneau reopened as a second arts theater screening first-run films, in competition with the Princess Theatre. So far both theaters seem to be thriving.

E. A. Corbett Hall

Address: 8205–114th Street
Style: English classical & modern renaissance
Architect: D. E. MacDonald & G. H. MacDonald
Date: 1929
Route: If you are still up for a bit more walking, return west
along 87th Avenue and turn south on 112th Street,
traveling past the east side of the Mackenzie Health
Centre to 82nd Avenue. Otherwise you can continue
north to 89th Avenue and return westward to
Saskatchewan Drive.

Compare this epitome of education buildings with many of the institutions dotted around the city, dating from the same period.

Built in 1929 as the center for all teacher training in the province, the
Edmonton Normal School operated only for three years before the
provincial government moved to close it in order to cut costs during
the Depression. The minister of education claimed that there was a
glut of teachers looking for work in the province and there was no
need to educate more. The normal school remained closed from 1932
to 1935.

After studying schools across North America, the architects had
based their design for the Edmonton Normal School on the "best" of
contemporary schools. The building is situated on a 6-hectare site and
shaped like a giant "E" facing southwest. The middle projection is the

longest and contains a gymnasium and an auditorium (which were later divided up for art studios). There was a basement cafeteria initially, but that also was converted to workshops. Designed to accommodate 500 education students, the building cost $590,000 in 1929.

Classical features displayed on the exterior include the twin arcaded entries topped with leaded glass windows and accessed through traditional wood doors. The balustraded roof is decorated with ornamental finials. The inside, although now significantly remodeled, still exhibits the projecting rotunda which was originally covered in ornate plaster moldings on the ceiling, and a gold and white dentilled frieze flanked by bay windows. Much of the interior has been remodeled, and contemporary fixtures have replaced the originals.

During World War II, the school was closed again from 1941 to 1945 to be used for the Royal Canadian Air Force's initial training squadron. The normal school moved to the Garneau School, where an addition was dedicated to its classrooms.

At the end of the war in 1945, the province handed over the teacher training program to the university, which renamed the normal school "the Education Building" until the Faculty of Education built its new building on 88th Avenue in 1963. This building became the home of the departments of extension, drama, and studio theater, and the School of Nursing and Rehabilitation Medicine in 1965.

In 1967, the building was again renamed after the director of the university's Department of Extension from 1920 to 1936. E. A. Corbett was also the founder and director of the Banff School of Fine Arts, helped to found CKUA Radio, was a director of the Canadian Association for Adult Education for fifteen years, and served on other national and local arts bodies. He was the author of several biographies and histories of Alberta. Corbett received an honorary doctorate of laws from the University of Alberta in 1963.

Extensive renovations of Corbett Hall in 1988 forced the relocation of all the departments using the building. The building reopened in 1991 as the exclusive home for rehabilitation medicine.

Highlands Tour

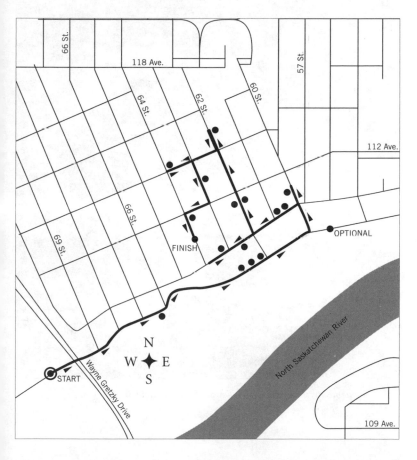

Highlands overlooks the river valley all along Ada Boulevard.

The Highlands community was developed in the building boom period between 1910 and 1914. Edmonton's population had been growing at a startling rate, up from 24,000 in 1904 to over 77,000 in 1914. Real estate developers William Magrath and Bidwell Holgate dreamed of an exclusive retreat neighborhood along the high, "delightfully situated" northern bank of the North Saskatchewan River. The name "Highlands" was chosen in a contest that was part of a well-planned publicity campaign in the Edmonton Bulletin, and the winner, 19-year-old S. Loughlin, carried off a prize of $50 in gold.

The new neighborhood was approximately five kilometers east of downtown Edmonton, and access to the neighborhood depended on a scheme to sponsor (i.e., subsidize to a maximum of $25,000) the expansion of the city's streetcar line along Pine (112th) Avenue to Irwin (63rd) Street. The developers also extended city services to the new development, ensuring that electricity, telephone service, and running water were available to those who built there.

The land was originally surveyed as river lots 30, 32, and 34, claimed by Hudson's Bay Company employee William Borwick and the brothers James and George Guillion respectively. In 1898, John A. McDougall purchased the Guillions' lots but he didn't start the sub-division of the land until 1910. Initially called McDougall Heights, the property was sold to Magrath and Holgate in 1911 for about $150,000. McDougall remained active in the early part of the development, as a silent partner—offering automobile rides to view the properties to interested purchasers brought in by Magrath and Holgate.

Like all real estate deals in the period, the transaction was mostly on paper, and as the economic times shifted, few of the parties involved realized their potential monetary gains. In the heady times of 1911, Magrath and Holgate continued to acquire property to the west of the Highlands subdivision with expectations of filling in all the land between there and the city.

The developers of the Highlands took care to ensure the standards of buildings, especially along the river valley lots, were of the highest quality. Low-density residential use was the norm for the majority of the neighborhood development. Although no restrictive covenant was placed on the property as in Glenora, the developers instead controlled the values by having the purchaser apply for a building permit of a specific value before the sale went through. A building restriction on the minimum value of the construction (at least $2,500) and a minimum lot size of 20 by 40 meters created a set of conditions that limited potential purchasers to the elite of Edmonton. On the first day of sales, approximately $35,000 worth of Highlands lots were sold.

More moderate housing was allowed farther back from the riverbank. From 1912, Magrath and Holgate built about two dozen houses "on spec" themselves at an average cost of $4,400 for resale. Fifty houses were built between 1911 and 1913. Magrath and Holgate also built a curling rink, commercial blocks (along the major roadways at 112th and 118th avenues), and a small office to change an empty feeling in the development. Within the large tract of land divided into 516 lots, it didn't make a great deal of difference to the feeling of wide open, undeveloped space.

The streets and avenues laid out in the neighborhood curved gently near the river to provide easy turns and broad vistas along Ada Boulevard (named after Magrath's wife) and Jasper (111th) Avenue. Other family members and friends of the developers found their names on streets, such as Adrian (McGrath's son) and Lake (Ada's maiden name). In 1949, Jasper Avenue between 53rd Street and 71st Street was renamed 111th Avenue, and between 69th and 75th Streets it was renamed Ada Boulevard, because of confusion. Many other street names had been earlier replaced following the numbering scheme adopted after the amalgamation of Strathcona and Edmonton.

Both Magrath and Holgate built mansions for themselves in the neighborhood, setting the tone for the development they planned. Other purchasers included several mine owners who appreciated the proximity to their businesses that flourished along the banks of the river (even under the houses at the east end of the Highlands) and in the nearby town of Beverly (later annexed to Edmonton).

Incidentally, the miners and other laborers in Edmonton appreciated the expansion of the streetcar line that eased their morning and evening commutes to and from the Beverly mines. The other development, which reflected the interests of the owners, was the establishment of the Highlands Golf Course on the tablelands below the neighborhood.

The collapse of the building boom during the First World War caused a serious setback to the growth of the neighborhood and the fortunes of Magrath and Holgate. Very little building occurred between 1915 and the mid-1940s, after which smaller, postwar housing projects during the late 1940s and 1950s filled in the gaps left from the earlier period. A community league was started in 1921 and began to provide the neighborhood with recreational opportunities (in the form of a lawn-bowling green and a baseball diamond). Economic downturns continued to challenge the growth of the league, but the cohesiveness of the community ensured its survival through tough times.

Another quiet period in development ensued during the 1960s until the neighborhood was rediscovered in the late 1970s and heritage-conscious families moved in to undertake restoration projects, restoring the community and saving it from threatened commercial development in the 1980s and 1990s. The neighborhood has an interesting mix of architectural styles and an eclectic history of residents and owners.

Some of the city's best-preserved, privately owned historic houses and streetscapes can be found in the Highlands. Because they are mostly private residences, they should be viewed from street. If you are interested, the Highlands Historical Foundation does occasionally offer tours (information on the foundation can usually be found at the commercial properties along 112th Avenue). Five neighborhood buildings have been provincially designated, including the Magrath, Holgate, Grierson (6124–111th Avenue), and Morehouse (11153–64th Street) residences and the Gibbard Block (5427–112th Avenue). Others are pending as their proud owners complete restoration work.

Concordia University College

Address: 7126 Ada Boulevard
Style: Gothic
Architect: Unknown
Date: 1925

The imposing military style building is the oldest on the Concordia University College Campus.

The Reverend Alfred Rehwinkel, pastor at St. Peter's Lutheran Church on 96th Street in the early 1920s, urged the Missouri Synod of the Lutheran Church to open a college for the education of young people, especially those interested in ministry, in western Canada. In 1921, he was allowed to start a school in the Caledonia Temperance Hotel (10875–98th Street), which opened initially with 35 students.

Rehwinkel was a popular pastor who was also very involved in the community. He urged the city to become involved, and served on the committee to celebrate the Queen's jubilee and was a founding member of the zoological society that was responsible for the development of the zoo at Borden Park on 112th Avenue.

With time and support from the synod, Rehwinkel was able to purchase land and mineral rights from the estate of John Fraser, who had homesteaded northeast of Fort Edmonton in 1871. The Fraser estate was bounded by 74th Street and 69th Street from the river to 118th Avenue. It was mostly bush until 1920 when Fraser died, and he had given away most of his land to friends. The city claimed the rest for taxes and then connected the sewer, water, and electric services properly. The four hectares purchased by Rehwinkel stretched from the top of the riverbank to 112th Avenue and cost $13,800. Along the edge of the bank ran a roadway named Ada Boulevard, stretching over the ravine on a little bridge into the neighborhood of Highlands, still underdeveloped in 1925.

Concordian students boarded with Highlands families and later in Schwermann Hall (named after the first president) and Founders Hall boys dormitory. The college went co-educational in 1941 for its Alberta accredited high school courses, and also trained men for the Lutheran ministry. Four houses were built on Ada Blvd to accommodate faculty in 1929. Those were demolished to make way for Capilano Freeway in the 1960s. When the City exchanged eleven lots along the river for some of the college lands along 112th Avenue they promised the school an exemption for taxes. The following year however, the City's attempts to charge taxes for the school lands resulted in a legal case which went all the way to the Supreme Court of Alberta which decided in the College's favour and then to the Supreme Court of Canada when the city appealed. Unfortunately, the city won that battle in 1934.

Construction on the Gothic structure, a popular style in those days for educational facilities, was begun immediately and the college opened on January 10, 1926. The first president of the college, from 1925 to 1954, was Rev. Albert Schwermann. Mrs. Schwermann prepared the meals for the students. Schwermann had been stationed at St. Matthew's Lutheran Church and School at Stony Plain, and he was a strong advocate of parochial education. Between 1942 and 1954, he was often a program speaker on CBC Radio's "Church of the Air," and he urged the University of Alberta to initiate a course in choral music under the direction of Richard Eaton (later of the Richard Eaton Singers) for choir leaders.

The college was somewhat negatively affected by the anti-German sentiment during the Second World War, despite the high level of enlistment in the armed forces from among the student body. The first building, which served as both residence and classrooms, was added to over the years until Concordia has become a small campus. A gymnasium/auditorium was added in 1953, a women's dormitory in 1956, and the Guild Hall in 1959. Increasing numbers of students forced the creation of a second south-side campus in the 1980s. In 1992, the Tegler Centre, the quadrangle chapel, and student council offices were constructed. The final piece was the high school on 112th Avenue added in the mid-1990s.

Highlands Golf Club

Address: Ada Boulevard & 67th Street
Date: 1929 (9 holes)
Route: Head east and cross the bridge over the Capilano Freeway to join up with Ada Boulevard in Highlands proper.

The entrance to the Highlands Golf Course is formal in multi coloured brick.

Built when the neighborhood was still very "rural," with market gardens and in some cases livestock being raised on neighboring pieces of land, the Highlands Golf Club members set out to make their mark on the farmland and forests lining the river valley.

Unlike in many new neighborhoods in the city, the developers of Highlands made sure that the residents did not have to wait for their recreational facilities. Besides golf, the community was furnished early with lawn-bowling greens, tennis courts, and skating rinks.

To finance the golf club, 100 shares were sold at $100 each with green fees for the year of $35 per couple. The cost of purchasing the land from the city, $2,000, proved too steep for the members; however, they did manage to convince the city to lease them the land for a long term. Construction began in the early summer of 1929 using horse-drawn equipment, and nine holes were completed before the fall.

The official opening, however, was in the spring of 1930 when Lieutenant Governor William Egbert and Mayor Ambrose Bury cut the ribbon. Stunt flyer Vic Horner tried unsuccessfully to drop golf balls during a flyby to start the play. Tea was served in a tent since although the pro shop was built, the unheated clubhouse was not completed until 1931. A second floor was added in 1938. Harry Shaw served as the first pro for the Highlands Club.

The course was altered somewhat with the construction of the Capilano Freeway, which eliminated the fourth tee and forced the reconfiguration of the other holes to accommodate the changes. Other difficulties, or interesting features, to the course are provided by the occasional sinkhole that opens up in the fairways. Since the course was laid out over the Premier Coal Mine shafts, which were drilled into the hill from the riverbank, the collapse of an old shaft or shifting of the surface on a filled-in pit can create a bit of an obstacle on the course.

The Henry Martel Park on the north side of Ada Boulevard just across from the entrance to the Highlands Golf Club is named in memory of one of the Highlands favorite golf pros.

Ash Residence
Address: 6256 Ada Boulevard
Style: Craftsman
Architect: Ernest Morehouse
Date: ca. 1913
Route: Continue east along Ada Boulevard past the inter-
    section with 63rd Street.

The beautiful landscaping adds much to the character of this house.

This was one of the 24 houses built by Magrath and Holgate from
plans of Ernest Morehouse to fill the vacant lots in Highlands and
encourage purchasers. They rented the house to Margaret Jane and
William Thomas Ash until 1921 when Mrs. Ash purchased it for
$10,400. William Ash and his brother, Sidney, were the proprietors of
the Ash Brothers Diamond Hall.

The Ashes stayed only another three years before the house was
sold to Otis H. Sprague, who kept it only another three years before
selling to Matilda and Philip Singer, who worked as a salesman for
the Singer Sewing Company. This time the sale took, and the house
remained in the Singer family's possession until 1962.

This house was one of the first properties in the neighborhood to have extensive landscaping done, made necessary because of the sloped front yard. The two-storey building has many Craftsman-style features including the wide, bracketed eaves, the wraparound verandah, and the open gable-roofed balcony on the second floor. With the pleasant vista and large sweep of yard, this was a very attractive location.

McGrath Mansion
Address: 6240 Ada Boulevard
Style: Georgian
Architect: A. E. Morehouse
Date: 1912

This is the Highlands signature residence.

William McGrath began building his development's signature residence in 1911 as a fourteen-room estate house with a matching coach house (see attraction no. 11 on the Highlands Tour) and an elegant drive which curved around the lot and under the colonnaded, covered front entrance, called a porte cochére. The building permit estimated the cost of construction at $30,000, but actual finished costs may have approached $85,000.

The red brick and wood-trimmed exterior has a wraparound verandah, a second-storey balcony, and a third-storey portico over-looking the extensive grounds covering ten lots. The 604-square-meter interior was decorated in the finest taste with oak paneling, linen wall coverings, and leaded glass windows. Imported English marble framed the fireplace in the vestibule, which had a three-meter-high ceiling. Many built-in features, such as cabinets and shelves, as well as a room-to-room intercom system, added beauty and value. Other pieces were imported from Europe to furnish this most distinguished address.

There was also a built-in swimming pool, a large kitchen and pantry, and a laundry in the basement all provided with water and heat from the large steam-heat boiler. The third storey contained a billiard room and five bedrooms. Five more bedrooms were on the second storey, and the house contained five full bathrooms.

McGrath was a businessman, originally from Belleville, Ontario, where he had been an exporter of cheese. Born in Peterborough about 1869, he married Ada Lake in 1894 and had one son, Adrian. In 1904, the family moved to Edmonton, where McGrath started in real estate with partner J. H. Hart. Hart sold his interests to Bidwell Holgate, another Ontarian, in 1909. McGrath was a Methodist and very involved in his church He was appointed superintendent of the Wesley Sunday school in 1907. He was also an avid sportsman, helping to organize the Highlands Curling and (Lawn) Bowling Club, serving as the first president of the Alberta Curling Association, and, in 1914, as president of the Edmonton Baseball Club. McGrath campaigned for mayor unsuccessfully in 1912, losing to lawyer William Short.

Together with Holgate, he developed several east-end neighbor-hoods including Bellevue, the Bellevue addition, and City Park Annex as well as having properties in Windsor Park and West Glenora.

McGrath died in 1921 after a lengthy illness. His fortunes were much reduced by the economic downturn, and although Ada and Adrian remained in the house until the 1930s, they were frequently unable to pay the taxes. The property was eventually seized by the city and sold for tax arrears. Mrs. McGrath and Adrian moved to another, more modest property the family owned on 62nd Street, and the two lived with her sister, Mrs. W. H. Hamilton, until Adrian's marriage.

The house was vacant from 1931 until 1937, when it was subdivided and rented out in suites. In 1935, Mrs. A. Bulmer-Watt was in residence as the "chatelaine" to care for the suites. The house was purchased from the city in 1948 by the Ukrainian Greek Catholic Church for the residence and offices of their bishop, the Most Reverend Neil Savaryn. The indoor pool was removed, and the space was converted into a library and archives. The billiard room became more bedrooms for visitors.

The mansion was declared an Alberta historic resource in 1975. When the church decided to downsize the bishop's residence in 1996, it was put on the market and listed at $1.1 million. It was estimated at that time that $500,000 of restoration work would be required.

Holgate Mansion

Address: 6210 Ada Boulevard
Style: Tudor revival, with Edwardian influences
Architect: Nesbitt & Morehouse
Date: 1912–13
Route: Continue east along Ada Boulevard to the Holgate residence

Bidwell A. Holgate was from Foxboro, Ontario. He and his wife, Mable, came to Edmonton about 1909 when he entered into a partnership with William McGrath in real estate. The Holgate family resided in this house until 1921 when they moved to another Highlands property at 6010 Jasper (111th) Avenue. Bidwell Holgate died in 1928, and his widow moved back to Ontario, to Belleville, in 1931.

This residence is a strong representation of the values and image the developers wished to project for the neighborhood.

Holgate's house, a Tudor revival mansion, is three storeys tall and has plenty of decorative wood trim emphasizing the central gable on the second floor, and above the entry and windows. Two shed-roofed dormer windows flank the central gable and bring light to the third floor. The interior was decorated with English arts and crafts designs and furnishings, including a hand-finished fresco on the ceiling. Another piece of artwork, this one a wall hanging, depicting the settlement of Canada in linen, hung in the main floor den.

The construction costs ran about $49,000 including $10,000 for the garage with living quarters on the second floor. The garage was demolished in 1962. The mansion contained twenty rooms, including eight bedrooms, and had three fireplaces.

The Holgate mansion was designated as a provincial historical resource in 1987.

Davidson Residence

Address: 5650 Ada Boulevard
Style: Foursquare
Architect: Unknown
Date: 1912
Route: Continue east along Ada Boulevard to the Davidson
Residence.

*Beautifully restored and maintained, this house is another excellent example of
the foursquare style in Highlands.*

This two-and-a-half-storey house had 22 rooms originally, including
a grand hall with detailed woodwork, maple floors, and three fireplaces. The symmetry of the square design is visible in the four identical gables extending out from the roof—although it is slightly
marred by the shed-roofed extension creating the enclosed sunroom
over the front entry.

Adam J. Davidson was one of the owners of the Bush Mine Coal
Company in Beverly, and he must have found this nearby neighborhood ideal for his morning and evening commute. The Bush mine was
one of the traditional coalmines, rather than a "gopher hole" mine dug
in from the riverbank. It had an 11.5-meter shaft that ran down to a

coal seam between 1.5 and 2 meters thick. A series of tunnels were dug into the coal seam, and the chunks of coal hauled into the central area and hoisted to the surface. Occasionally blasting was done to break farther into the coal bed. There was no rail spur to the mine, unlike at the nearby Humberstone mine, so the coal was shipped to Edmonton in horse-drawn wagons. The hoist for the coal was also horse-powered.

A second Bush coalmine was added in 1921, at the outskirts of the Highlands, and Magrath and Holgate were investors in the scheme. The digging moved northwest from Ada Boulevard right under the eastern edge of the Highlands. In 1928 Davidson leased the mine and went dairy farming and it was eventually closed and turned into a gravel pit in 1944.

The Davidson house was of a typical foursquare style with four gables protruding from the roof; however, the addition of the closed-in balcony with the shed rood over the verandah has altered the profile. Mr. Davidson's daughter, Cora Bell, married Glen Wilson, and they resided in the house until 1981.

Holgate Residence II

Address: 6010–111th Avenue
Style: Georgian
Architect: probably E. Morehouse
Date: 1913
Route: Farther down the boulevard are larger, modern houses. When you come out on 50th Street, there is Uncle Ed's café and the Mundare sausage house. If you do not continue to the end of Ada Boulevard, turn north at the next corner, travel one block, and return westward on 111th Avenue.

The first resident of this house, which was probably one of the 24 built by Magrath and Holgate in 1913, was Vincent Hunt, the musical director at Alberta College. Ken McKenzie purchased the house in 1916 and remained here for six years. He was a teacher at Victoria and MacDougall high schools during this period.

This style harkens back to a statelier age and lifestyle.

After the real-estate fortunes of Magrath and Holgate dissipated in the aftermath of the bust of 1913, the war, and the economic downturn that followed, the Holgates had to economize, and they moved to this smaller house in 1922. After Mr. Holgate's death in 1928, his widow, Mable, remained here until 1931 when she returned to Ontario.

The features of the house that represent the simplified Georgian style include the columned portico over the entryway and the sidelights on either side of the door. The shutters on the lower floor windows with decorative cutouts seek to give the windows a wider appearance. Note the fieldstone retaining wall and its gateposts with the old Jasper Avenue address carved in the stone.

Sheldon Residence
Address: 6018–111th Avenue
Style: Craftsman bungalow
Architect: Unknown
Date: 1915
Route: Continue west along 111th Avenue.

In a more modest line this residence is of smaller scale and uses more unpretentious materials such as the cobblestone retaining wall.

Carleton and Bessie Sheldon were owners of a coal mine nearby to this house. Between 1907 and 1944, there were seventeen active coalmines in the Edmonton area although other short term or seasonal gopher mines (dug in a few feet from the riverbank) were excavated during the same time. The Sheldons resided here from 1915 until 1950.

The bungalow of the prewar period was not necessarily a one-storey building, but rather an architectural style that was open and airy with large overhanging eaves to create shade. The craftsman styling includes use of natural materials and colors such as the green cedar siding which is original to the house. The wide verandah beneath large overhanging eaves provides shade in the summer for an extra outdoor room.

This house received provincial designation as a historical resource in 1997.

Ward Residence
Address: 11125–60th Street
Style: West Coast or California bungalow
Architect: A. S. Morehouse
Date: 1912
Route: Continue west along 111th Avenue.

A delightful feature of this style is the open and shady porch on the second level.

This building is another example of another popular bungalow style. Though classed as a bungalow, it is a two-storey house with a large useable attic. There are four bedrooms on the second floor and a three-piece bathroom. Two screened porches, one at the front and one at the back, overlook the street and the yard. Downstairs there was a large parlor containing a redbrick fireplace with a green tiled hearth, a dining room, and a kitchen and pantry, which were fronted by the large verandah across the width of the house.

In the basement of this self-sufficient and fully equipped house were the large coal-burning furnace for central heating, a cistern for rainwater collection (although the house was hooked up to the city's water and sewerage systems), and a cold cellar for storage of vegetables. The house was also originally wired for electricity.

Harry and Muriel Ward originated in Hamilton, Ontario, but had owned a hardware business in Morinville prior to coming to Edmonton. They raised four children in this house, and one of them, Henry, purchased a house from Magrath and Holgate in March 1913. He remained in the Highlands until the 1960s. Harry died in 1949, but Muriel remained in the Ward House until 1974.

Grierson Residence

Address: 6124–111th Avenue
Style: Queen Anne
Architect: Unknown
Date: 1912
Route: Continue west on 111th Avenue.

Walter Armstrong, a grain buyer, bought this property from Magrath and Holgate as an investment in 1912. They continued to hold the mortgage on the property until it was sold to Mrs. Annie Grierson in 1916. The house was rented out in 1914 and 1915. The Grierson family moved into the house in 1922 and remained until 1972. The next owner was James McGregor and then in 1977, Charles Rees, who carried out renovations to the interior.

From the turret room to the wrap-around verandah this house is built for romance.

Annie was married to Walter Grierson, brother to Edmund Grierson, who built the Alberta Hotel, owned the Queen's Hotel, and served as city councilor. Grierson Hill is named for the more famous brother.

Typical features of the Queen Anne style include a "complex roofline" with several levels. The octagonal tower, arched windows, and a swept dormer on the front roof are also common. The wrap-around verandah follows the curve of the tower, giving it an interesting sweep around the corner of the house.

Carriage House
Address: 6229–111th Avenue
Style: Georgian
Architect: Ernest Morehouse
Date: 1913

An excellent example of the style, its hard to believe this was initially the storage building for carriages.

Built originally as the carriage house for the Magrath mansion, this structure matched the design of that building. It was constructed of a wood frame with a brick veneer, but the decorative hoods and modillions link the structure to the mansion. At $6,000 to construct, it was slightly less flashy than Holgate's $10,000 garage. Extensive alterations have been done to transform this into a separate dwelling, although it was used for years to house the carriages and later the cars of the mansion owners. The upstairs has always been for residential use, for the staff of the Magraths and later owners.

Harry Cox, Magrath's chauffeur, lived in the Carriage House from 1914 to 1924. It was rented out to various tenants from 1925 until it was sold in 1933. The two west-facing parking bays were replaced with large bay windows in the 1940s, and in 1990, architect Robert Spencer designed the addition. (A line visible in the roof slate indicates where the changes were made.)

The house is now 275 square meters, in red brick with carved wood detailing including soffits with dentils (tooth-shaped decorations), a central pediment, an archway over the entrance, and

Georgian-style windows. Renovations in the 1950s added a main-floor family room and an upstairs master bedroom as well as a covered porch and a brick patio at the rear of the house. The interior has original dark-stained oak hardwood and 2.7-meter-high ceilings. There is an L-shaped living/dining room, a breakfast room, a laundry room, and a three-piece bathroom on the main floor, and four bedrooms and a four-piece bathroom upstairs. The original basement was undeveloped.

Although once a lowly carriage house, this building was listed for sale in 1981 at $280,000.

You can also see the rear of the Magrath mansion from this side and the new garage which was built after the Carriage House was severed from the property. It was designed in the same Georgian style as both houses.

Baker Residence

Address: 6318–111th Avenue
Style: Foursquare
Architect: Unknown
Date: 1914

The taste of the developers of the Highlands is shown in the use of the setting of each residence to improve its "curb-appeal".

This house was built for Herbert Baker and his family in 1914, and it was his second home in the Highlands. Baker came to Edmonton to take over the management of the Massey Harris Company dealership in 1910. Born in Yorkshire in 1866, Baker came to Canada in 1882 and joined Massey Harris in Toronto the following year. He made his way up through the company, married Grace T. Willis in 1889, and was sent to manage the Winnipeg store in 1904.

The Bakers were members of the United Church in the Highlands, and Herbert served on several boards including the Edmonton Exhibition Association, the Edmonton Industries Committee, and the Chamber of Commerce. After Herbert's retirement from business life, he let his interest in city beautification lead him into public life in civic affairs. He was elected alderman in 1927, serving until 1933 and chairing the finance committee with distinction during that time. The family built and moved into 6274 Ada Boulevard after the election.

This house was bought subsequently by the Robert Marshall family of Crown Paving and Construction.

The asymmetrical aspect to this house is caused by the addition on the east side of the two-storey extended bow, which enclosed a sunroom and an upper-storey porch.

Chown Residence

Address: 11141–62nd Street
Style: Foursquare
Architect: Ernest Morehouse
Date: 1912
Route: Turn north up 62nd Street to view the Chown and Humphreys residences.

This was one of the "spec" houses built by Magrath and Holgate to encourage sales of their lots. It was the most costly on Grace (62nd) Street, listed at $4,800, and it was purchased by Russell Chown, who moved from Belleville, Ontario, in 1912 to join his family who were already in Edmonton. Chown Hardware had been established in 1906 and by 1912 had two stores. Russell's brother Leroy also lived in the Highlands, a block away at 11145–63rd Street. In fact, 116th Avenue was originally named Chown Avenue on the development maps.

The use of this common style in the area, and indeed on this street, ensures that the house fits in well with its neighbors.

The economic downturn around 1914 affected the business badly, and by 1916 the Chowns had liquidated their stores. All the family but Russell left in 1916. Russell had been working since 1914 for the city's stores and works department, but he was let go in 1917. He became a traveling salesman for a few years before unemployment again claimed him, although he did work as a laborer between 1923 and 1924. His fortunes did not improve, and he and his family probably returned to Ontario soon after that.

Magrath and Holgate's company foreclosed on the mortgage in 1924 and converted the house into two suites, causing extensive interior changes.

The building was designated a registered historic resource in 1993.

Humphreys Residence

Address: 11142–62nd Street
Style: Foursquare
Architect: Unknown
Date: 1912
Route: Turn to face the house on the west side of the
street.

The symmetry of the style give the house a pleasing appearance as well as allow light into all the interior spaces.

This is another of the Magrath Holgate houses, and the first house in the Highlands to receive a building permit from the city. The contractor was L. A. Webb, and it cost the Magrath Holgate Company $3,500 to build on the $1,500 lot.

Herbert Baker paid $1,500 for the property in August 1912 and lived here until 1914, when he moved around the corner. The house was then rented to Horace Leonard Humphreys in 1916. Humphreys was a teacher and later the principal of McCauley School. He bought the house in 1922 and continued living there until his death in 1936.

His daughter, Erica, married Adrian Magrath in the 1940s, and they moved into the house next door at 11136–62nd Street, which was also the home to Ada Magrath. The house may have belonged to Adrian or to his uncle William Hamilton.

After the Humphreys vacated, the house was rented to Nathan Eldon Tanner, a provincial MLA and minister of lands and mines in 1939.

Distinguishing features of this minimally decorated house are the diamond-shaped windows, the bellcast roof, and the bracketed eaves. The verandah is a replica of the original, which was torn down in the 1970s. A new sunroom around the side was added when the verandah was rebuilt. The caragana hedge is original to the house.

Route: Continue north across 112th Avenue and proceed up 62nd Street. You will pass the Highlands Community League Hall at 11333–62nd Street.

The Highlands Community League started on this property, which was originally a lot held by Magrath and Holgate and loaned to the curling club they founded in 1912 because of their love of the sport. They built a $9,000 curling rink on the northeast corner of 113th Avenue and 62nd Street. The Magrath Holgate Company held onto the land until 1922 when it was taken over by the city for tax arrears. The city later acquired most of the rest of the block in a similar fashion and decided to reserve the block for parkland.

The Highlands Parent-Teacher Association was formed soon after, and it attempted to establish various recreational programs for the children in the community. As the community league movement grew, it was a natural move to convert the association into the Highlands Community League, which formed in 1921. In the following years they built bowling greens and a baseball diamond, and skating rinks alternated with tennis courts according to the season. A. U. G. Bury, later Mayor Bury, was on the executive.

Problems with their lease and the effects of the Great Depression delayed plans to build a better clubhouse until the 1940s, when materials for the building were donated by Adby Demolition from lumber reclaimed from an internment camp in southern Alberta. The building was named the Highlands Community League Memorial Centre for local soldiers lost in war. The 1912 clubhouse was removed in the 1950s, and the second building, with change rooms on main floor, a members' lounge, and a caretaker's residence above, was begun in 1954 and completed in 1957.

Highlands Junior High School

Address: 11509–62nd Street
Style: Collegiate Gothic
Architect: George Turner
Date: 1913–20
Route: Continue north on 62nd Street to the School.

This style of school, popular in the inter war years must have impressed the students with a sense of privilege and solemnity.

As part of the annexation agreement between the Highlands and the City of Edmonton struck in 1911, the Edmonton Public

School Board promised to build a secondary school in the neighborhood. The Highlands school district was actually formed in 1910 out of Beverly, which was closer than the nearest Edmonton School district. The construction of Highlands School commenced in 1913; however, due to the onset of World War I, there were no funds available to finish the school for several years.

The school shell was left unoccupied until 1916 when the first storey opened for limited use. Prior to opening in 1916, classes were held in three wood-framed temporary buildings on the grounds. One was later used as the janitor's residence. In 1915, the students were encouraged to organize a patriotic garden project to help support the local war effort. The building, which originally held seventeen rooms, was not completed until 1920. The second floor of the new school was used as Edmonton's first teachers' college from 1920 to 1923.

Constructed of brick and sandstone, the two-storey institution was a duplicate of the King Edward School which was completed in 1913. The Edmonton Public Schools architect, George Turner, turned out a number of these Gothic-styled buildings with crenellated rooflines and imposing central towers over the arched entryway. A trapdoor access to the tower was reached through the second-floor vice principal's office. Inside, wood paneling lined the foyer with its terrazzo flooring, marble stairs, and leaded glass windows. Over the interior doors, transoms allowed light into classrooms from the halls. The original coal-fired boilers were replaced with gas during the 1950s renovation. Few original details remain today.

Initially the completed construction cost $210,722. The school was expanded in 1958 when five classrooms and new offices were added to increase the capacity to 550 students in grades 7 through 9. A further $70,000 in renovations was carried out in 1970.

Owens Residence

Address: 11227–63rd Street
Style: Foursquare
Architect: Garnett Meiklejohn (contractor)
Date: 1912
Route: Continue west from the school on 113th Avenue to 63th Street. Turn south and go halfway down the block to the Owens house.

While architecture is interesting, this residence shows that the stories of the people who resided in them is often a fascinating tale.

Built by the original owner, Garnett Meiklejohn, also known as "the Lumberman" because of his business, this foursquare-style building cost approximately $2,500 in 1912. Meiklejohn built the house as an investment property and rented it to the Owens in 1914. Herbert Owens was a retired sea captain who came to Edmonton in 1908 with his wife, Eda. Owens worked as a weather station manager and so constructed a meteorological observatory with an 18-meter red tower holding a rotating wind gauge and another observatory platform in the backyard.

Herbert enlisted during World War I, and he died in a prisoner of war camp in 1917. Eda assumed his meteorological duties and, as a widow, continued on in the position after his death. The house was sold to the Duncan family, but Eda Owens continued to live in the house until 1944.

Eda Owens was the first woman to hold the post of weather station manager in Canada. There were 26 instruments to be read starting at 5:40 a.m., and over 100 weather stations sent daily weather reports to her in Edmonton. From those, she made two daily reports and one weekly report to Toronto. Despite that it was exceptional for married women to work (the war changed that somewhat, though even then women were usually restricted to nontechnical jobs), Eda thrived in the position. She developed an international reputation, attracting visitors from many countries, including aviators, academics, and explorers. The weather station was closed in 1943 when Eda retired. She died in 1957. Her biography, *Eda the Weatherlady,* was written by Phyllis Patterson, her granddaughter.

The foursquare style is symmetrical with four main rooms on the main floor. The Owens house had a wraparound verandah, and the exterior was finished with wood siding and shingles. Interior details such as original maple floors added beauty to this simple structure. The home was lovingly restored after Jim and Sandra Storey purchased the house in 1980. They spent over ten years recreating the prewar ambience. The house was designated a provincial historical resource in 1993.

Highlands United Church
Address: 11305–64th Street
Style: English Tudor revival
Architect: William Blakey
Date: 1923
Route: Return northwards to 113th Avenue and continue west to 64th Street.

Little of the original church can be seen except from the sides of the building. Highlands United Church, ca. 1925.
CITY OF EDMONTON ARCHIVES EA 10-511

A Methodist Sunday school was started in 1911, using the classrooms of the wood-frame Highlands school. Eventually the group of people who started to teach the Highlands children would form a congregation that would eventually become Highlands United Church. In 1912, they decided to build their own church, and Mr. Magrath generously provided a site on 64th Street. First the congregation built a parsonage with an unfinished main floor that could be used as a worship space.

E. W. Morehouse, also a Methodist, designed the house/church and supervised its construction, which was completed by December 1912. That building at 11317–64th Street, served as the manse for the church for many years after the new church was built, receiving a major facelift in the 1950s.

With the large number of Methodists moving into the Highlands community, it was soon discovered that the church would not hold them all. By 1913, they had relocated services to the local curling rink on 62nd Street. The new church, a wood-frame, clapboard-covered structure which cost about $3,000, less than most houses in the neighborhood, was built by volunteers from the congregation. It was dubbed the "little white church" and served for church and Sunday school (for which two extra rooms were added in 1914) until 1927.

In 1923, the congregation again thought about expansion and built a brick and concrete basement as the foundation for a new church to accommodate the families of the 500 children registered in their Sunday school. They hired architect W. G. Blakey, who designed a church similar to but larger than his 1921 Christ Church Anglican design. The new church was a version of Gothic revival with a steeply pitched roof with cross gables and an entrance porch with a hipped roof. Its exterior was finished in stucco and half-timbering. Inside, exposed scissor trusses support the roof and lend an air of loftiness to the interior. The church was completed in 1927. In the intervening years the Methodists became part of the United Church of Canada and the new building was called the Highlands United Church.

A notable addition to the church is the memorial window, added in 1953 at the new south entrance. The attached hall blocks the view of the old church, which can best be seen from the side.

Route: If you like you could make a short detour north from the church to see the McLuhan house. Otherwise turn south on 64th Street and cross 112th Avenue before turning west to 65th Street.

Note: The McLuhan residence at 11342–64th Street was the home of Marshall McLuhan, Canadian media guru. He was born in 1911 and lived in this house with his parents from 1912 to 1918. His parents purchased the land in 1912 and obtained a permit to build a $3,000 house. Their architects were Nesbitt and Morehouse, and the contractors, Bailey and Berry, built the rugged Craftsman bungalow with its exposed beams, a low-pitched roof, and large front porch over a cast-concrete foundation. The McLuhans left for Winnipeg in 1918, but retained ownership until 1923.

Sometime after they left, in about 1929, the house was rented to Walter Husband, a salesman for a national drug and chemical company and a relation of Herbert Husband, the proprietor of the drugstore in the Gibbard Block (1926–44). He purchased the house in 1943 and sold it in 1956.

Marshall McLuhan received his PhD from Cambridge in 1934 and taught English at various American colleges before moving to the University of Toronto in 1944. He specialized in language and perceptions and the influence of mass media on culture. McLuhan died in Toronto in 1980.

Gibbard Block

Address: 6423–112th Avenue
Style: Classical Revival
Architect: Ernest Morehouse
Date: 1913
Route: Continue south to 112th Avenue and west to 65th
Street.

A landmark for those who pass through the Highlands, the Gibbard block's history of revitalization is also a symbol for the heritage preservation of the neighborhood.

Although it was technically located just outside the original boundary of the Highlands, Magrath and Holgate wanted to build this residential and retail block to increase the neighborhood's sustainability without compromising its exclusive residential quality. They interested an investor, William T. Gibbard of Nipanee, Ontario, who contributed about a quarter of the $90,000 cost. For his investment, the building bore his name. Gibbard was a successful furniture dealer in Ontario and was obviously looking for new opportunities for his wealth in the west.

The new building was announced in the *Edmonton Journal* and described as having the latest in architecture, comfort, modern equipment, and convenience. The Gibbard Block contained nine suites on the upper two storeys and two storefronts on the main level. A central gas plant provided cooking fuel, and each suite had a telephone and hot running water. Residents included salesmen, teachers, lawyers, packing plant workers, policemen, ministers, and bank clerks. Many of these individuals, after having a taste of life in the Highlands, moved into nearby houses as they prospered. Similarly, many of the shop's proprietors did the same.

The three-storey building is clad in Redcliff brick from southern Alberta and features many classical features such as pilasters, brackets on the cornice, contrasting sills, and keystones.

The building was sold in 1926, and various owners and tenants worked in and inhabited the building, subdividing the retail space. Carole and Ernst Eber first rented one of the spaces in 1979, then gradually began to purchase first the retail spaces and then the entire building by 1985. They dreamed, restored, and converted the disparate parts into a restaurant called La Boheme and a bed and breakfast operation.

The Gibbard Block was designated a registered historic resource in 1992.

Morehouse Residence
Address: 11153–64th Street
Style: Georgian revival
Architect: Ernest Morehouse
Date: 1912
Route: Continue south on 64th Street.

Although responsible for some of the most spectacular examples of architecture in this neighborhood, the owner of this lot chose a family friendly style for his own home.

Ernest Morehouse was born in Ontario in 1871 and educated in Toronto at the Polytechnic School. After graduating in architecture in 1892, he worked for various contracting businesses, building factories in the United States and Canada. One of the contracts led Morehouse and his family, wife Minnie and two children, to Edmonton in 1910. He went into partnership with Arthur Nesbitt in an architectural firm.

Soon Morehouse was designing houses for the real estate team of Magrath and Holgate in their new development at the Highlands. He was responsible for the Magrath and Holgate mansions as well as the residences of Ash, Chown, and Atkinson. He also designed his own residence in the Highlands, the Gibbard Block, and several commercial blocks in the area, as well as most of the 24 speculative properties Magrath and Holgate erected in the neighborhood to make the development look more prosperous and encourage sales of their lots.

Morehouse's own residence was much more modest than Magrath's and Holgate's houses, probably costing only $4,500. It is designed in the symmetrical foursquare style with one major room on each side of a central hallway and staircase. Interesting features include the bay window topped with the hip-roofed verandah and the balcony over the main entrance. The interior was finished with lovely details such as brass fixtures, beveled glass, fine woodwork, and stenciled patterns on the walls. Technical features included a master switch for all the upper-floor lighting in the master bedroom.

The house was sold to James Ross, a city lawyer, in 1922. The Morehouse family left Edmonton for Detroit in 1929, possibly hoping that a better living for architects could be found in the larger center.

The Morehouse Residence was designated a registered historic resource in 1987.

Route: Return south to Ada Boulevard to complete the circuit.

Glenora Tour

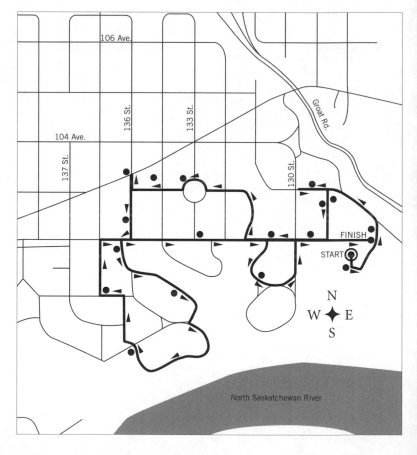

The name of the Glenora neighborhood probably derives either from a descriptive combination of the words *glen* and *or*—a valley of gold, since there was gold panning going on in the area ravines and river valley—or from a place in either Quebec or Ontario, a mill on the LaChine Canal or a village near Pictou. Both were known to the developer of this community, though he did not explain his rationale for naming Glenora.

River valley from St. George's Crescent viewpoint.

The land on which this neighborhood was built originally belonged to Malcolm Groat and his wife, Margaret Christie Groat. Malcolm Groat came from Scotland to the Hudson's Bay Company's Fort Edmonton to take charge of the gardens and livestock, being a farmer by birth and inclination. When the Hudson's Bay Company sold its lands in the northwest to the Canadian government in 1869, Groat was one of the first to take up a homestead, on river lot 2, just west of the HBC reserve around the fort. He married the chief factor's daughter, Margaret Christie, in 1870, but remained with the company until 1878 when he bought another large parcel of land to the west of his homestead, giving him over 400 hectares in all. In today's Edmonton, the land stretches from 121st Street to 149th Street between the river and 111th Avenue. The Groats had nine children.

Malcolm and Margaret were among the first settlers to live outside Fort Edmonton. Their first house was a cabin at 132nd Street and Stony Plain Road. They raised cattle and horses as well as growing wheat and barley. With his sons, Malcolm also started a cartage business hauling goods east and west, to and from the fort. When other settlers arrived in the area, the Groats were influential in developing the community. Groat sat on the first school board and donated his land for churches (Roman Catholic and Anglican). The city's first doctor, George Verey, also had a home and small farm in the river valley, east of the Groat Bridge on land given to him by Malcolm Groat.

By 1903, growth in the city had made the land valuable for more than farming. The Groats subdivided their land and sold the majority of it to a developer named William J. Tretheway, a lawyer from Ontario. The price was $100 per acre (equaling roughly $40 per hectare). The survey of the area produced lots of 15 by 45 meters on the symmetrical pattern, except where the Groat Ravine and the river valley allowed for graceful arrangements on curving circles and crescents. The avenues were named and the streets numbered (although most also had informal names), following the pattern established farther east in downtown Edmonton.

Tretheway realized that distance might prove a barrier to selling his lots, so in late 1903 he and a partner, R. P. Inglis, offered to buy the charter for the streetcar company that had been granted to the city in 1893. In 1904, Edmonton was incorporated as a city and had extended the city limits to 127th Street. Some of the Groat estate was therefore within the city limits before the neighborhood was developed. There was no streetcar yet, however. With a $10,000 deposit and a promise to build three kilometers of track by 1905, Tretheway and Inglis were allowed to purchase the charter. They purchased equipment, but before the end of 1905 had defaulted on their company with no track laid. The city then bought most of their equipment, and Tretheway began selling off his lots to another developer, James Carruthers from Montreal.

Between 1902 and 1912, Carruthers and Round and Company (headed by father and son partners, James and George Carruthers, and H. B. Round, an employee of the HBC) acted as real estate agents in Montreal, Winnipeg, and some American cities. Carruthers was born in 1853 of Scottish parents in Toronto, and educated there. Through his company, James Carruthers and Company, he was a member of several grain exchanges in North America, which earned him the nickname "the Grain King." He also had interests in finance and transportation.

The company bought the block of lots from 124th to 142nd streets, from north of the river to 111th Avenue, from William Tretheway about 1908. Carruthers also purchased lots in Westmount, a neighborhood he intended to market to young professionals. Glenora, however, was to be an exclusive enclave for the wealthy.

In 1908, the city finally began the construction of the streetcar line along Jasper Avenue to 121st Street. In 1909, James Carruthers offered to donate $25,000 to the city to build a bridge across the Groat Ravine since access to Glenora was hampered by the ravine's depth. (Carruthers was later reimbursed for that gift.) The ravine bridge was erected of concrete and steel materials, but was thereafter known as the "Iron Bridge." To ensure that the bridge was built twelve meters wide instead of the usual six meters, Carruthers also promised to donate the ravine proper and some other land to the city for parks in 1912, after the bridge was completed. The city built paths and footbridges there, and planted trees throughout the park, which was used as a nursery for the city's tree program. The Groat Ravine Park was used for years as a promenade and for recreational activities in the winter.

The other impediment to development was the tracks of the Edmonton, Yukon and Pacific Railroad spur line, which crossed the area from about 123rd Street to join the Canadian Northern line at about 106th Avenue. It took many more years before the trains were rerouted and those tracks were taken up.

The city annexed the rest of the Groat property in 1910. The streetcar crossed the Groat Ravine after the city annexed out to 142nd Street, and the bridge was under construction in late 1910 and completed in 1911. Under the Carruthers and Round land company, the exclusive neighborhood of Glenora was ready for development. To ensure the select type of development Carruthers foresaw, in 1911 he requested a city bylaw to enforce a caveat on development between Connaught Drive and 142nd Street containing several assurances about the types and placement of homes and restricting commercial development in Glenora. Depending on location within the development, home costs had to exceed $3,000 to $5,000, the houses had to sit back from the street at least eight meters, and be single family dwellings. No trade or business was to be carried out in any building within the caveat area.

The only serious challenge to the caveat was brought forth in 1949 by the Toronto Dominion Bank. The challenge was eventually successful in the courts, and a bank was built on the east side of 142nd Street over the protests of neighbors.

Many of the streets in the Glenora development were named after British royalty and nobility, especially those with connections to Canada. It was, perhaps, a way of selling to the wealthy of eastern Canadian and British descent, the respectability of the neighborhood. For example, 130th Street was called King's Road, and 104th Avenue was MacKenzie Avenue. Other names, such as Wellington, Alexander, and Churchill, will remind you of English history as you tour.

From 1912 to 1932, a stub line of the Edmonton Radial Tramway operated between 142nd Street and 124th Street. (After 1932, a bus covered the route.) Called the "Toonerville trolley" like the tram in a popular American cartoon of the day, the streetcar's ride fare was five cents and was paid upon entry at the rear of the trolley. Passengers disembarked from the front. There was no heat provided in the earliest trolleys, although the driver eventually got a coal heater and then an electric heater in the vestibule, and small pipes carried some of the heat back to the passengers.

Regular drivers on the route included Bill McLellan and Bob Chambers, who were colorful characters and about whom many tales were told (see Tony Cashman's *Best Edmonton Stories)*. Later, Bert Berry took over on the route. Drivers would often wait for passengers coming from their homes, but not necessarily from the 124th Street stop. They would, however, take a long stop outside McCray's garage (now a restaurant and pub just east of the bridge) so passengers who missed at 124th could catch up.

Groat Estates still exists on the east side of the Groat Ravine. The last Groat home is an impressive brick two-storey structure that was originally surrounded by eight hectares for Groat's horse breeding business. A large stable for the transport company's horses was erected at 125th Street and 101st Avenue overlooking the river and Groat Ravine. Malcolm Groat died the year after the house was completed in 1912. His wife, Marguerite Christie Groat, remained in the house for another ten years until her death on December 22, 1922.

By 1912, the population of Edmonton had reached about 31,000, and the western border of the city was ripe for real estate sales. Unfortunately, for Carruthers and other real estate speculators, the Hudson's Bay Company chose that year to open up the lots on their reserve for sale and glutted the market with real estate. Speculation was rife but actual development meager, especially with the outbreak of war in 1914. Although lots west of 136th Street were sold to potential owners, most property there reverted to the city after the real estate bust of 1913. The area was not extensively developed until the 1950s.

Carruthers also played a part in Edmonton's aviation history. He presented an airplane (a Curtiss JN–4 biplane) to the government (apparently several national businessmen did) for military training in Ontario. After the war, the plane was presented to the city. Named *The Edmonton,* it was used by Wop May and George Gorman in exhibition flights. It is now in the Aviation Hall of Fame at the Reynolds Alberta Museum in Wetaskiwin.

Before the Iron Bridge spanned the Groat Ravine, settlement tended to be closer to Stony Plain Road, where there was at least a footbridge. After 1911, development increased along 102nd Avenue as well. A second, decorative bridge was built over the second ravine on 102nd Avenue as a 1930s work project.

By 1914, Stony Plain Road was paved to 127th Street, but remained a mud track from there, all the way out to 142nd Street. It served mostly the horse and wagon traffic—farmers bringing produce to market and First Nations people. There was a wooden bridge over the ravine and a wooden walkway from the bridge to 133rd Street. The walkway then turned south to serve the houses there. Before World War I, the fields north of Stony Plain Road were often used for campsites by First Nations people who came into town to trade. There was a water trough at 127th Street and Stony Plain Road for their horses. A city dump was located north of Stony Plain Road at about 106th Avenue and 132nd Street until about 1940.

The land from St. George's Crescent to 142nd Street south of Stony Plain Road was mostly shrub and brush until the late 1920s. The Capital Hill area (just west of St. George's Crescent) was initially called Hog's Back. Full of hiking trails through the bush to the riverbank, it became a popular place for Glenora residents to ride horses and walk.

The city took an option to buy the land in the Groat Flats in 1922, and several Chinese market gardeners sublet for many years. Mr. Lee Hong had a garden on the western section where the Groat Road is today, and he supplied the small grocery stores in the West End along 124th Street and Stony Plain Road.

The area between 136th Street and 142nd Street, south of 102nd Avenue, grew rapidly after the oil discovery at Devon in 1947. Edmonton's population increased greatly from the war years on, as did the demand for new housing. The railway tracks were removed from the Groat Estates and a road built along the Groat Ravine to open up the area north of Glenora for development. In 1949, the Glenora Community League was formed under the presidency of Fred Purkis. The skating rink was moved from the Glenora School to land given to the league near the Westminster School, north of Stony Plain Road on 135th Street, and the league built a community hall there the next year.

While the status of the Glenora neighborhood that Carruthers and Tretheway envisioned has certainly remained, there is a high degree of mixed housing in the area. Recent developments have apparently broken the caveat in several locations, and heritage homes are constantly under threat of demolition and replacement by "monster houses," especially on the riverbank and ravine crescents.

Glenora has been the neighborhood of premiers, lieutenant governors, mayors, and aldermen as well as businessmen, bishops, and maybe a few not so well-off and saintly citizens. In certain quiet crescents, the historic feel of the neighborhood with its imposing trees and diverse architecture still lingers to make Glenora a most attractive community.

Government House
Address: 12845–102nd Avenue
Style: Jacobethan revival
Architect: Richard P. Blakey
Date: 1913

Unlike Calgary, Edmonton has only a few sandstone buildings like Government House.

In 1909, in order to finance the building of the Iron Bridge, Carruthers sold close to twelve hectares just west of the Groat Ravine to Wellington Crescent, from the riverbank to 102nd Avenue, to the provincial government for a home and garden for the lieutenant governor. The government paid $33,571 for the property.

The three-storey mansion was designed by R. P. Blakey of the provincial architect's office in 1910 under the direction of the provincial architect Allan Jeffers, and was completed in 1913. The palatial style is called Jacobethan revival, and it is a spin-off of the Tudor revival style, popular at the turn of the century. Typical features of the style include raised gable ends and bays, and double-hung bow windows with crenellated parapets above them. The pillared entrances are topped with balconies.

Constructed of steel and concrete, it is faced with sandstone quarried from around Calgary. Stonemasons were imported from Scotland to work the stone onsite. Government House is Edmonton's only sandstone dwelling. Originally there was a conservatory on the west side, but it was removed during World War II when the house was converted into a convalescent hospital. There were extensive gardens and trees planted on the grounds, and a stable and carriage house built closer to the river. It was later converted to a garage and then to government greenhouses. The cost of the house was $100,000; with furnishings and landscaping of the extensive grounds, the total cost rose to $350,000. Lieutenant Governor G. H. V. Bulyea opened the house on October 7, 1913. Through the following years, extravagant entertainments were often held in the house including annual levees for New Year's, elegant government receptions, and banquets and social and charitable events hosted by the lieutenant governors and their spouses.

Lieutenant governors who resided at Government House included G. H. V. Bulyea (1913–15), Dr. R. G. Brett (1915–25), Dr. William Egbert (1925–31), William L. Walsh (1931–36), Philip C. H. Primrose (1936–37; died in office), and John Campbell Bowen (1937–50).

In 1938, during the term of Lieutenant Governor Bowen, a dispute arose between him and the government of the day about the constitutional power of the lieutenant governor. The Social Credit government enacted legislation that would have severely restricted the ability of the media to report the news, especially as it concerned the government. Many people thought it was censorship, and there was considerable opposition (outside of the House). On advice of counsel, the lieutenant governor refused to sign the bill, in essence refusing to give royal assent. The Socreds thought the appointed official did not have the right to forestall the wishes of the elected Legislative Assembly. They retaliated by cutting off funds to the office of the lieutenant governor, including his secretary's salary, his transportation, and the expenses for running his residence such as water, power, and the telephone.

To be fair, there had been years of wrangling about the expense of running Government House, especially during the Depression, and the dispute was a convenient excuse for curtailing costs. (The United Farmers government had tried to pass a motion to shut down Government House and abolish the office in 1925, but failed.) Bowen was housed first at the Hotel Macdonald and then in temporary quarters offered by supporters (General Griesbach and Horace Harvey) until the issue of the housing allowance was settled, after the Social Credit government was defeated.

Government House was vacant from 1938 to 1942. The furnishings were sold at auction in 1942 at a fraction of their actual cost From 1942 to 1944, Northwest Airlines used the building as a residence for between 150 and 200 of their staff. In 1944, it became a convalescent home for wounded WWI veterans, and they remained in residence until 1950. In 1951, the building was purchased by the federal government's Department of Veterans Affairs for $350,000 and converted into a home for disabled veterans.

In 1964, the grounds to the north were chosen as the site for the Alberta Centennial project: the erection of the Provincial Museum and Archives. There was some opposition to the project by neighbors on Wellington Crescent, especially to the plan to build a tower restaurant overlooking the river. The project was completed, without the tower, by 1967 when Government House was returned to the province. Extensive renovations were carried out on the house to create a conference center for the Alberta government.

In the meantime, subsequent lieutenant governors solved their housing problems in a number of ways. John J. Bowlen (1950–59) built his own home in the Capital Hill neighborhood. J. Percy Page (1959–66) lived at 10312–133rd Street on the Alexander Circle. Dr. J. W. Grant MacEwan (1966–74) purchased three lots for an official residence at 56 St. George's Crescent (previously the "summer" property of Horace Harvey, chief justice of Alberta and the man who had advised Bowen not to sign the act which had him expelled). The architect for that bungalow was John Rule of Rule Wynn and Rule.

The home was subsequently used by lieutenant governors Ralph Steinhaurer (1974–79), Lynch Staunton (1979–85), Helen Hunley (1985–91), Gordon Towers (1991–96), and Bud Olsen (1996–2000). Lieutenant Governor Lois Hole (2000–   ) declined to live in the house, preferring to stay in her home in St. Albert. The house remained vacant, until in 2004 the government demolished it.

After World War I and through the Depression years, there were numerous other nonofficial residents on the Government House property, especially below the stable and carriage house in the river valley. Many unemployed men lived in the ravines from Groat Ravine to Miner's Flats, near today's Laurier Park. Some built cabins out of scrap lumber or cut down the bush in the area. "Hank the Hermit" (described by some as a religious fanatic) got permission from the city to clear out some trees and build a cabin, where he lived for ten to twelve years. Others just tunneled into the riverbank. Some tried their hand at sluicing for gold in the streams and the river.

The coach house was a suitable outbuilding for the fine house it served.

Art Ford was probably the most notable hermit who lived in the riverbank. He was quite a public figure, well known by the construction crews building the Groat Bridge in 1957. Art criticized their work, predicting that high waters on the North Saskatchewan would wipe out their pylons, which did happen.

Also on the grounds is the residence of the lieutenant governors' chauffeur. The address is 12903–102nd Avenue, but the house is located at the back of the museum's parking lot. The same architects as for Government House, A. M. Jeffers and R. P. Blakey, designed this Tudor-inspired, rectangular, wood-frame building. It has a stucco and brick exterior, arched windows, flared verge boards (ornamental boards hanging from a projecting roof), and the typical half-timbering associated with Tudor houses.

The first occupant was John Colwill, chauffeur, coachman, and gardener to Lieutenant Governors Brett and Egbert. Stables were located behind and below the house in the ravine. If you look over by the west side of the house, you will see that the south façade is built downhill two storeys. It has one of the best river valley views in the city.

Ferris Residence

Address: 12704–102nd Avenue
Style: Craftsman
Architect: Unknown
Route: Head east of Government house and north out of the Provincial Museum grounds, crossing 102nd Avenue using the pedestrian crossing light.
Date: 1911

Dr. Ferris built (actually his brother was the builder) this brick mansion across from the Government House gates in 1911. Dr. Ferris came to Edmonton in 1902 and married Grace Swanzey, a teacher from Ontario, in 1904. Ferris was a leading city physician. He served on the public school board and the first University of Alberta senate. He was a Presbyterian and a Mason, a member of the Edmonton Club and the country club, a polo player, a golfer, and a hunting enthusiast.

The eye-pleasing symmetrical façade fronts this large family friendly mansion.

In 1914, he went overseas as a medical officer for 66th Battalion, which was disbanded in England soon after its arrival. Dr. Ferris was reassigned to Stancliff Military Hospital for the remainder of the war. He received a Military Cross for his work with prisoners of war.

His wife also went to England. Grace Ferris was the first Canadian woman to be involved with military canteens. She served as a teacher at the Westminster Technical School on canteen management, and traveled all over England and Ireland setting up canteens. On her return to Edmonton, Mrs. Ferris brought an enthusiasm for the YWCA concept, and she became involved in that organization here.

Dr. Ferris was promoted to lieutenant colonel after his return to the city. In 1921, he was made commandant to No. 6 Casualty Clearing Station and medical advisor to the Department of Soldiers' Civil Re-Establishment.

Dr. Ferris died of a heart attack while attending a function at Government House in 1927. His widow continued to be active in civic affairs. She was a founding member of the Local Council of Women in 1908, the Women's Canadian Club, the International Order of Daughters of the Empire (serving as regent of the Beaver chapter), and she worked for the children's home and YWCA. Mrs. Ferris was also a school trustee from 1930 to 1936. She died in 1962.

Between 1963 and 1990, the house was the Western Canadian headquarters for the Catholic order of St. Alphonsus, a group of Redemptorist fathers who lived and worked in the building. It has since been the property of a large family who appreciate the house's history and amenities.

This house is wood frame, faced with stucco between half-timbering and clinker brick, including the three corbelled chimneys. It has a large gabled roof with overhanging eaves, showing notched verge boards at the ends of the gables. The large central gable dormer is typical of the Craftsman style, as is the front verandah and the large brackets under the roof. The front door is original to the house. There was at one time a gasoline storage tank under the garage to ensure the doctor always had a full tank in case of emergencies.

The layout is square, and it rises two and a half storeys. The house contains twenty rooms including six bathrooms. On the first floor is a vestibule, sun porch, a hall to the garage (which was originally converted to medical offices and a waiting room), the main entrance hall, the living room, dining room, bathrooms, kitchen, and a back porch. The second floor houses the master bedroom with an off-suite bath and sitting room, an off-suite sun porch, a laundry room, bathrooms, and three other bedrooms. The third floor has the two remaining bedrooms. In the basement are another laundry, a family room, the boiler and mechanical rooms, and a small nanny suite.

Originally the interior was furnished in dark-stained oak wainscots and maple floors, some of which remain. Alterations and renovations have seen modern replacement windows, although there are some original leaded glass windows in leaded frames. The hot water heating system has been supplemented with a small forced-air unit for the basement suite and family room.

Goodridge Residence

Address: 10226 Connaught Drive
Style: Craftsman
Architect: Unknown
Date: 1915
Route: Continue east around the corner and north onto
Connaught Drive.

The Craftsman Style was very popular before the First World War.

Connaught Drive was probably named after Prince Arthur, first Duke of Connaught and Strathern (1850–1942), who was governor general of Canada from 1911 to 1916. Connaught Drive runs parallel to the Groat Ravine, which at one time was less overgrown than it is today.

Although it was wooded, the city and neighbors kept the bushes back and the paths through the ravine cleared. Villa Avenue boys flashed Morse code messages with flashlights attached to flags across the Groat Ravine to their friends on Connaught Drive, according to stories told by previous inhabitants of the ravine houses. There was a local hockey team that played on the wide road intersections along Connaught Drive called the Connaught Rangers.

Cross-country skiing was also a popular activity on the trails that ran along the Groat Ravine. Access paths came up into Glenora at Connaught Drive. It was known also as Promenade Park, and in the summer there were walking and pony trails. Two saddle clubs serviced the area riders: the Connaught Hunt Club and the Edmonton Saddle Club, which had been organized by H. G. Munroe of the Hudson's Bay Company land sales office. On Sunday afternoons, the members "hunted" for picnics that had been transported by car to a secret place somewhere on the river.

The three heritage houses along this first section of Connaught Drive were all built in 1915 and all listed on the city's municipal register of historic resources ("B" list). The listing comes either because of a historic association with a significant Edmontonian, or for its architectural merit. On this street, in most cases both criteria apply.

At 10226 Connaught Drive is the Goodridge residence—a fine example of a Craftsman-style bungalow constructed of clinker brick and stucco over a wooden frame. The house is one and a half storeys with a large central gable and half-timbering on the gable ends. It has a large wraparound verandah, and the overhanging roof is supported by square columns on brick piers and covered in a brick skirt. Other typical features for the style include the bay window, lintels, and lugsills. A sunroom was added to the southeast side. The historic person attached to the house was former chief justice of the Alberta supreme court Horace Harvey, who owned the house during the 1920s.

The next house, no. 10236, was purchased by C. V. Jamieson, a physician, in 1920. The most famous resident was Vincent Dantzer, an economist and lawyer who served the city as alderman (1963–66) and as mayor (1966–69). The Dantzer family resided in this house between 1965 and 1970. It also is of 1915 vintage, a two-and-a-half-storey house in the foursquare style. It is a brick house with a bellcast roof, dormers, and a balcony on the second floor over a single-storey, flat-roofed addition.

Hard as it is to believe, the next house, no. 10242, was repossessed by the Merchants Bank (later the Bank of Montreal) when the builder defaulted on payments for this and another house in the vicinity. The house's first resident was William Brown, general superintendent of the Canadian National Railway in 1915; however, the house was only rented to him. When the bank took possession of the two houses, they offered Frank Pike, the new manager of the Edmonton branch of the Bank of Montreal, his choice for a home. Newly arrived from Wetaskiwin where he had been since 1900, Pike originated in Newfoundland. This house probably appealed to him because of its style and brick construction. The Pike family lived here until 1941.

Built in 1915, the Pike residence is also a two-and-a-half-storey, square, brick house. The gable-hip roof has wood shingles, gable dormers, and a decorated cornice. The pedimented main entry with columns and the two-storey bay window are classically inspired features sure to inspire confidence like the bank Mr. Pike served.

Newell Residence

Address: 10304 Connaught Drive
Style: Georgian revival
Architect: Unknown
Date: 1911
Route: Turn left and follow the road around the corner
briefly to reach the Newell house on the north side.

Camby Foster Newell (1883–1958) was a lawyer and King's Counsel in the firm of Emery, Newell, Ford and Lindsay. He came to Edmonton from Ontario to practice law with the firm of Beck, Emery and Dubuc in 1903. He was involved in the United church and several social and athletic clubs, and served on the board of Alberta College and the Royal Trust Company.

After his first wife died, he married Dr. Mildred Folinsbee, one of Edmonton's first women doctors. She worked as a doctor for 35 years, then retired to take a job with the public health department. She was president of the Canadian Federation of Medical Women twice (in 1941 and in 1957) and the health convener for the National Council of Women. The couple had no children themselves, and they adapted this house to their lifestyle and entertaining needs. Dr. Folinsbee was also an artist.

A revival of a classical style gave an air of respectability and consequence to houses in upscale neighborhoods.

The house contains 375 square meters of living space, but the interesting alteration was the placing of the billiard room or ballroom on the third floor—a space usually reserved for the nursery and the maid's rooms.

A typical feature of this style of architecture is a symmetrical composition with classical details. The building is usually of square configuration with the rooms around a central hallway. There is a central entrance with a paneled door capped by a porch which is supported by columns. The dormers have a pediment (or a triangular gable)—in this case, a broken pediment—and jut out from the hipped roof. The chimneys are also placed symmetrically, usually at both ends of the roof. This house also has a wraparound verandah and an enclosed sunroom to the west, a popular addition on many houses in the neighborhood.

The White House

Address: 10360 Connaught Drive
Style: unknown
Architect: G. H. MacDonald
Date: 1913
Route: Continue west along 103rd Avenue to the corner of
130th Street. The white house is on the south east
corner of this intersection.

An architect's house will frequently be interesting for the style rules it breaks.

The house is a wood-frame, two-and-a-half-storey house with beveled siding and an irregular gabled roof with internal, symmetrical chimneys. There is a screened verandah with turned columns and a balcony above with French doors. There are both gable and shed additions to the house. The surrounding hedge and trees make the house quiet and inaccessible, but a good view can be had from the gate.

George Heath MacDonald (1883–1961) originated in Prince Edward Island. He had trained as a draftsman in the office of architect Percy Nobbs in Montreal and with his uncles, who were contractors. Getting on with Dominion Iron and Steel Company in Nova

Scotia, he met an architect named Hervert Alton Magoon, who was designing buildings for the company.

By 1902, Magoon was in private practice, and in 1904, he moved to Edmonton MacDonald came with him, to be his assistant while finishing high school. After graduating high school, MacDonald enrolled at McGill in architecture in 1907 and graduated in 1911, returning to Magoon's firm as a junior partner. He met his wife, Dorthea Heustis, in Edmonton, and they were married in 1913. He designed the White House as a wedding gift.

During the First World War, MacDonald served the federal government as a munitions supply supervisor and moved the family to Montreal and Toronto. MacDonald returned to Edmonton between the wars, but found little lucrative work for architects during the Depression. In 1921 he sold the White House and built a smaller house in the neighborhood (at 10318–130th Street) to reduce expenses. During the Second World War, he designed airport hangers and aviation buildings for the Northwest Staging Route (a series of airfields built from Edmonton to the northwest to assist the American Government to transfer airplanes to Russia to shift the balance of airpower for their allies fighting the Germans).

Together with Magoon, MacDonald was responsible for the design of many city buildings, including Corbett Hall (with D. E. McDonald in 1929), Robertson Wesley Church (ca. 1946), St. Joseph's Auxiliary Hospital (1948), and the Federal Building (1955).

John Mason Imrie, publisher of the *Edmonton Journal,* bought the white house from MacDonald in 1921. It was under his jurisdiction that the *Journal* took on the Social Credit government to oppose the legislation restricting the freedom of the press (that resulted in the ousting of the lieutenant governor from Government House). The articles on the issue won the *Edmonton Journal* a Pulitzer Prize in 1938.

Martyn Residence

Address: 10334 Connaught Drive
Style: Tudor revival
Architect: Ernest Litchfield (contractor)
Date: 1928
Route: Turn to the west to view the Martyn house across the
street.

This style is particularly appropriate for a neighborhood which celebrates its English traditions.

Ernest Litchfield was a contractor who worked in the Glenora area between 1928 and 1930. It is unknown whether he worked with an architect or simply built from stock plans and adapted them. He tended to buy up two or three lots on a street and build a group of houses at the same time. The houses tended to have themes. There are several "English cottages" and a group of "Spanish influence" houses (although one has been extensively altered) within a six-block radius in this section of Glenora. Other Litchfield houses can be found at nos. 13110, 13114, and 13118 on 103rd Avenue and at nos. 46, 70, and 92 on St. George's Crescent.

Built for Angus and Bernice Martyn in 1928, this is an early example of one of Litchfield's English-style "gingerbread" houses, and it is both alone on this street and a slightly larger (two-storey) version than usual for Litchfield houses.

The shingles are laid to resemble a thatched roof and that the stucco exterior resembles the daub and wattle exterior of old English cottages. The details in this building were well done. The windows have leaded glass panes, and the steep, pitched gable roof is typical of the style. The interior likewise included softly tinted molded plaster and quarter-cut oak floors edged with black walnut. Interesting alterations to the design include the built-in garage, a modern kitchen with a Frigidaire and gas range, and construction techniques that took advantage of the new principles of insulated walls and ceilings. The house was heated originally with a gas furnace and water radiators, a relatively new innovation in the neighborhood.

As you head south toward 102nd Avenue again, you cross Glenora Crescent, which was named, or renamed, in 1947 or 1948. The name appeared in the original Tretheway design, but the houses were given street addresses equivalent to 130th and 131st streets, between 103rd and 104th avenues as the road twists south. Most houses along the crescent were built between 1938 and 1947.

Griesbach Residence

Address: 12916–102nd Avenue
Style: Foursquare
Architect: Unknown
Date: 1922
Route: The next stop is back eastward along 102nd Avenue.
The foursquare style exhibits a symmetrical layout with four relatively equal-sized rooms around a central entry. The Griesbach residence is built in brick and has an open, columned verandah at the front, paired with an enclosed sunroom off the parlor, with arched windows on the lower floor. The roof is hipped and has symmetrically placed corbelled brick chimneys, with a hip dormer at the sides, and the cornice shows

double lentils. There is an attached double garage and a brick wall around the perimeter of the yard. The house has approximately 275 square meters of space. The owner in the 1990s allowed it to be redecorated for open houses for a charity fund raiser.

One of the most popular mansions on 102nd Avenue—well visited during Charity Open Houses.

William Antrobus Griesbach was born in 1878 at Fort Qu'Appelle, Saskatchewan. His father was Arthur Henry Griesbach, a lieutenant colonel of the North-West Mounted Police who came from a British military background and who was the first man issued a Mounted Police badge when the force was formed in 1873. The Griesbachs were transferred to Fort Saskatchewan, the headquarters for the NWMP in 1883.

William was sent to the Anglican St. John's College in Winnipeg in 1891, and he returned to study law in 1895. Like his father before him, he took up a military career. He enlisted when the Boer War started in 1899, serving until 1901 when he returned to start his own law practice in Edmonton. He was also successful in real estate and business dealings in the insurance and investment field. Because of his business acumen, he was encouraged by family and friends to run for public office, and he attempted unsuccessfully to become an alderman in 1903. He was more successful in 1905.

Griesbach married Janet McDonald Lauder, or Jennie, in 1906. She was the daughter of James and Hannah Lauder, owners of the first bakery in Edmonton and centers of the Scottish community in town. The Lauder sons and daughters were well-rounded, well-liked individuals who were involved in sports and had professional lives. One of Jennie's brothers was the fire chief, and Jennie had been the first telephone operator for Alex Taylor's telephone company. One of her sisters married Jennie's boss, telephone company manager William Ormsby. The year after his marriage, in 1907, Griesbach ran and was elected "Edmonton's Boy Mayor," when he was only 28 years old.

When World War I started, Griesbach, a lieutenant in the 19th Alberta Dragoons, volunteered for service with the rest of the men. He was named in December 1914 to command the 49th Battalion and within a month had recruited the 1,000 men required, setting a record which still stands. The Edmonton regiment, the 49th, served well in Europe, seeing action including on Vimy Ridge and at Passchendale. Griesbach returned home as a brigadier general at 39 years of age.

After the war Griesbach was promoted again to major general and was elected to the House of Commons as the member for Edmonton West. He served one term, then was appointed to the Senate from 1921, serving until his death in 1945. The Griesbachs loaned their house temporarily to the lieutenant governor in 1938 after the Social Credit government shut off the power at Government House (the Griesbachs were in Ottawa at the time). Mrs. Griesbach sold the house after her husband's death.

Ramsay Ravine

Address: access down Churchill Crescent, north of 102nd
Avenue

Route: Turn west and proceed along 102nd Avenue. Cross
the bridge over Ramsay Ravine and look over the edge.
Head north along Churchill Crescent until you see the
access on the right, if you wish to walk down the ravine.

The bicycle path along Ramsay Ravine runs to the river valley.

Churchill Crescent was probably named for Winston Churchill's father, Lord Randolph Churchill, rather than for the British prime minister, who had not really come into his glory at the time the streets of Glenora were named.

The ravine was named for James Ramsey, of the Ramsey Department Store, who built a house on St. George's Crescent before Glenora was really established.

The 102nd Street Bridge over the Ramsay Ravine was built in 1932 as a public works project for the unemployed in the city. It is made of cast cement complete with the spindle work in the center of the central portions. Even though it is a utilitarian structure, the style so suited the neighborhood that when the city suggested building a more modern bridge here, the community insisted that the old plans be used to create a new version of the old bridge. The city did, including the 1932 date-plate on the northwest side of the bridge.

The river valley walking trails can be accessed from this location, leading to the river near Government House Park at the base of the Groat and McKinnon Ravines. The trails were paved in 1988, after some neighborhood discussions. If you decide to take this short four-block detour, do take care, protect the environment, and watch for speeding bicycles.

Bradley Residence
Address: 13115–103rd Avenue
Style: Foursquare
Architect: Unknown
Date: 1913
Route: Continue west along 103rd Avenue, which was formerly named Peace Avenue.

Built in 1913 for the Charles H. Bradley family, this frame and brick irregular two-and-a-half-storey house is a good example of four square style architecture. The bell-case hip roof with wood shingles is broken by gable dormers and has two corbelled chimneys. There is also a gabled two-storey addition at the rear. The wraparound verandah with paired tapered columns leading up to the main entry has semi-elliptical sidelights beside the doors and an elaborate keystone voussoir above. The house is on the City of Edmonton's "B" list of municipal historical resources.

Typical of many houses in this part of Glenora the wrap around verandah was a pleasant gathering place for family and friends in the evenings.

Charles Bradley was the general manager for Swift's meat packers. He and his family lived in this house for almost twenty years. In 1931, Mrs. Myrtle Bradley, his widow, leased the house A. S. Ramsey, a department manager for the Ramsey store after whose family the ravine is named.

Note: The house at 10325–132nd Street was built in 1914 for the Reverend Arthur and Mrs. Emily Murphy, one of several houses the couple owned in the city. He was an Anglican minister, then serving in loco temens for Christ Church, just east of 124th Street on 102nd Avenue. The congregation had lost two ministers in rapid succession and thought a temporary replacement for six months might help them while they conducted a proper search for a minister. Murphy then served a variety of other parishes in the city and surrounding countryside.

Mrs. Murphy was, of course, an interesting woman in her own right. She was the first woman magistrate of a juvenile court in British Empire, a journalist, author of the Janey Canuck series, a suffragette and progressive, a campaigner for women's and children's rights, and later a member of the "Famous Five" women who brought the Person's Case to the British Privy Council. The house has been significantly altered on both the exterior and interior—but it is interesting to know that the Murphys lived in this neighborhood, too.

Alexander Circle

Address: 133rd Street & 103rd Avenue
Date: 1953
Route: Continue west along 103rd Avenue.

The circle provided these homes with their own parkland, which increased their value and cachet in this exclusive neighborhood even more.

Before the circle fountain was built, the Alexander Circle was used as a hockey rink in the winter. In the summer it was turned into a rugby pitch, although there was a lamppost in the center surrounded by grass and flowers. By 1952, the nearest neighbors were tired of replanting the flowers after the kids had trampled them, and they suggested eliminating the playground by creating a fountain. Led by Douglas Jones, fourteen residents petitioned the city and paid $5,000 for a fountain to be built. Originally it had several water jets which shot up and in from nozzles around the perimeter. In the evening it was lit by underwater lights.

Around the circle are some examples of pre–WWI houses. Several have been extensively renovated and altered, but some retain their historic value. Number 8 Alexander Circle (previously 10239–133rd Street) was built on the site that James Carruthers had chosen for his own home. In the end, Carruthers did not build nor come to live in Edmonton. This foursquare house was built in 1911 or 1912 with clinker brick and stucco. Interesting features include the second-storey bay window and the wraparound verandah with turned columns

Number 7 (previously 10241–133rd Street) was built by George Eaton in 1915. Another foursquare-style building, this one is an irregular rectangular shape because of the addition and the two-storey sunroom to the west. This house is also on the municipal historical resources "B" list.

Page Residence

Address: 16 Alexander Circle (formerly 10312–133rd Street)
Style: Georgian revival
Architect: Unknown
Date: ca. 1915

John Percy Page came to Edmonton to teach, and he spent 40 years with the Edmonton Public School Board as a teacher and a principal. He taught and then served as principal of McDougall Commercial High School, where he founded and coached a girls' basketball team. The Commercial Grads became world famous, playing 522 career games between 1915 and 1940, of which they won 502 for a 96-percent winning average. They played in four Olympics as exhibition only.

This residence was home to one of many city and provincial politicians who chose to live in Glenora over the years.

Maude Roach Page was a strong supported of Percy Page's work, helping as chaperone and translator during international competitions and world tours. She had come to Edmonton with her family in 1912, and she lived in the Lemarchand Manor when it was first built. She was an active member of the Women's Canadian Club and sat on the YWCA board.

In 1938, when Percy retired from teaching, he got involved in provincial politics and was elected president of the Edmonton Constituency Party which replaced the defunct conservative People's League of Alberta. He ran as an independent candidate for the provincial Legislative Assembly and served four terms as opposition between 1940 and 1948 and as a Progressive Conservative from 1952 to 1959. After his retirement from politics, he was appointed as the eighth lieutenant governor of Alberta, serving from 1959 to 1966. He and his wife lived in this house for part of that time.

John Percy Page died in 1972, and Maude, in 1978.

The house is threatened with demolition in 2004.

Glenora Electrical Substation

Address: 135th Street & Stony Plain Road
Style: Moderne
Architect: Unknown
Date: 1956
Route: Continue west along 103rd Avenue towards 135th
Street. Turn north towards Stony Plain Road.

This substation was more of a showroom than a working facility in its early years.

To the north of the schoolyard is an Epcor (formerly Edmonton Power) building which looks somewhat like it was built on stilts. In 1956, it was used as a showpiece for household electric appliances. The back portion of the building had the utilitarian function of being a switching station for electricity.

The moderne design used twelve sheets of plate glass around the south and east sides of the building to create an open display space, elevated from the roadway. In these windows, the electric company displayed the latest in labor-saving kitchen and laundry appliances, and hired female staff to illustrate the ease of their use to Glenora residents walking or driving by. The interior of the showroom was elegant and inviting, having terrazzo floors and sparkling white furnishings. It was the epitome of everything modern.

Several complaints were lodged with the city, since Edmonton Power was a municipally run utility. Some believed that the $33,195 cost for the building, plus extra for all the electrical equipment inside, was a bit extravagant. Eventually the showrooms were closed and the windows replaced with walls, except for the upper quarter which was still glassed in for light.

Glenora Elementary School
Address: 13520–102nd Avenue
Style: Arts & Crafts
Architect: Rule Wynn & Rule
Date: 1940
Route: Return south along 135th Street to view Glenora
School from the south side of 102 Avenue near St.
Georges' Crescent.

This school fits into its neighborhood better than many traditionally designed educational facilities would have.

The first Glenora School was built in 1918 at 128th Street and Stony Plain Road. It was a two-storey building with a small cinder playground. As the neighborhood grew, especially after the First World War, the school became overcrowded. In 1931, the school board recommended building a new school on city land between 102nd and 103rd avenues. It was specified that the exterior should harmonize with the neighborhood. It was to accommodate 279 students in grades one through six (with a ratio of 39.8 students per teacher). The old school was moved in 1941 (now it is a church and gospel club on Stony Plain Road), although it was pressed into service again for grades one and two during the late 1940s and 1950s, when the second Glenora School became overcrowded due to the postwar boom.

The new Glenora School was designed by Rule Wynn and Rule in an English style to fit with the neighborhood. Like many of the houses in the area, it displays brick on the lower half, and half-timbering and stucco infill above. There are wide gables at the ends of the roof and in the central part of the school. It cost $55,000 and was constructed to allow for additions in a similar style. Unfortunately, the large gymnasium which was added on the north side in the 1970s was of a generic concrete block style rather than a sympathetic addition.

The new school was opened in 1940 by Edmonton Public School Board chairman A. E. Ottewell. The ravine that emerges by St. George's Crescent on the south side of 102nd Avenue originally began in the school's front yard. It was very much appreciated by the children as a natural playground. Frequently, however, it was difficult for the teachers to find students after recess and return them to class.

Miss Draper was the first principal at this school, followed by J. Stockwell. He actually lived in the old school because of the difficulty with finding accommodation during the Second World War. Stockwell is responsible for clearing and leveling the schoolyard and eliminating the access to the ravine.

The Bulletin House

Address: 13501–102nd Avenue
Style: Moderne
Architect: Ernest Litchfield
Date: 1936

Route: Continue south along St. Georges' Crescent stopping first at the corner to view the Bulletin House.

Often judged to be an oddity in this neighborhood, this house represented the way of the future in 1936.

As Edmonton and the rest of Canada began to move out of the Depression, the *Edmonton Bulletin* sponsored this "modernistic home of tomorrow" to illustrate "what could be done to meet the demands for modern homes at low cost and suited to the rigours of the Canadian climate and within the means of the average family." In a campaign to help bolster the Edmonton economy and to encourage the real estate market, the newspaper paid $5,000 to design and build this home.

Typical aspects of the moderne design included the use of glass windows along the edge of the building, and sometimes around the corners, use of glass block (rather than brick) as a structural element, and, of course, the flat roof. People came by the carloads to view the way of the future, but few really appreciated the style.

This house has been significantly altered from the original, including the addition of the shed-roofed front entrance, the bay window beside the door, and the attached garage, but some of the essence of the original still exists.

Graenon

Address: 36 St. George's Crescent
Style: Tudor
Architect: Catalogue house
Date: 1914
Route: Continue south along St. Georges' Crescent following the curve of the ravine.

This house has so much character it even has a name, Graenon.

George Bligh O'Connor was a lawyer originally from Ontario. He was educated at Osgoode Hall in Toronto and called to the bar in Ontario and in Alberta in 1905. O'Connor partnered in the firm of Griesbach, O'Connor and O'Connor from 1904 to 1940. He was appointed King's Counsel in 1913. At the request of the federal government, he served on several boards and commissions including being the chair of the Wartime Labour Board (1944) and the Royal Commission that enquired into wages for coalminers. He was appointed chief justice of the Supreme Court of Alberta.

Hannah Margaret O'Connor was a journalist and sometime theater critic for the *Edmonton Bulletin*. She was a charter member of the Canadian Women's Press Club and came west in 1913 with the club on a tour to meet western members. She met George O'Connor here, and they married within a year.

Mrs. O'Connor chose the plan for her house from the catalogue of a Virginia architect. Her brother W. A. Fairlie and his partner W. Morrison built the house in 1914, the second house in the otherwise wilderness of west Glenora. It was the only house Morrison and Fairlie ever built, for soon after it was completed they enlisted in the services and were killed in the First World War. The house was a Tudor style with overlapping gables, a steep gabled roof resembling a thatched roof, tall and narrow windows, and large chimneys. It cost approximately $10,000 and contained about 290 square meters of space. Mrs. O'Connor named it Graenon, from the Irish Gaelic word meaning "a sunny place."

The O'Connors had one daughter, Margaret (Peggy), who served with the British Intelligence Service during World War II for the spy called Intrepid, doing all kinds of interesting jobs around the world. After the war she returned to the University of Alberta and worked as a librarian for 23 years, unable to tell the stories of her wartime experiences until recently. She married Gerrald Farnell, a bomber pilot, after the war in 1946, and they had four sons. Her father died in 1957, but her mother remained at Graenon until her death in 1966. The Farnells then took up residence, and Peggy Farnell lived in the house until 1997—keeping the house in the family for 83 years.

On the 40th anniversary of Glenora School in 1984, Mrs. Farnell was approached to write and publish a history under the auspices of the Old Glenora Historical Society. It was an instant hit and sold out almost immediately. It was updated and reissued in 1999 for the 50th anniversary of the Glenora Community League.

Ramsey Mansion

Address: 65 St. George's Crescent
Style: Tudor
Architect: Magoon and MacDonald
Date: 1914
Route: Continue south and then west along St. Georges'
Crescent.

*Like many houses in Glenora the Ramsey mansion has been altered and added
to so that little of its original character remains.*

The first house on St. George's Crescent was built by James Ramsey,
of the Ramsey Department Store (established in 1911). The house was
built at 65 St. George's Crescent (formerly 9920–135th Street) in 1914
at a cost of $20,000. Magoon and MacDonald were the architects.
Ramsey was elected alderman and served from 1915 to 1921. His store
was purchased by the T. Eaton Company in 1928. He lived in the house
until 1929, and in 1931, he rented the Bradley House on 132 Street.

The Ramsey Mansion was then occupied by James McKinnon,
MP, who also had a ravine named after him. Lieutenant Governor
John Campbell Bowen lived in the house temporarily between 1938
and 1947. It was loaned to him by McKinnon while he was in Ottawa.

In the 1980s, Herbert T. Richards, architect, made major alterations and converted the coach house to a garage and study for the new owner, Pat Bowlen. Later, Edmonton Oilers hockey franchise owner and financier Peter Pocklington lived in this house.

Blakey Residence

Address: 13526–101st Avenue
Style: Moderne International
Architect: William Blakey
Date: 1946
Route: Turn north and take the road to the right as you come past the Ramsey mansion to 101st Avenue where you will turn left to reach the Blakey house on the next corner.

Skillful and loving restoration and repair can maintain a heritage house even as the years pass.

William George Blakey was an British-trained architect who came to Canada and Edmonton in 1907. His brother Richard, who was also an architect, was working for the office of the provincial architect. William joined that office for a year and then transferred to the office of Roland Lines, who had a very prosperous and busy practice. Blakey remained with Lines until the beginning of the First World War, when both men enlisted. Blakey returned in 1919 and started his own practice, but Lines did not. In 1925, Richard joined his brother in the growing firm and they took on several partners over subsequent years.

Blakey built this house for $9,000 in 1946 for his wife, Carrie. It has several moderne features such as corner windows, the emphasis on the horizontal (which is helped visually by the flat roof), and the smooth texture of the walls.

Blakey was an architect of considerable talents and not stuck on this style only. Although the Roxy and Garneau theater buildings partake of the moderne and art deco styles, Blakey also designed more classical styled structures such as public schools, the Anglican Christ Church, and the Highlands United Church as well as the downtown Masonic Temple.

As you return north to 102nd Avenue along 136th Street, watch for another example of the moderne style at 10123–136th Street. This was the design of Macdonald and Macdonald, also built in 1946, for Louis and Muriel Hyndman for $11,000.

Hyndman was born in Edmonton in 1904 and attended the University of Alberta for law. He practiced with Field and Field from 1926, rising to the position of master of chambers of the Alberta courts between 1968 and 1986. His civic interests led him to serve on the school board and the zoning appeal board. Their son, Lou, became the provincial treasurer in Peter Lougheed's Conservative government.

Northwestern Utilities House

Address: 13224–102nd Avenue
Style: Unknown
Architect: Unknown
Date: 1932
Route: Return north to 102nd Avenue and go east back
	towards the Provincial Museum and Government House.

Northwestern Utilities showcased their new gas appliances in this Glenora house.

Another house built in Glenora for advertising purposes, this bungalow was built by Northwestern Utilities in 1932 to demonstrate the use of gas in heating and cooking. The house was open to the public for several years until the use of gas was established in the city. Then it was sold and continues as a private residence at the present time.

Freeman / Brintnell Residence

Address: 23 Wellington Crescent
Style: Foursquare
Architect: unknown
Date: 1923
Route: Proceed east back toward the Provincial Museum
and Government House. Tweedsmuir Crescent and
Wellington Crescent which circle around on the south
side of the avenue were named for British nobility.

Churchill Freeman had this house built in 1923. Freeman had built another house in Glenora but moved to this location when

Wellington Crescent was opened up. Rich interior details included an inlaid wood floor in the front hall and arched mahogany French doors. The second owner was Leigh Brintnell, who lived here between 1937 and 1967. Brintnell was a bush pilot and owner of several air transport companies.

Often Glenora residents built second homes in the neighborhood, like this one, as their needs changed rather than move away.

After the Second World War, Brintnell received an Order of the British Empire medal for his work with the Commonwealth Air Training Plan. He developed flying camps in Europe for training and assisting airmen. Just before the war, he also started Aircraft Repair Limited at Blatchford Field (Edmonton's first official airport), which serviced aircraft using the Northern Staging Route over Russia during the war.

Back in the Canadian north, Brintnell was involved in air surveying and mining exploration, especially exploration for radium. He started MacKenzie Air Service to provide cargo and passenger service to the mines. He eventually took a major role in Canadian Pacific Airlines.

Route: Return around the crescent for some striking views
of the river valley, and then continue into the Provincial
Museum parking lot.

Edmonton
Cemetery Tour

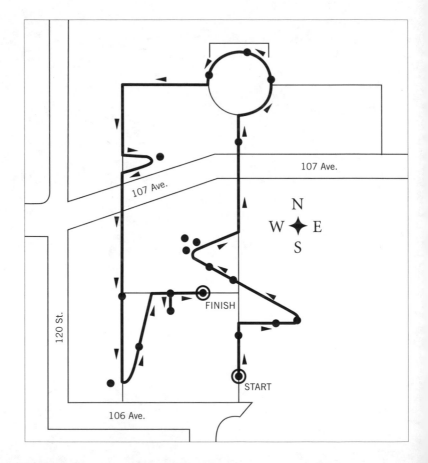

The history of the Edmonton Cemetery Company began in 1886 when a group of Edmonton businessmen applied for a charter for a limited dividend company to acquire land for use as a cemetery. Other cemeteries existed in and around Edmonton, but they were informal family plots on private land or associated with churches.

As the town began to grow, it was becoming imperative that more formal arrangements should be made. The Hudson's Bay Company was willing to donate 2.4 hectares of land for the cemetery, since Richard Hardisty, chief factor of the fort, was a member of the board of directors of the Cemetery Company. A meeting was held in February 1886 to strike a charter for the company, divide and sell stocks, and elect directors. Any profits of the company were to be used for beautification of the grounds and maintenance of the graves. Approximately 4,000 gravesites were laid out on the grounds south of today's 107th Avenue, west of 116th Street.

For the first few years, records were not well kept so the order and numbers of internments are not available. It is supposed that a number of transfers from other burial sites were made, since some of the stone predate the Cemetery Company's formation. After 1915, the company was reorganized and the records management improved. Larger numbers of internments and plot sales were occurring, and better bookkeeping became necessary.

By the end of the First World War, the company was beginning to realize it would need to expand to be able to stay in business and meet the demand for plots. There was also a need for a place to remember the veterans of the war. The city agreed to the expansion, and the company worked with the Commonwealth War Graves Commission, the Department of Veterans Affairs, and the Department of National Defense, as well as the Last Post Fund, to provide a proper burial for all veterans.

As part of the expansion, the company agreed to provide plots for veterans free of charge within the military field of honor. Plans were made to erect the 6.7-meter Cross of Sacrifice in the center of the field—a facsimile of the crosses erected in Europe. The bodies of several soldiers were re-interred in the Edmonton Cemetery's military area. A further expansion in 1924 swapped land for free graves for members of the North-West Mounted Police and the Canadian Legion. At that point, the extra land was across on the north side of 107th Avenue.

In 1929, the company was approached to build a mausoleum, which they did, completing it in 1930. The cemetery had then grown to include sixteen hectares of land. One further expansion between 107th and 108th Avenues, west of 120th Street, was allowed for a second military field in 1938, but the city refused any further expansion. St. Joachim's Cemetery lies directly to the east of the southern and oldest portion of the Edmonton Cemetery. No division is made between the cemeteries, but the stones do change orientation from one cemetery to another.

By 1964 the city was making plans to assume control of the Cemetery Company, spurred by provincial legislation to eliminate private ownership of cemeteries. The mausoleum was making a profit for the company at that time, there were still graves and crypts left to sell, and a $135,000 memorial trust was turned over to the city to cover the maintenance costs of the graves.

There is a great deal of public art in a cemetery. Many of the stones are beautifully carved; many have a great deal of symbolism hidden in their illustrations and messages. Edmonton's cemeteries have really been set up as parks, and they are places of peace and rest more than some cemeteries in older cities, where there can be some scary places and some unusual sayings on the stones. Colors, sizes, shapes, and the choices of pictures or images on the stones can tell us a lot about who the deceased was, or what their families thought about them.

Young Family Mausoleum
Dates: 1915
Location: A–9–27 through 31
Style: 6 family crypts
This is a private, or family, mausoleum which contains six crypts or spaces for the entombment of an individual's remains. There is only

one of these in the Edmonton Cemetery, and although the structure was erected in 1915, the spaces are not all filled.

This family mausoleum has a variety of decorative motifs; vines and striated columns.

The mausoleum was built for W. Young, who died in October 1915, and a Hannah Young was also entombed in here in 1928.

The classical details of the structure include the two columns supporting the pediment that bears the family name. Draperies carved on either side of the name provide a simple decoration. The columns are supported on large pedestals which bear the date of construction.

James Powell Family

Dates: various
Location: A–14–0001 through 0012
Style: Sculpture-draped figure
Route: Turn north and follow the path to the angel statue.

Statues such as this are rare for the Edmonton Cemetery.

The Powell family has nine internments around this central statue—an Italian marble carving of a woman with beautiful draperies. Another statue, a juvenile angel to the right of this one, has been seriously damaged by weather and perhaps vandalism.

The Powell family derived their fortune from real estate dealing, not unusual among pre–World War I entrepreneurs in Edmonton. The ability to keep the fortune during the Depression period was what separated the good businessmen from the bad.

Statues for grave markers come in a variety of shapes and sizes, although the majority are of angels in both young and adult forms; of saints, including the mother of Jesus; and of Jesus himself. Carved marble statues are rare these days because of their fragility and their vulnerability to cracking in our harsh climate. Bonded marble is more popular now; it consists of Carrara marble powder mixed with resin and poured into a cast of the desired shape. Once the bond sets, it has the same appearance as marble, but it is impermeable to water and will hopefully last longer.

Dr. Herbert Charles Wilson

Dates: 1859–1909
Location: A – 35 - 0005
Style: Celtic cross on vertical tablet
Route: Head east over the grass to find the large, white
Celtic cross tablet marker of Dr. Wilson.

Dr. Wilson was born and educated in Ontario. He came to Edmonton in 1882 as Edmonton's third physician. Since he had also trained in pharmacy, he ran a drugstore below his medical office. He returned to Ontario to marry Miss Emily Lee in 1884 before returning to Edmonton to settle. The Wilsons had three children.

Dr. Wilson was elected to the Northwest Territorial Council in 1885, defeating Frank Oliver and sitting until 1888 when the council was abolished. He returned to assembly in 1890 as first speaker, but was forced to retire in 1891 due to poor health. He served as president of the Edmonton Liberal Association and the Alberta Medical

Association, and as a director of the Edmonton Cemetery Company. In 1898, he returned to politics, this time defeating John A. McDougall for the mayor's chair, and later serving as an alderman from 1905 to 1907. Dr. Wilson died of a stoke in 1909.

Elaborately carved stones tell a story about the people they remember.

His son Charles worked as a lawyer with Henwood and Harrison until he enlisted with the 19th Alberta Dragoons in 1914. He served with the 49th Regiment and was killed in Flanders in June 1916. A great sportsman, his obituary appeared on the sports page, where his previous accomplishments in rugby, football, and other athletics had been applauded.

Charles's mother and Dr. Wilson's wife, Charlotte, is remembered with a small stone facing the large rough-hewn tablet on which an intricate Celtic cross is carved.

Susan Little

Dates: 1865–1912
Location: A – 60 – 4
Style: Brick cairn
Route: Turn slightly southeast to discover the Little cairn.

This cairn was as much an advertisement for the Little Brick Company as a labour of love.

James Little and Sons operated the Edmonton Brickyard Company in the river valley. When Susan Little died in 1912 at age 47, her husband, James Little, erected this cairn from his bricks. It is the only brick cairn in the cemetery, and it stands over 2.4 meters tall. At Mrs. Little's funeral, over 50 carriages attended at her graveside. She was quite a popular woman and active in many Edmonton organizations.

The ashes of John Lawrence Little were later placed in the same plot. Despite the grave being planned as a family plot (with space reserved for other family members), James Little is interred in the mausoleum with space for his second wife.

The construction of cairns is associated with a variety of northern neolithic peoples, and it seems to have remained a common method of marking graves, or actually creating a grave in places where there was a great deal of rock and perhaps not a lot of loose soil for an in-ground burial. The practice seems to be associated with Scottish heritage. This particular version is a more formal construction than most cairns and might almost be construed as a monument rather than a cairn.

Malcolm Groat & Marguerite Christie Groat

Dates: 1836–1912; ca 1940-1922
Location: C-24-2
Style: Pillar
Route: Return westward to the roadway and slightly north past the intersection.

Malcolm Groat came from Scotland to the Hudson's Bay Company's Fort Edmonton. He came to take charge of the gardens and livestock, being a farmer by birth and inclination. When the HBC transferred its lands in the northwest to the Canadian government in 1967, Malcolm Groat was one of the first to take up a homestead, on river lot 2, just west of the HBC reserve land around the fort. He married the chief factor's daughter, Marguerite Christie, but remained with the company until 1878, when he bought another large parcel of land to the west

This family memorial lists the names of several people buried around the marker in the family plot.

of his homestead, giving him over 405 hectares (from present-day 121st Street to 149th Street between the river and 111th Avenue).

Malcolm and Marguerite were the first settlers to live outside Fort Edmonton, and they raised cattle and horses as well as growing wheat and barley. With his sons, Groat also started a cartage business hauling goods east and west, to and from the fort. His brother-in-law John Norris had a neighboring river lot. Eventually they subdivided their land, sold the majority of it to a developer from Montreal, James Carruthers, and it became the exclusive neighborhood of Glenora. Groat Estates still exists on the east side of the Groat Ravine, above which the last Groat home was erected, overlooking the river.

Malcolm Groat died the year after the house was completed, in 1912. His wife, Marguerite Christie, who bore nine children, died on December 22, 1922.

The pillar is a popular marker or monument. It is tall enough to capture attention and is easily found, and the sides are flat to allow for carving memorials.

William Griesbach & Jennie Lauder Griesbach

Dates: 1878–1945;   ca. 1980-1950
Location: C–26–0018
Style: Vertical tablet with arched cap
Route: Continue onto the grass, heading slightly north and west to near a large spruce tree for the Griesbach and Taylor markers.

William Antrobus Griesbach was born in Fort Qu'Appelle, Saskatchewan. He moved with his family to Edmonton and started to study law in 1883. Coming from a military family, he obtained a commission in the Canadian Mounted Rifles regiment and enlisted in 1899–1900 to go to South Africa for the Boer War. He was award-ed the Queen's Medal, with four bars. Returning to Edmonton, he began his own law practice in 1901.

Designed to allow room for lots of information, the vertical slab memorial can be valuable for historians and genealogists.

He ran unsuccessfully for the town council in 1903 and again, successfully, in 1904. In 1905, he attempted to win a seat in the provincial house but was defeated. He married Janet Scott McDonald Lauder in 1906 and was elected mayor the following year. He was 29 years old and was referred to as the "Boy Mayor." A captaincy in the 19th Alberta Dragoons was obtained in 1908, and at the outbreak of the First World War he was asked to recruit soldiers for the front. In ten days he had raised enough men for a western regiment, which would become the 49th Regiment, or the Loyal Edmonton Regiment.

In 1917, Griesbach was promoted to brigadier general, and he became the inspector general of the army in western Canada until his resignation in 1945. In the same year, he was elected to the House of Commons in Ottawa, defeating the incumbent Liberal Frank Oliver. In 1921, he was appointed to the Senate and worked to provide services for veterans.

Jennie (Janet Scott McDonald) Lauder was the first telephone operator hired by manager A. W. Ormsby of the Edmonton Telephone Company (he later married her sister Margaret). She was an avid and talented sportswoman, skating at the Royal Glenora; a member of the Victorian Order of Nurses and president of the Florence Nightingale Auxiliary; and a member of the Independent Order of the Daughters of the Empire, the Women's Canadian Club, Girl Guides, and the Young Women's Conservative Club.

The exploits of Mr. Griesbach's father are detailed on the other side of this stone.

This vertical tablet marker has a cap with the family initial engraved on both sides in Gothic text. The black granite is a highly durable stone and can be intricately etched with a laser.

Alex Taylor
Dates: 1854–1915
Location: C–26–11
Style: Obelisk
Route: Turn north for the Taylor stone.

This style of memorial marker is ancient.

Alex Taylor came to the Edmonton area in 1877 with the telegraph. In conjunction with Frank Oliver, he used the information that came in over the telegraph to publish the *Edmonton Bulletin*. The next challenge was to start a telephone company in 1884. Eventually the town of Edmonton purchased his system. An electrician, Taylor started the first electric light company in the town as well, and his wife Harriet was his primary stockholder. This company was also purchased by the city. Taylor worked as a postmaster and as clerk of the supreme court. He also served as a school board trustee and a director of the Cemetery Company. A school was named after him in honor of his years of service with the school board.

Taylor lost his first wife, Harriet Marsh, and later married his sister-in-law. Both of his wives are recorded on this obelisk, as is one of his sons.

The stele is a pillar with a pyramid-shaped top. It is a classical marker deriving from the Roman period.

William Short

Dates: 1866–1926

Location: C–35–0001

Style: Large slab

Route: The next monument is slightly northwest of the Taylor stele.

William Short was born in Ontario in 1866 and was educated there, studying law. He came to Alberta in 1889 to article with Senator Lougheed in Calgary between 1891 and 1894 when he was admitted to the Alberta bar.

After coming to Edmonton, Short joined the firm of Short, Cross, Biggar and Ewing, among others, and was the author of the city charter, which was adopted in 1904. Short was active in community groups, as a Mason, a chairman of the Edmonton Board of Trade, and an enthusiastic motorist who purchased one of the first cars brought into the city. He married Henrietta McMaster in 1900, and they had two children.

The use of symbols, such as the Alberta Rose, can provide information about an individual's life as well as words.

Short was elected mayor of the town of Edmonton, serving from 1902 to 1904, when Edmonton was incorporated as a city. He was reelected as mayor of the City of Edmonton for the term of 1904–05, and again in 1913.

This vertical table is elongated and has the Alberta rose carved into the top.

Wilfred May

Dates: 1896–1952
Location: C–44–4
Style: Horizontal tablet
Route: Continue in a northwesterly direction to the May and
Oliver markers.

This horizontal slab is used to display the names of several family members.

Wilfred Reid "Wop" May was a flyer in World War I who won the distinguished flying cross for his war service. His nickname derived
from the inability of one of his younger siblings to pronounce his
first name. He was one of the few pilots who survived a battle with
the infamous Red Baron. After the war, May continued to fly, still
into danger, but mostly in the Canadian north delivering the mail,
freighting passengers and supplies and occasionally saving lives, like
the time he flew diphtheria serum to Fort Chipewyan in 1929
through terrible weather conditions in an open cockpit plane.

May was instrumental in establishing an airfield in Edmonton
in 1936 and founded the Edmonton Flying Club. The City of
Edmonton named Mayfair Park (now renamed Hawrelak Park for
William Hawrelak, the former mayor) in his honour.

The rest of May's family are named on the stone as well. Family stones such as this are extremely valuable for genealogical research.

Frank Oliver

Dates: 1853–1933
Location: C-28-0010
Style: Horizontal tablet
Route: Turn east to discover the Oliver stone.

Another impressive horizontal memorial has more detail carved along the perimeter.

Frank Oliver was a journalist when he came to Edmonton in 1878. He had worked for newspapers in Toronto and Winnipeg before venturing to this frontier outpost, but for five years after arriving in Edmonton, he operated a grocery store.

In 1880, he became partners with Alex Taylor to bring the telegraph wire-service news to the masses through the power of the press. Their newspaper was the *Edmonton Bulletin,* published until 1951. The paper helped launch Oliver's political career, carrying him to his position of minister of the interior in Laurier's cabinet from 1905 to 1911.

The Edmonton Public School Board and the City of Edmonton named a school and then a community in honor of their best booster.

Cemetery Office

Location: Just inside the north-side gates, at approximately 117th Street

Route: Return east to the roadway and proceed across 107th Avenue, cautiously at the crosswalk. Stop at the south end of the cemetery office to read the plaque.

The City's Cemetery offices provide a number of services to families.

The cemetery office is staffed only occasionally; however, a map of the cemetery is posted in the front window to assist visitors in orienting themselves and finding their plots.

Every plot in the cemetery can be located by a three-part identifier. Along the roadways, cast-iron markers with letters help visitors locate the sections. Within the sections are numbered blocks, and within each block are numbered plots. The individual identifiers of the graves can be obtained by calling the cemetery office at

Beechmount, or by doing a search on the municipal cemeteries website. (See details in appendix).

On the south side of the cemetery office is a plaque listing the company officers and directors. Note that a number of fathers and sons took this responsibility as a family commitment.

Robert Dykes & Edgar Allin Families

Dates: various
Location: L-39-01: L-14-0002
Style: Vertical cross & horizontal slabs
Route: Continue northward along the path toward the mausoleum.

This family requires two monuments for their members.

The expansion across to the north side of 107th Avenue was accomplished with the cemetery company's acceptance of a number of conditions. Because several of the residential neighbors had objected to the cemetery taking over more land, the company had to promise to restrict the size of monuments and to ensure at a certain percentage were flush to the ground. In the case of the Dykes family marker, the six-meter cross, these regulations were obviously not followed. Perhaps the fact that the Dykes family owned the marble and granite company had something to do with their monument's size.

The majority of memorials on the north side of the cemetery are smaller than on the south side – however, the Dykes cross is an exception.

In the case of the Allin family markers, the limit of one stone to a family was ignored, perhaps because of the lapse of time between the burials or because different branches of the family insisted on their own markers. The Allin family were important in the medical profession, having come to Edmonton to assist in the setting up of the Royal Alexandra Hospital and then opening their own clinic in Oliver. Despite being in competition with the University Hospital, the Allin family still lived in Garneau and associated with many of the university personnel.

Cathedral of Memories Mausoleum

Dates: 1932
Location: north side of 107th Avenue at 117th Street
Style: Beaux-Arts
Architect: William Ralston
Route: Continue around the circle to the mausoleum.

The classical style mausoleum is a rarity in Western Canadian cemeteries.

Built in 1932 by Canadian Mausoleums Limited, the Cathedral of Memories was one of only a few mausoleums constructed across western Canada.

The word *mausoleum* comes from the name of the Persian king Mausoleus, whose widow erected a magnificent tomb for her departed husband. The structure is designed with neoclassical details such as the ionic columns and the simple pediment over the entrance topped by a palm frond finial and two more pediments at the end of the wings. The Cathedral of Memories mausoleum is faced with Tyndall limestone from Manitoba, in which you can see fossil remains.

Some controversy and the lack of familiarity with the practice of "above-ground" internment made the decision of the Edmonton Cemetery Company to erect this mausoleum quite radical. The building was used for a few years as a temporary place of burial for the winter months, but many people found the idea attractive. There are places for 450 burials on two levels and columbarium niches found inside.

Several interesting families and individuals have their resting places within the mausoleum, including the Reverend Arthur and Mrs. Emily Murphy, Dr. Twillegar and his family, and John Percy Page and Olive Page.

Around the base of the mausoleum are platform memorial markers, which cover the interred ashes of cremations. In the center of the circle to the south of the mausoleum are columbaria, in which ashes in urns may be stored in niches.

Gladys Muttart & Merrill Muttart

Dates: ca. 1902-1969; 1904–1970
Location: N–27–0005 & 0006
Style: Horizontal slab with geometrics
Route: Continue westward around the circle to the Muttart stone.

The Muttarts were prominent members of the business community in Alberta and Saskatchewan for many years. They were married in 1927 and had two children. The Muttarts owned several businesses relating to housing, engineering, lumber, and construction, including Gladmer Developments and W. I. Muttart Industries.

The black granite stones can be shaped into a variety of forms and is easily etched with different decorations.

In 1953, the Muttarts created a foundation that would make philanthropic donations to various charities to improve their ability to help people within the community. Gladys Muttart was heavily involved in assisting people with diabetes like herself. She helped form the Canadian Diabetic Association and assisted in creating a camp for diabetic children. Other charitable activities kept her busy, including the YWCA, the Alumni Association of the University of Alberta, and the National Council of Women. Mr. Muttart's activities included serving on a number of boards of colleges and of the University of Alberta.

Their foundation continues making grants today, and notable public facilities which have benefited include the Muttart Conservatory and the Muttart Hall at Alberta College.

The Muttart black granite headstone is unusually eloquent, bearing not only the names and dates of the deceased but also a Baha'i invocation, added by their son, and the logo of the Muttart Companies, the cluster of trees representing their involvement in the lumber business.

Children's Section

Dates: various

Location: Along 107th Avenue; northern edge of sections C & D

Style: Various; white marble/granite

Route: Turn right onto the road which leads west to the second military field of honor. Turn left and proceed to the fence on 107th Avenue, and veer off the path to the left to find one of the children's sections.

Children's sections are often the most poignant places in the cemetery.

In places along the edges of the cemetery there are clusters of small, white marble gravestones in various shapes, but most often bearing a likeness of a lamb, a winged cherub, or a baby. In many cases the stones are placed close together. These are the graves of infants and young children.

The white stones and the depiction of small animals and angels remind the visitor of the innocence and vulnerability of children.

In most cases where children died before their parents, the family was unprepared and no "family plot" was ready to receive the remains of the child. Most cemetery companies would offer a half-sized (and reduced price) gravesite, situated among other children's graves, to the bereaved family.

Occasionally the visitor will notice in one section that a number of deaths occurred within the same year. Often when epidemics struck a community, they carried off the very young and the very old in great numbers. In such times the children's section of the cemetery could fill rapidly. In Edmonton, smallpox and measles struck in 1907, the Spanish influenza in 1918, and polio in 1925 and 1941.

Cross of Sacrifice & Military Field of Honor

Dates: 1922
Location: Between F & G sections
Style: Cross monument & regulation vertical tablets
Route: Cross over 107th Avenue again, heading southward, and continue along the roadway through the first military field of honor until you find the Cross of Sacrifice.

Military fields of honor were constructed in many Canadian cemeteries by the War Grave Commission following the first and second World Wars.

Created by the expansion of the Edmonton Cemetery in 1921, this military field of honor was dedicated by Lord Byng, Governor General of Canada, and the officials of the War Graves Commission.

The six-meter Cross of Sacrifice in the center of the field is a replica of those placed in the military graveyards in Europe and the Middle East where Allied troops were buried.

The headstones are provided to servicemen and veterans of any branch of the Canadian armed forces and allied forces. They are uniform in terms of size and style of carving. The top of the stone displays the insignia of the soldier's branch of the armed forces, or a religious symbol. Beneath that appears the soldier's name, rank, and battalion or division. Below that is a space where family members can add an epitaph or quotation. Stones are placed, regardless of rank, in straight rows and columns, as all soldiers buried there made a similar sacrifice for their country.

Some rows are dedicated to North-West Mounted Police veterans, and two to nursing sisters. Those are found at the easterly edge of the field of honor, along the south side of the roadway.

Northern Alberta Pioneers & Old Timers Association (NAPOTA) Cairn

Dates: ca. 1930s
Location: F section
Style: Fieldstone cairn
Route: Continue south along the path from the Cross of
Sacrifice until you see the fieldstone cairn on the right.
The Northern Alberta Pioneers and Old Timers Association was founded in 1894 to preserve the history of the city of Edmonton and the memories of "old timers." Membership was conveyed only on individuals who had been in Edmonton before 1885. Later the name was changed to "Pioneers and Descendants," and the year restriction stretched to 1905.

In the 1930s, during the Depression, the association became concerned that some of its members—founding members of the community—were often unable to provide a suitable monument for themselves and their families when they died. A deal was negotiated with the Edmonton Cemetery Company for a number of grave plots, which were sold to association members at a discount.

Fieldstone is an elegant material for a cairn.

In 1932, the association hired C. C. Batson, a mason with the construction firm of Batson and Pheasey, and a member of the association, to create a suitable monument for the center of this group of graves, and in 1935, a like one for the nearby Catholic cemetery. The cairn is constructed of local stones capped with red granite. It stands two meters high and has a foundation of similar depth.

The grass markers laid around the cairn represent some of the earliest inhabitants of Edmonton and their descendants.

David McQueen

Dates: 1854–1930
Location: 8–14–E
Style: Horizontal granite tablet
Route: Return northward along the roadway until you see the McQueen stone on the right.

The family has inset the bronze medallion from the first War into their memorial.

David George McQueen was a Presbyterian minister who was trained in Toronto, Ontario, and accepted a call to minister in Edmonton in 1887. He came to serve the First Presbyterian Church of Edmonton and remained as its pastor for 43 years. His job responsibilities included offering services in four outlying communities— which often meant taking three to five services on a Sunday and traveling on horseback between the churches or homes where the services were offered.

Besides his pastoral duties, McQueen served as the first moderator of the Edmonton Presbytery (a local administrative unit) and as moderator of the Synod of British Columbia and Alberta in 1907. His local public service included serving on the board of the Edmonton Cemetery Company, as a member of the University of Alberta senate, and as inspector of schools for the Northwest Territories (before Saskatchewan and Alberta were formed into provinces).

McQueen was married to Catherine Robertson of Ontario, and they had seven children, several of whom are listed on the family monument. Note the bronze medallion in the lower left corner—it depicts the sacrifice of Alexander McQueen, who served as a lance corporal in the Princess Patricia Canadian Light Infantry and died in June 1916. His brother James was wounded in battle the following year during his service with the 63rd Battalion (later the 49th or Loyal Edmonton Regiment.)

David McQueen was a much loved and respected member of the Edmonton community, even outside his church. Reportedly more than 2,000 people attended his funeral in 1930.

P. C. H. Primrose

Dates: 1864–1937
Location: E-34-0012
Style: Large, vertical, serpentine-topped tablet
Route: At the Cross of Sacrifice, turn right and follow the road eastward until you reach the last row of the military field of honor. Turn right to visit the Primrose monument.

Philip Carteret Hill Primrose was born in Halifax in 1864 to a United Empire Loyalist family. He studied at Royal Military College in Ontario, graduating in 1885, and immediately joining the North-West Mounted Police as an inspector.

Inspector Primrose was transferred to the Saskatchewan division, and he spent thirteen years in various Alberta and Saskatchewan posts (Wood Mountain, Calgary, and McLeod). In 1898, he was sent to the Yukon, where he spent four years during the

Klondike Gold Rush. In 1902, he returned to McLeod as superintendent and remained there until 1913. Also in 1902, he married Lily Deane, daughter of Major Richard Burton Deane (NWMP) of Calgary. Mrs. Primrose had been born in England and came to Canada as a child. She followed her father as he moved about the west with the force, to Regina in the early 1880s, followed by Lethbridge in 1887. The Primroses had two daughters and one son.

Although shaped like the other War Graves' Commission stones the size of this memorial marks it as something special.

Primrose was called to Regina in 1913 to head the newly established criminal investigation branch. He was reassigned in 1915 to Edmonton as police magistrate, a post he held with honor until 1935 and his retirement from the force.

In 1936, the Government of Alberta recognized his years of work for justice in the province and appointed him lieutenant governor. Unfortunately, Primrose was in poor health, and he died six months later of a heart attack at the age of 73.

His was the only viceregal burial ceremony in Alberta (since he died in office). The stone monument sits among other members of the North-West (and later the Royal Canadian) Mounted Police in the military field of honor. His wife Lily is interred here as well.

Richard Secord

Dates: 1860-1935
Location: B-T-0012
Style: Horizontal tablet
Route: Continue eastward along the roadway and you will
  see the family markers of Richard Secord and John
  McDougall.

Compare the traditional horizontal tablet with the stone memorial beside it.

Richard Secord was from Ontario. He was a great-grandnephew of
the famous Laura Secord. He arrived in Edmonton in 1881 and took
a number of jobs in succession including carpenter on the first
schoolhouse, town site surveyor, and, between 1883 and 1887, teacher
in the school. He operated a trading post for John McDougall for two
years before becoming his partner in 1897.

Secord also had political aspirations, and he served as a member
of the Territorial Assembly from 1902 to 1904 (before Alberta was
made a province).

The Secord-McDougall partnership was also responsible for
building the Empire Block on Jasper Avenue and 101st Street for their
financial business offices.

John A. McDougall

Dates: 1854–1928
Location: B–W–0012
Style: Obelisk
Route: Continue eastward to the next family gravesite with the large gray obelisk.

John Alexander McDougall came to the Edmonton area in 1879 to trade independently with the native peoples, in competition with the Hudson's Bay Company. Three years later he set up his own store and soon lured Richard Secord, the local school teacher, to be his partner. The business prospered, and two more stores were built as more space was required. Secord traveled throughout the northwest as a buyer and representative, and the company was soon involved in other activities.

Many of the prospectors who traveled through Edmonton on their way to the Yukon in 1897 and 1898 left town after being "outfitted" by McDougall and Secord. When the Treaty Commission left to negotiate settlements with the northern First Nations bands, McDougall and Secord followed and were able to develop large holdings of real estate in prime agricultural territory because of their trade in Métis scrip.

As well as his business interests, McDougall had political aspirations. In 1894, he was elected alderman. He followed that up with a run for the mayor's chair in 1907, in which he sat for one term. In 1909, McDougall and Secord took on financial and mortgage businesses and succeeded in those as well. Both men built substantial homes in the center of the city along 100th (Victoria) Avenue, which have since been replaced with high-rise buildings. McDougall was a member of hospital boards, the Edmonton Chamber of Commerce, and the Board of Trade, sat on the Edmonton Exhibition Association board and was a member of the first University of Alberta senate.

The McDougall family, many of whom are buried in this family plot, partook of the highest levels of social commerce in the city as well. One of the benefits of their wealth was the ability to travel, and they finished the education of their children in the European style known as the Grande Tour. Each of their children accompanied their parents on a world cruise—some to Europe, others to the Orient—where the cultures and commodities of the world were sampled. The McDougall family accumulated a vast number of goods from these trips, including artworks, furnishings, and collectibles such as weaponry and textiles, much of which was donated to the Provincial Museum of Alberta on the death of the last surviving son, Edmund McDougall.

This large family plot has a number of flat stones around the obelisk.

Glossary

balustrade – A railing with supporting balusters (pillars or columns supporting a handrail).

bellcast roof – A roof whose cross-section looks like a bell, with curved edges at the bottom.

clinker brick – A form of brick overbaked in an old-style kiln which resulted in discoloration, causing it to be rejected by most brick makers. Occasionally sold more cheaply than other types of bricks.

corbel – A bracket which projects from the building and supports a cornice, arch, or oriel. Also, an overlapping arrangement of brick or stone in which each course extends farther out from the vertical of the wall than the course below (it steps up and out from the wall or around the chimney).

cornice (aka crown molding) – Any crowning projection; in classical architecture, the third or uppermost portion of an entablature resting on the frieze.

Craftsman-style bungalow – Usually one and a half storeys; not a modern one-storey bungalow.

dormer – A structure projecting from a sloping roof, usually housing a window.

gable – The triangular portion of a wall between enclosing lines of a sloping roof.

half-timbering – A construction method in which vertical and horizontal timbers make up the frame of a wall, which is then filled in with lath and plaster, mud or clay, stone or brick.

hip roof – A roof that slopes inward on all four sides.

iconostasis – The partition between the sanctuary and the nave in Eastern rite churches.

keystone – The central stone, sometimes carved, which holds the central place in an arch or vault; the central voussoir in an arch.

lintil – A supporting wood or stone beam across the top of a window or door.

lugsill – A projecting piece of a sill which is either for decoration or support.

mansard roof – A roof with two slopes on each of four sides; the lower slope is usually steeper and may hide the upper slope. Frequently gables protrude from the lower portion of the roof, allowing light into the space which can then be used for extra rooms or an attic. The term is derived from the name of French architect Francois Mansard (1598–1666), who revived this roof style.

modillion – An ornamental bracket used in a series to support the upper part of a cornice.

pediment – A triangular gable across a portico (porch), door, or window.

pilaster – A shallow, rectangular column projecting from a wall, pretending to be a pillar.

reliquary – A special box or casket used to keep safe relics such as bones or teeth of saints.

vergeboard (aka bargeboard) – A board, often carved, which is fixed to the projecting edge of a gable roof.

voussoir – One of the wedge-shaped bricks forming the curved part of an arch or vault.

wainscot – A decorative or protective facing such as wood paneling.

References

Cashman, Tony. *The Best Edmonton Stories.* Edmonton: Hurtig
    Publishers, 1976.

Farnell, Margaret O'Connell. *Glenora.* Edmonton: Old Glenora
    Historical Society, 1984.

Hawker, Peter. "A Historical Walk of Early Edmonton," ms. City
    of Edmonton Archives, 1990.

Herzog, Lawrence. Various "Our Heritage" articles in *Real Estate
    Weekly,* 1998–2003.

Herzog, Lawrence, and Lowe, Shirley. *Life of a Neighborhood:
    Edmonton's Oliver District, 1870 to 1950.* Edmonton: Oliver
    Community League, 2002.

Hesketh, Bob, and Swyripa, Frances, eds. *Edmonton: The Life of a
    City.* Edmonton: NeWest Press, 1995.

Lowe, Shirley A. and Yannish, Lori. *West Side Story.* Edmonton:
    The 124th Street and Area Business Association, 1991.

MacGregor, J. G. *Edmonton: A History.* Edmonton: Hurtig
    Publishers, 1967.

Mair, Alex. *Gateway City: Stories from Edmonton's Past.* Calgary:
    Fifth House, 2000.

Merrett, Kathryn Chase, *A History of the Edmonton City Market,
    1900-2000: urban values and urban culture.* Calgary:
    University of Calgary Press, 2001.

Pyszczyk, Heinz. *Archaeology Guide and Tour of Greater Edmonton Area*. Edmonton: Provincial Museum of Alberta and Archaeological Survey of Alberta, 1996.

Shute, Allan. *Riverdale: From Fraser Flats to Edmonton Oasis*. Edmonton: Tree Frog Press, 1992.

Architectural resources

Alberta Historic Sites Service maintains an historic building inventory at their offices at the Old St. Stephen's College (8820-112 Street, Edmonton) – this contains information on all buildings designated as provincial heritage resources. See blue pages in the Edmonton Telephone directory for the current listings.

City of Edmonton Planning and Development Department, and specifically the Office of the Heritage Planner, maintains a municipal historic resources list which lists the locations, dates, architects and other pertinent information about buildings considered of important historical value—the list is divided into A and B class resources (A being of more significance—and over which the city planners will take more interest in the case of proposed alteration or demolition. See blue pages in Edmonton Telephone directory for current listings.

Harris, Cyril M., ed. *Illustrated Dictionary of Historic Architecture*. New York: Dover Publications, 1977.

Research resources

City of Edmonton Municipal Cemeteries – Search for City of Edmonton Cemeteries on your search engine and follow the links to "search Edmonton Municipal Cemeteries."

About the Author

Kathryn Ivany's first job at the Provincial Museum of Alberta launched a career in the study and interpretation of Alberta's natural and human history. Educated at the universities of Alberta, Calgary and Cambridge, she has pursued historical subjects for over twenty years as a public historian, and has acted as a consultant researcher and writer to neighborhood groups, not-for-profit agencies and archives and museums.